Learn C and Save Your Job

Computer Books from QED

Systems Development
The Complete Guide to Software Testing
Developing Client/Server Applications
Quality Assurance for Information Systems
Total Quality Management in Information Services
User-Interface Screen Design
On Time, Within Budget: Software Project Management Practices and Techniques
Managing Software Projects: Selecting and Using PC-Based Project Management Systems
From Mainframe to Workstations: Offloading Application Development
A Structured Approach to Systems Testing
Rapid Application Prototyping: The Storyboard Approach to User Requirements Analysis
Software Engineering with Formal Metrics

Information Engineering/CASE
Practical Model Management Using CASE Tools
Building the Data Warehouse
Information Systems Architecture: Development in the 90's
Enterprise Architecture Planning: Developing a Blueprint for Data, Applications, and Technology
Data Architecture: The Information Paradigm

IBM Systems Software
REXX in the TSO Environment
REXX Tools and Techniques
The MVS Primer
Cross System Product Application Development
TSO/E CLISTS: The Complete Tutorial and Reference Guide
MVS/JCL: Mastering Job Control Language
MVS/VSAM for the Application Programmer
Introduction to Cross System Product
CICS: A How-To for COBOL Programmers
CICS: A Guide to Performance Tuning
CICS Application and System Programming: Tools and Techniques
CICS: A Guide to Application Debugging

OS/2
OS/2 2.0 Workplace Shell: The User's Guide and Tutorial
OS/2 Presentation Manager Programming for COBOL Programmers
Micro Focus COBOL Workbench for the Application Developer

AS/400
AS/400: A Practical Guide for Programming and Operations
AS/400 Architecture and Applications: The Database Machine

VSE
VSE/SP and VSE/ESA: A Guide to Performance Tuning
VSE JCL and Subroutines for Application Programmers
DOS/VSE: CICS Systems Programming
DOS/VSE: An Introduction to the Operating System

UNIX
UNIX C Shell Desk Reference
The UNIX Industry: Evolution, Concepts, Architecture, Applications, and Standards

Management and Business Skills
The Disaster Recovery Plan
Controlling the Future: Managing Technology-Driven Change
How to Automate Your Computer Center
Mind Your Business: Managing the Impact of End-User Computing
Understanding Data Pattern Processing: The Key to Competitive Advantage

VAX/VMS
Rdb/VMS: Developing the Data Warehouse
Network Programming Under DECNet Phase IV and V
VAX/VMS: Mastering DCL Commands and Utilities

Database
Client/Server and Distributed Database Design
Third-Wave Processing: Database Machines and Decision Support Systems
Database Management Systems: Understanding and Applying Database Technology

Database — DB2
QMF: How to Use Query Management Facility with DB2 and SQL/DS
SQL for DB2 and SQL/DS Application Developers
DB2: the Complete Guide to Implementation and Use
Embedded SQL for DB2: Application Design and Development
DB2: Maximizing Performance in Online Production Systems

Database — ORACLE
ORACLE: Building High Performance Online Systems
How To Use ORACLE SQL*Plus

QED books are available at special quantity discounts for educational uses, premiums, and sales promotions. Special books, book excerpts, and instructive materials can be created to meet specific needs.

This is Only a Partial Listing. For Additional Information or a Free Catalog contact
QED Publishing Group • P. O. Box 812070 • Wellesley, MA 02181-0013
Telephone: 800-343-4848 or 617-237-5656 or fax 617-235-0826

Learn C and Save Your Job

C for COBOL Programmers

Kenneth Pugh

A Wiley–QED Publication
John Wiley & Sons, Inc.
New York • Chichester • Brisbane • Toronto • Singapore

Designations used by companies to distinguish their products are often claimed as trademarks. In all instances where John Wiley & Sons, Inc. is aware of a claim, the product names appear in initial capital or all capital letters. Readers, however, should contact the appropriate companies for more complete information regarding trademarks and registration.

This text is printed on acid-free paper.

© 1993 by John Wiley & Sons, Inc.

All rights reserved.

This publication is designed to provide accurate and authoritative information in regard to the subject matter covered. It is sold with the understanding that the publisher is not engaged in rendering legal, accounting, or other professional services. If legal advice or other expert assistance is required, the services of a competent professional person should be sought. FROM A DECLARATION OF PRINCIPLES JOINTLY ADOPTED BY A COMMITTEE OF THE AMERICAN BAR ASSOCIATION AND A COMMITTEE OF PUBLISHERS.

Reproduction or translation of any part of this work beyond that permitted by section 107 or 108 of the 1976 United States Copyright Act without the permission of the copyright owner is unlawful. Requests for permission or further information should be addressed to the Permissions Department, John Wiley & Sons, Inc.

Library of Congress Cataloging-in-Publication Data

Pugh, Kenneth.
    Learn C and save your job : C for COBOL programmers / Kenneth Pugh.
      p.   cm.
    Rev. ed. of: C language for programmers. c1989.
    Includes index.
    ISBN 0-471-58807-5
    1. C (Computer program language)   I. Pugh, Kenneth. C language for programmers. II. Title.
    QA76.73.C15P827   1993
    005.13'3—dc20   93-3391
                                                                                                 CIP

Printed in the United States of America

10 9 8 7 6 5 4 3 2 1

Dedication and Acknowledgments

This book is dedicated to my wife Leslie Killeen, who has endured many years of computer talk, and to Nameless, our cat.

I would also like to express my appreciation to Jim Hines for reviewing the COBOL programs in this book, and my thanks to the X3J11 committee for standardizing the language.

Contents

1 Introduction 1
    History of C 1
    COBOL and C Examples 2
    COBOL and C Comparison 2
    Mistakes and Errors 9
    Summary 9

2 Data Types, Variables and Operators 11
    Data Types 11
        Declaration *12*
        Names *13*
    Constants 15
    Initialization 16
    Expressions 16
    Operators 16
        Arithmetic Operators *17*
        The Assignment Operator *17*
        Shorthand Assignment Operator *18*
        Increment and Decrement Operators *19*
        Type Conversions *19*
        Precedence of Operators *20*
    Statements 21

vii

Compound Statement 21
Null Statement 21
Comments and White Space 22
printf and scanf 23
#define 25
Sample Programs 25
Summary 28

3 Control Flow 29

if Statement 29
Test Expression 30
Relational and Equality Operators 30
Test Expression Explored 34
if-else and Compound if 35
while Statement 38
do-while Statement 39
for Statement 41
break Statement 42
switch Statement 43
Sample Programs 46
   Date Check *46*
   Averaging Program *51*
   A Guessing Program *51*
Summary 59

4 Functions 61

Function Definition 61
Function Names 65
Function Prototypes and Parameter Checking 65
   Call by Value *66*
   Call by Reference *67*
   Return Values *67*
   void Return Type *68*
   Implicit Function Calls *69*
   Library Functions *69*
A Sample C Program 69
main and exit 70
Variable Storage Classes 70
   Local Variables—Auto and Static *77*
   External Variables *77*
   Externals and Multiple Source Files *80*

	Sample Programs 81	
	Date check *81*	
	Averaging Program *89*	
	Summary 89	
5	**Arrays** **91**	
	Declaration and Use of Arrays 91	
	Initialization *93*	
	Sample Functions *95*	
	Transitioning to C Arrays 96	
	Array Restrictions *96*	
	Arrays and Functions *98*	
	Sample Averaging Program *101*	
	Strings *105*	
	Functions and Strings *105*	
	String Length *107*	
	Other String Functions *108*	
	String Literals *109*	
	Input and Output *111*	
	Arrays of Character Arrays *112*	
	Summary 114	
6	**Input and Output Functions** **115**	
	Formatted Output 115	
	Format Specifiers 118	
	Formatted Input 119	
	String Conversion *122*	
	Character Input and Output 122	
	Standard Redirected Input and Output 123	
	Sample Functions 124	
	Print Date *124*	
	Summary 126	
7	**Structures** **127**	
	Comparison between COBOL and C FIELDS 127	
	Templates 129	
	Initializing Structures *133*	
	Functions and Structures *134*	
	Hierarchies *138*	
	Packages *140*	

Unions 142
Example Functions 143
Example Program 143
Summary 150

8 Pointers 151

Introduction 151
Pointers and Data Types 154
Function Parameters 155
Pointers and Structures 159
Pointers and Unions 162
Pointer Errors 163
Null Pointer.. *164*
Void Pointers 164
Example Program 164
Summary 164

9 Preprocessor 167

Preprocessor Commands 167
The #define Statement *167*
The #include Statement *170*
Conditional Compilation *171*
Enumeration Variables 172
typedef Statement 175
Summary 178

10 File Input and Output 179

COBOL File I/O 179
C File I/O 182
File Positioning.. *190*
Formatted File Operations *191*
Binary Files Versus Text Files 191
Character Functions 192
Pre-opened Files 193
Example Functions *193*
Summary 201

11 The Rest of the Story 203

Variables and Functions 203
Scope of Names *203*
Static Externals and Functions *204*

  Data Types and Constants 204
    Data Types. 204
    Numeric Constants 205
    Character Constants 205
  Conversion 207
    Register Types 208
    Type Modifiers. 209
    Bit Pattern Constants 209
    Bitwise Operators 210
    Conditional Operator 210
    Comma Operator. 211
    Logical AND/OR 211
    Cast Operator 212
    Precedence and Associativity 212
  Control Flow 212
    The goto Statement 212
    The continue Statement 214
  Pointers 215
    Pointers and Allocated Memory 215
    Pointer Arithmetic. 216
    Strings and Pointers 216
    Arrays of Pointers 217
    The Arguments argc and argv 217
  Additional Preprocesser Statements 219
    #define with Tokens 219
    Conditional Compilation Directives. 220
    Quoting and Token Concatenation. 220
    Other Directives 220
  Summary 221

A **Comparison of COBOL and C** **223**
  COBOL and C Equivalents 223

B **Function Listing** **225**
  Library Names 227
  Header Files 231
  Library Usage 236
    stddef.h 236
    errno.h 237
    float.h. 237
    limits.h 239
  Mathematical Functions 239

CONTENTS

- *math.h* 240
  - *Trigonometric Functions* 240
  - *Regular Functions* 240
  - *Arc Functions* 241
  - *Hyperbolic Functions* 241
  - *Exponential Functions* 242
  - *Floating Point Numbers* 243
  - *Miscellaneous* 243
- Input/Output Functions 244
  - *stdio.h* 246
  - *File Manipulations* 247
  - *File Errors* 250
  - *File Buffering* 250
  - *File Positioning* 251
  - *Formatted I/O* 253
  - *Character I/O* 261
  - *String I/O* 263
- General Utility Functions 265
  - *stdlib.h* 265
  - *String to Number Conversion* 265
  - *Random Number Functions* 267
  - *Memory Management* 267
  - *Sorting and Searching* 269
  - *Integer Arithmetic Functions* 270
- String Handling 271
  - *string.h* 271
  - *Copying* 271
  - *Concatenation* 271
  - *String Comparison* 272
  - *String Search* 273
  - *Miscellaneous* 275
  - *Memory Functions* 275
- Date and Time 277
  - *Timing* 278
  - *Time Conversion* 278
- Character Handling 280
  - *ctype.h* 280
  - *Character Conversion* 280
  - *Character Testing* 280
- Environment 282
  - *stdlib.h* 283
- Diagnostic 284
  - *assert.h* 284

	Non-Local Jumps	284
	setjmp.h	*284*
	Signal Handling	286
	signal.h	*286*
	Variable Arguments	287
	stdarg.h	*288*
	Internationalization Issues	289
	Characters	*289*
	Supporting Functions	*290*
	Header File	*290*
	Locale	*291*
	Collation Sequence	*291*
	Time Transformation	*292*
	Monetary Information	*293*
	String Operations	*294*
C	**Linking and Compiling**	**297**
	Multiple Source Files	299
D	**Bits, Bytes and Numbers**	**303**
	Bit Values	303
	Sign extension	304
	Shifts	*304*
	Memory Locations	*305*
E	**Summary of C**	**307**
	Data Types	307
	Integer Types	*307*
	Floating Point Types	*308*
	Void Type	*308*
	Enumerated Type	*308*
	Type Modifiers	*308*
	Aggregates and Derived Types	*309*
	Operators	312
	Statements	313
	Simple	*313*
	Compound	*313*
	Functions	315
	Preprocessor	315
	Keywords	316
	List of Keywords	*316*

       List of Symbols and Their Meanings *317*
       Scope of Identifiers *318*
       Linkage of Identifiers *319*

F   ASCII Chart **321**

       Bibliography 327
       Guide to Magazines. *328*

Preface

C has become a popular language among programmers because it is quite portable. A program written in ANSI C can run without significant alteration on a variety of machines, ranging from embedded controllers to massive parallel processors.

C for Cobol Programmers is designed to ease the transition of programmers coming to C from COBOL. This book uses the ANSI COBOL 1985 standard as the basis for all comparisons with C, and assumes that the reader is familiar with programming in COBOL and, in particular, with the END-IF, END-PERFORM, and EVALUATE statements. The version of C presented in this text is the ANSI standard C (ANSI C) adopted in September 1988, compatible with most compilers used today.

Good programming style is better taught by example than by explicit lists of guidelines. All examples in this book follow a common style. For example, the sample programs use descriptive variable names such as "sum" and "result" rather than "s" or "r," because those who must subsequently understand a program will more readily understand descriptive names.

Many features of C permit the programmer to code operations in several ways. This multiplicity of styles can be confusing even to experienced C programmers, let alone beginners. I have therefore relegated the use of rare syntax features to footnotes and limited to some extent the applications of those features presented in this book. A few features that are unique to C appear in later chapters. More detailed information on programming in C is available in my book *All on C* or other advanced texts.

Experienced C programmers may be slightly taken aback by an approach to using C that so closely resembles COBOL. A COBOL programmer can write a program in C using many of the concepts found in a COBOL program. Only after several months' experience with C should a COBOL programmer attempt to use advanced features of C. I have recommended this approach to thousands of programmers with apparent success.

Most programmers today need not be concerned with saving a few microseconds of computer time. The increased speed of computers achieved over the past decade will easily compensate for most inefficiencies caused by the programmer's choice of features in a given programming language. How quickly a program may be interpreted by other programmers is far more important these days than how quickly it can be executed. Code should be written so that it can be read like a novel—albeit a somewhat mechanical sounding novel.

Most programs contain few routines, if any, that are executed repeatedly enough to make speeding them up worthwhile. *C for Cobol Programmers* therefore avoids complicating the explanation of the language with efficiency considerations that are seldom, if ever, needed. Techniques for improving efficiency may, however, be found in *All on C* or other advanced texts.

Style is a matter of how you use C to write code. The most important aspect of style is picking a convention and sticking with it. Consistency will enable anybody reading your code to determine easily what you intend it to do. C permits you to create unintelligible expressions and unreadable code. If you discipline yourself to follow a certain style of writing, your programs will be both more readable and more maintainable.

Style involves visual appearance, appropriate usage of code, and clarity. Using adequate white space and following indentation guidelines makes the code easy to read. A consistent style with few **goto**s and **returns** makes tracing a program's flow easy. Names and comments should be long enough to be understandable, but short enough to ensure that they will be read.

The maxim KISS (Keep it simple, stupid) applies as well to C as to many other facets of life. Though your definition of simple may vary based on your experience, I recommend sticking to simple coding techniques throughout your programming career. The maintenance programmer who will follow in your footsteps must be able to understand your code and is bound to have less experience than you in the language. Using complex techniques will make your code harder to read.

The sample programs in this book use a common style for white space, indentation, and names, and are intended as starting points for writing your own programs.

Kenneth Pugh
Durham, NC
Compuserve 70125, 1142

1
Introduction

Programmers use C to write programs ranging from simple calculators to complex operating systems. This chapter introduces some key features of C by comparing a simple COBOL program to an equivalent C program.

HISTORY OF C

The C programming language has a long history. Its ancestor, Basic Combined Programming Language (BCPL), was developed by Martin Richards in 1967. Ken Thompson refined BCPL into a language called B. Dennis Ritchie produced an enhanced version of B called C in 1972. C was developed as a high-level language with close ties to assembly language. Many C commands could be represented with single machine instructions on the PDP-11, the first machine on which C was implemented. The C compiler was subsequently ported to other machines, notably the IBM 370 and the Honeywell 6000.

When personal computers were first developed, many of the early programs for them were written in assembly language and BASIC. However, C proved to be an excellent language for developing programs on personal computers. Because the speed of C approaches that of assembly language while its high-level constructs make developing maintainable code easy, the use of C has spread to such diverse machines as the Apple II and the Cray supercomputers.

The X3J11 committee of the American National Standards Institute was formed in 1983 to standardize C. The resulting standard was adopted in 1988, and practically every C compiler in use today complies with this standard.

COBOL AND C EXAMPLES

Throughout this book a number of comparisons are made between programs written in COBOL and equivalent programs written in C. Unless otherwise noted, these programs perform basically the same operations. To keep all of the programs functionally equivalent, the first few programs accept values from the console and display results on the console, although these forms of input and output are not the norm for COBOL programs. File input and output will be covered in its own chapter.

COBOL AND C COMPARISON

As procedural languages, COBOL and C have many similarities. Because they were developed for dissimilar purposes, however, they also have several important differences.

Both languages have numeric and character variables and require variable declarations. COBOL has both DISPLAY (external) and COMP (internal) formats, and permits computations with numeric variables expressed in either format. However, C has only the internal form for numeric variables. Numeric data in external form must be converted to internal format before being used in computations.

Both COBOL and C have the standard arithmetic and logical operators. In addition, C includes bitwise operators that can act on individual bits in an integer.

Standard flow control constructs are a part of both languages. The conditional execution (IF), looping (PERFORM WHILE) and selection (EVALUATE) features of COBOL are present in C with slightly different names and syntax. These are covered in the chapter on Control Flow.

The number of reserved words in C is less than one-tenth the number in COBOL. Both languages present a slight problem in that the presence or absence of certain punctuation—the period in COBOL, the semicolon in C—can significantly alter the meaning of a program.

The most significant difference between the languages is in the area of input and output. COBOL provides a variety of options (PICTUREs) for formatting variables. C does not provide input and output formatting operations as part of the language, but rather as functions that are part of a standard library. The formatting options in C are not as complete as those provided by COBOL.

The manner in which programs are organized in COBOL and in C differs significantly. COBOL programs tend to be more inclusive. Paragraphs and subprograms in COBOL perform operations that separate functions perform in C. All paragraphs in the PROCEDURE DIVISION share the variables in a COBOL program. In C, these variables tend not to be shared, but passed as parameters to called functions.

C programs may appear much more complex than COBOL programs, partly because of the terseness of C's syntax and also occasionally because of the variable names the programmer has chosen. In addition, expressions may be significantly more complicated in C than in COBOL. However, C can be written in a manner that is as readable as COBOL code.

The programs in Examples 1.1 and 1.2 give an overview of basic differences and similarities in syntax between COBOL and C by exploring a simple problem. Assume that employees at HiTech Corporation fall into one of three categories, designated 1, 2 and 3. Each category has a minimum and a maximum salary. Examples 1.1 and 1.2 check whether the salary for a particular person in a given category falls within the proper range.

Example 1.1. COBOL program to verify whether a given employee's salary falls within the proper range.

```
IDENTIFICATION DIVISION.
PROGRAM-ID.
    PROGRAM-1-1
```

```
ENVIRONMENT DIVISION.

DATA DIVISION.

WORKING-STORAGE SECTION.

    01 EMPLOYEE-SALARY PIC S9(8)V99.
    01 EMPLOYEE-CLASS PIC 9.

    01 EMPLOYEE-SALARY-COMP COMP-2.
    01 EMPLOYEE-CLASS-COMP COMP.

PROCEDURE DIVISION.

101-EMP-CLS.

    COMPUTE EMPLOYEE-CLASS = 1

    PERFORM UNTIL EMPLOYEE-CLASS EQUAL 0

        DISPLAY 'ENTER CLASS: '
        ACCEPT EMPLOYEE-CLASS WITH CONVERSION
        DISPLAY 'ENTER SALARY: '
        ACCEPT EMPLOYEE-SALARY WITH CONVERSION

        MOVE EMPLOYEE-SALARY TO EMPLOYEE-SALARY-COMP
        MOVE EMPLOYEE-CLASS TO EMPLOYEE-CLASS-COMP

        IF EMPLOYEE-CLASS-COMP EQUAL 1
            IF EMPLOYEE-SALARY-COMP < 10000.00 OR
               EMPLOYEE-SALARY-COMP > 100000.00
                DISPLAY 'SALARY OUT OF RANGE'
            END-IF
        END-IF

        IF EMPLOYEE-CLASS-COMP EQUAL 2
            IF EMPLOYEE-SALARY-COMP < 100000.00 OR
               EMPLOYEE-SALARY-COMP > 1000000.00
                DISPLAY 'SALARY OUT OF RANGE'
            END-IF
        END-IF
```

```
            IF EMPLOYEE-CLASS-COMP EQUALS 3
                IF EMPLOYEE-SALARY-COMP < 1000000.00 OR
                   EMPLOYEE-SALARY-COMP > 10000000.00
                    DISPLAY 'SALARY OUT OF RANGE'
                END-IF
            END-IF
    END-PERFORM.
102-PROGRAM-END.
    EXIT PROGRAM.
```

In Example 1.1, the two MOVE commands that transform DISPLAY (or ASCII) values to COMP and COMP-2 values are not necessary because in COBOL the computation the program requires could take place in DISPLAY form. The program was coded in this way to reinforce the fact that COBOL variables may have both an external (DISPLAY) form and an internal (COMP) form. This differentiation in forms is more apparent in C.

Example 1.2. C program to verify whether a given employee's salary falls within the proper range.

```
#include <stdio.h>
#include <stdlib.h>
void main()
    {
    /* Declarations */

    double employee_salary_comp;
    int employee_class_comp;

    /* Executable */

    employee_class_comp = 1;

    while (employee_class_comp != 0)
        {
        printf("Enter class: ");
        scanf("%d", &employee_class_comp);
        printf("Enter salary: ");
        scanf("%lf", &employee_salary_comp);
```

```
        if (employee_class_comp == 1)
           {
           if (employee_salary_comp < 10000.00 ||
                 employee_salary_comp > 100000.00)
              {
              printf("salary out of range\n");
              }
           }

        if (employee_class_comp == 2)
           {
           if (employee_salary_comp < 100000.00 ||
                 employee_salary_comp > 1000000.00)
              {
              printf("salary out of range\n");
              }
            }

        if (employee_class_comp == 3)
           {
           if (employee_salary_comp < 1000000.00 ||
                 employee_salary_comp > 10000000.00)
              {
              printf("salary out of range\n");
              }
           }
        }
   exit(0);
   }
```

The C program appears shorter than its COBOL equivalent. No IDENTIFICATION or ENVIRONMENT DIVISIONS are needed. Symbols are used in place of words. The == operator replaces EQUAL. Braces ({ and }) group statements to be executed in a **while** loop or an **if** condition.

Another prominent difference is that the C version has only computational variables, defined in the declarations following the initial brace. The **printf** function converts from internal (COMP) format to ASCII (DISPLAY) format, while the **scanf** function converts in the reverse direction. As in COBOL, all variables in C programs must be declared. Variable names in C are lower case, following the standard C convention.

The remainder of the C program consists of statements that have direct counterparts in the COBOL program's PROCEDURE DIVISION, except for slight syntactical differences.

Let us look at each portion of Example 1.2 in detail. The first two lines are **#include** statements. These tell the compiler to read the file named between brackets, **<stdio.h>**, and **<stdlib.h>** and include its contents in this file; it is similar to COPY BOOK in COBOL. The information in **stdio.h** is used by the **scanf** and **printf** functions later in the program, and **stdlib.h** is used by the **exit** function. Even if the **#include** statements were omitted, most compilers would accept the remaining code. However, certain compilers may provide warnings such as "prototype for scanf not found" and "prototype for printf not found."

The line **void main()** is the first source line executed when the C program is run, and is equivalent to the COBOL PROCEDURE DIVISION's first line. Opening and closing braces begin and end the body of **main**, which is equivalent to the content of COBOL's DATA DIVISION and PROCEDURE DIVISION. In **main**, declarations come first, followed by executable statements. The first executable statement ends the declarations. The lines /* **Declarations** */ and /* **Executable** */ are comments included to help you understand the program and are ignored by the compiler.

Just as in COBOL, all variables in C programs must be declared. The **double** variable in C is the same as COBOL's COMP-2 (double precision floating point), and **int** is the same as COMP (binary integer).

The assignment **employee_class_comp = 1** works like the COMPUTE statement. The value of the expression on the right-hand side is put into the variable on the left-hand side.

The **while** statement in C works like PERFORM UNTIL in COBOL with the test condition inverted. The body of code enclosed by braces will be performed while the test is true. While **employee_class_comp** is not equal to 0, the loop will repeat.

Like the DISPLAY statement in COBOL, the **printf** function in C displays the string enclosed by double quotes on the console.

The new-line character **\n** causes the next character to be output in the first column of the following line on the terminal.

The **scanf** function inputs characters from the terminal, converting them to internal format according to the format string enclosed in quotes. Use the format string %**d** to input **int** variables and %**lf** to input **double** variables. The symbol **&** provides the address of a variable, and is needed on variables passed to **scanf**. These functions are discussed in more detail in the Input and Output chapter.

The **if** statement in C works like the COBOL IF. In Example 1.2, braces enclose blocks of code in a manner similar to the way in which IF and END-IF group statements in COBOL. Since each block of code is only a single statement, the braces in Example 1.2 are not required, but are included to match the END-IF groupings in Example 1.1. The symbol || in C stands for OR.

Note that both the **while** and the **if** statements use braces around the statements they control. You may use a closing brace as either an END-IF or an END-PERFORM. The C compiler matches each closing brace in a program with an opening brace, proceeding in inverse order. In Example 1.2, the braces enclosing the **if** statements match up, so the next to the last closing brace matches the opening brace of the **while** statement, and the last brace matches the one immediately after **main()**.

The **exit** function returns a value to the operating system, similar to the RETURN-CODE in COBOL.

An example of the program in execution follows. The user types the characters in italics in response to each prompt.

```
Enter class: 1
Enter salary: 34543.
Enter class: 2
Enter salary: 34.
salary out of range
Enter class: 0
```

To compile Example 1.2, enter the statements into a source with your editor and then follow your compiler's instructions or refer to those in Appendix C. If your program compiles and links without any errors, but does not run as shown above or produces the wrong answer, check your source file carefully against the listing above.

MISTAKES AND ERRORS

You can learn a good deal by making mistakes. When you have run Example 1.2 successfully, try experimenting with it in different ways. For example, when the program asks for a number, type some garbage input such as "XYZ". The program may either respond that your salary is out of range or go into an endless loop. The input routine **scanf** was told to expect an integer number and a floating point number. As **scanf** read your keystrokes and found nothing that it could interpret to be a number, it assigned no value either to **employee_salary_comp** or to **employee_class_comp**.

If no value is assigned to a variable, then the variable retains its previous value. If no value was ever assigned to the variable, its value is whatever happened to be in its memory location when the program started. This is usually an unknown or garbage value that causes the program to produce incorrect output. In the case of Example 1.2, the value of **employee_class_comp** would be 1, the value assigned to it originally.

Certain errors you make may not cause the compiler to give an error message. Instead, the program may either give incorrect answers or hang up and freeze. In this case, the only way to continue is to restart the entire computer system. To see the results of a common error beginning C programmers make, you may wish to make a copy of your source file and try compiling it after deleting the **&** before **employee_class_comp** or **employee_salary_comp** in the call to **scanf**. The chapter on input and output explains the reasons for the results produced by this error.

SUMMARY

- A C program consists of at least one module named **main**, comprised of declarations and executable statements. The first executable statement in **main** marks the end of the declarations.
- A C program may compile but not run, or it may run but contain errors not detected by the compiler.
- C program flow can parallel that of a COBOL program.
- C does not provide for DISPLAY format numeric variables.

2
Data Types, Variables and Operators

The data types in C correspond to COMPUTATIONAL or internal variable types in COBOL. The operations that C can perform on variables include the usual arithmetic operations. Both COBOL and C programs are made up of sequences of statements. However, the requirements for source column alignment of these statements are much more relaxed in C than in ANSI COBOL.

DATA TYPES

COBOL has DISPLAY or external variables using PICTURES composed with X and 9. These variables are defined in terms of ASCII (or EBCDIC) characters (bytes). COBOL also uses COMPUTATIONAL or internal variables to represent numbers, and these variables have equivalents in C. For example, COMP and COMP-2 in COBOL are equivalent to **int** and **double** in C.

An **int** may contain only whole numbers, usually from −32767 to +32767.* The **double** holds noninteger numbers ranging in absolute value between 10^{-38} and 10^{38} with at least ten decimal digits of significance. As noted in Chapter 1, you must use functions in C

---

*This range is for two byte **ints**. The ranges given for each data type are the minimum ranges set forth in the ANSI C standard. Some computers and compilers have larger ranges. Check your compiler's manual for its particular limits.

to convert from internal to external format in order to display the value of an arithmetic variable. The **printf** output function is one of the functions that convert internal format to external. Conversely, the **scanf** input function and others perform the conversion from external to internal format.

Another C data type, **char**, works in much the same manner as a COBOL variable expressed by a PICTURE X statement. However, in COBOL, strings work like variables with multiple Xs in the PICTURE, while, in C, strings are not simple variables but rather arrays of **char** variables, which are explained in the chapter on Arrays.

While **char** variables in C usually contain characters, they may also be treated as integers stored in a single byte. You can do arithmetic with **char** variables, but not the decimal arithmetic that COBOL uses. Instead, C performs binary arithmetic on **char** variables using the internal value of the character assigned by the American Standard for Information Interchange (ASCII) or the Extended Binary Corded Decimal Interchange Code (EBCDIC).

Declaration

All variables in C must be declared, just as in COBOL. To declare a variable, the variable name is preceded by the type of data it represents.

data-type variable-name;

Consider the following COBOL declarations:

```
01  MONTH  PIC 99 COMPUTATIONAL.
01  DAY    PIC 99 COMPUTATIONAL.
01  YEAR   PIC 99 COMPUTATIONAL.

01  SALARY COMPUTATIONAL-2 .
01  A-FLAG PIC X.
```

Compare these with their corresponding C declarations:

```
int month;
int day;
int year;
```

```
double salary;
char a_flag;
```

You may declare multiple variables of the same type in the same statement by separating the variable names with commas, using the format

```
data-type variable-name, variable-name;
```

The preceding **int** variables could be declared in a single statement as:

```
int month, day, year;
```

Names

Certain names, called *reserved words* because the language reserves the right to use them, may not be used as variable names. Table 2.1 provides a list of words reserved in C. Note that this list is much shorter than the 400 or so reserved words in COBOL.

Variable names can be any combination of letters (upper or lower case), digits, and underscores, but they must begin with either a letter or an underscore. The ANSI standard suggests that names beginning with an underscore may become reserved words in the future, so you should limit yourself to beginning names with a letter only. Conventionally, names of variables are in lower case characters. Avoid using hyphenated variable names of the sort used in COBOL as these are not legal in C. Use the underscore instead of the hyphen.

Names must be unique within their first 31 characters. The compiler accepts names longer than 31 characters, but the extra characters will be ignored. Names that are spelled the same way but have letters in different cases are treated as two different names. For example, the expressions

```
int month;
int Month;
```

declare two different variables. If you refer in your program to a third form of the name (e.g., **MONTH**), the compiler would report the variable as undeclared or undefined. The two declarations:

Table 2.1. List of key words in C.

Key words	Usage
auto	storage type
break	control flow (in **for, while, do-while, switch**)
case	control flow (in **switch**)
char	data type
const	data type modifier
continue	control flow (in **for, while, do-while**)
default	control flow (in **switch**)
do	control flow
double	data type
else	control flow (with **if**)
enum	data type
extern	storage type
float	data type
for	control flow
goto	control flow
if	control flow
int	data type
long	data type modifier
register	storage type
return	control flow (in function)
short	data type modifier
signed	data type modifier
sizeof	built-in operator
static	storage type
struct	aggregate data type
switch	control flow
typedef	data type declarator
union	aggregate data type
unsigned	data type modifier
void	data type
volatile	data type modifier
while	control flow

DATA TYPES, VARIABLES AND OPERATORS **15**

```
int a_very_long_variable_name_greater_than_32_characters;

double a_very_long_variable_name_greater_than_32_characters_a;
```

would produce a message that you had redeclared the variable **a_very_long_variable_name_greate**.

You may be tempted to type everything in upper case, as in:

```
INT INTEGER_VALUE = 1;
```

but while **int** is a reserved word, INT is not. Thus the preceding expression is not a declaration. To declare the variable write:

```
int INTEGER_VALUE = 1;
```

Note that **INTEGER_VALUE** is a different variable from **integer_value**.

CONSTANTS

A constant is an unchanging value used in an expression. An **int** constant is a number without a decimal point. A **double** constant is a number with a decimal point. A **char** constant is an alphanumeric character enclosed in single quotes. For example:

```
32     int constant
32.2   double constant
'A'    char constant (ASCII value 65)
```

To represent characters that are not printable, C uses an escape sequence consisting of an escape character, the backslash ('\'), followed by a second character. The most common escape sequence is '**\n**', the new-line character.

String constants are enclosed in double quotes and are not the same as **char** constants. Strings will be discussed in the chapter on arrays. For now, simply bear in mind that the character constant **'A'** is not equivalent to the string constant **"A"**.

INITIALIZATION

You can initialize a variable in a C declaration using a procedure similar to the VALUE portion of a COBOL declaration. If you choose not to initialize a variable, its value may be either 0 or garbage, depending on the variable's storage class (see the chapter on functions). To initialize a variable, add an equal sign and the appropriate value after the variable name.

data-type variable-name = value;

Examples

```
COBOL:    01  MONTH  PIC 99 COMP VALUE 3.
          01  SALARY COMP-2 VALUE 99.5.

C:        int month = 3;
          double salary = 99.5;
```

EXPRESSIONS

An expression in C is any combination of variables, constants, and function calls connected by operators. Expressions may look like the values to the right of a COBOL COMPUTE statement, or they may be much more complicated. Examples of expressions are:

```
COBOL:    MONTH
          MONTH + 1
          YEAR - 3

C:        month
          month + 1
          year - 3
```

The value of an expression can be assigned to a variable, passed to a function, or used to build a more complex expression.

OPERATORS

C provides the operators found in COBOL and has several others not shared by COBOL.

Arithmetic Operators

The arithmetic operators, add, subtract, multiply, and divide, work in C just as they do in COBOL. While C has no exponentation operator, it does provide an integer modulus operator (%) that yields the remainder when one number is divided by another. There are also unary plus and unary minus operators (**+** and **−**) that allow you to code, for example, **+month** or **−month**. The basic arithmetic operators in C appear in Table 2.2.

Table 2.2. Arithmetic operators in C.

Expression	Yields
month	value of **month**
month + 1	value of **month** plus 1
year − 3	value of **year** minus 3
salary * 1.05	value of **salary** times 1.05
salary / .95	value of **salary** divided by .95
7 % 3	1

The Assignment Operator

The assignment operator in C works like the COBOL COMPUTE statement, taking the value of the expression to the right of the equal sign and putting it into the variable to the left.

```
COBOL    COMPUTE MONTH = MONTH + 1
         COMPUTE YEAR = YEAR - 3

C        month = month + 1
         year = year - 3
```

Unlike the COBOL COMPUTE, the result of an assignment operator in C has a value of its own, the value that has been assigned, which may be used in an expression (see Table 2.3). Although this property is useful, it can cause the novice C programmer to make many errors. Throughout most of this book, the assignment operator appears by itself. To make it a statement equivalent to the COMPUTE statement, add a semicolon.

Table 2.3. Sample expressions using the assignment operator.

Expression	Operation	Value of Expression
month = 3	value of 3 put in **month**	3
month = 3 + 2	value of 5 put in **month**	5
month = (year = 3)	value of 3 put in **year**	3
	value of 3 put in **month**	
month = (year = 3) + 2	value of 3 put in **year**	5
	value of 5 put in **month**	

The expression to the right of the assignment operator may need to be converted to the same data type as the variable to the left. If the value does not fit, then the excess is not transferred, but no execution error occurs. Table 2.4 summarizes the results that may occur when such conversions of data types take place.

Table 2.4. Results of conversions of data types in expressions with the assignment operator.

Left-hand side	Right-hand Expression	Conversion
double	**int**	Value converted to **double**
int	**double**	Truncates fractional part
		If number too big, result undetermined
char	**int**	High-order bits eliminated

Shorthand Assignment Operator

C offers several assignment operators that work like ADD, SUBTRACT, MULTIPLY, and DIVIDE. The variable to the left of the operator is added to, subtracted from, multiplied by, or divided by the expression to its right. These shorthand operators include +=, −=, *=, /=, and %=. Like the assignment operator, they also have a value that may be used in an expression:

```
COBOL    ADD 3 TO MONTH
         MULTIPLY DAY BY 2
```

```
C          month += 3
           day *= 2
```

Increment and Decrement Operators.

For incrementing and decrementing a variable by 1, C provides the prefix and suffix operators, which function like the add and subtract shorthand assignment operators with an implicit value of 1 on the right-hand side.

```
COBOL      ADD 1 TO MONTH
           SUBTRACT 1 FROM DAY

C          month++    /* or */ ++month
           day--      /* or */ --day
```

There is a significant difference between the prefix and the suffix versions of these operators. The prefix operator acts *before* the value is used in an expression, whereas the suffix operator acts *after* the value is used in an expression. Table 2.5 shows the results the two alternatives produce. If you always use these operators in expressions by themselves. This usage is a strongly recommended guideline.

Table 2.5. Results using prefix and suffix increment and decrement operators.

Original Value of day	Expression	Value of day Used in Evaluation	Value of Expression	After Evaluation Value of day
5	**10 + day++**	5	15	6
5	**10 + day--**	5	15	4
5	**10 + ++day**	6	16	6
5	**10 + --day**	4	14	4

Type Conversions

When operands of different types appear in expressions with a binary operator such as + or *, certain automatic conversions are

20 C FOR COBOL PROGRAMMERS

invoked that change the operands from one type to another. These conversions ensure that the processor is able to perform the indicated operation. If a **char** type is used in an expression, it is converted to an **int** type. If an **int** type appears on one side of an operator and a **double** appears on the other, then the **int** is converted to a **double**. If you had the variables:

```
int month;
double salary;
char character;
```

then the following automatic conversions would occur:

Expression	Result
character + 1	value of character converted to int; result is int.
month * salary	value of month converted to double; result is double.

Precedence of Operators

Just as in COBOL, operators in C expressions have an order of precedence. In expressions without parentheses, certain operations are performed before others. When two or more operators of

Table 2.6. Precedence of Operators

Operator		Associativity
++	increment	right to left
--	decrement	
-	unary minus	
+	unary plus	
*	multiplication	left to right
/	division	
%	modulus	
+	addition	left to right
-	subtraction	
=	assignment	right to left
op=	shorthand assignment	

equal precedence occur in an expression, the associativity is left to right, except as shown in Table 2.6. You can use parentheses to alter the evaluation of the expression.

STATEMENTS

A statement is an expression followed by a semicolon. Compare, for example:

```
Expression                  Statement

2 * 4 + 7                   2 * 4 + 7;
month = 7                   month = 7;
next_month = month + 1      next_month = month + 1;
```

Statements are executed in sequence, unless they are subject to control flow (**if**, **while**, etc.).

Compound Statement

A compound statement is one or more statements surrounded by braces.

```
{
statements
}
```

A compound statement may be used anywhere a single statement appears. Typically, a compound statement is used as the body of a loop (**while** or **for**), or as a set of statements controlled by an **if**.

The statements in a compound statement in C work like the COBOL statements between an IF and an END-IF or a PERFORM and an END- PERFORM (see COBOL Example 1.1 and C Example 1.2).

Null Statement

A null statement is simply a semi-colon by itself, used as a placeholder.

```
;
```

COMMENTS AND WHITE SPACE

Comments are treated as white space by the compiler. The compiler ignores comments when it translates the program. Just as in COBOL, comments in C are used simply as explanations to human readers. Unlike COBOL comments, C comments may appear on lines that contain executable code. Comments start with a slash–asterisk (/*) and end with an asterisk–slash (*/). Although comments do not nest, some compilers permit them to do so.

```
/* anything */
```

White space consists of characters that are mostly ignored by the compiler. These characters include the space, tab (horizontal and vertical), form feed, and new-line characters, and comments. Because the compiler tends to ignore these characters, C is a more free-form language than COBOL, which has strict alignment requirements.*

In C, you could write the statement

```
next_month = month + 1;
```

as:

```
next_month
  =
  month
  +
  1
  ;
```

You should try to keep a standard convention, such as one line to a statement, or your programs may become unreadable. However, blank lines can separate portions of code, even if comments are not appropriate.

---

*As defined by ANSI, COBOL Standard alignment requirements include:
    SEQUENCE NUMBER, Columns 1–6, Line number
    INDICATOR AREA, Column 7, Continuation or comment
    AREA A, Column 8, Divisions, sections, paragraphs (A margin)
    AREA B, Column 12, COBOL text (statements) (B margin)

DATA TYPES, VARIABLES AND OPERATORS   23

Key words, names, and constants must be separated from one another by white space. For example:

```
double salary;   cannot be written as doublesalary;
int day;         cannot be written as intday;
```

PRINTF AND SCANF

The functions **printf** and **scanf** are covered in detail in the chapter on Input and Output and Appendix B. The following brief description of these functions is given to enable you to input and output values of variables in your programs. The forms for calling these functions are:

```
printf("format-string",0-or-more-values....);

scanf("format-string",address-of-a-variable);
```

The **printf** function simply prints the characters in the *format-string* unless the string consists of or includes one of these specifiers:

Specifier	Data type
%lf	double
%d	int
%c	char

When one of these specifiers is present in the string, **printf** outputs the corresponding value in the list. The data type of that value should agree with the data type you specify in the format string. The character \n in the format string forces a new line on the terminal. For example, given the declarations

```
int month = 5;
int day = 8;
double salary = 13.;
char character = 'A';
```

the following calls produce the output shown.

24 C FOR COBOL PROGRAMMERS

Call	Output
printf(" Welcome to C");	Welcome to C
printf("\n Welcome\n to C");	Welcome
	to C
printf("\n Month is %d", month);	Month is 5
printf("\n Month is %d Day is %d", month, day);	Month is 5 Day is 8
printf("\n C is %c", character);	C is A
printf("\n Salary is %lf", salary);	Salary is 13.000000

When you use **scanf**, the format string must contain one of the specifiers. The data type of the variable corresponding to the address given should agree with that of the specifier. The address operator **&**, explained in detail in the chapter on pointers, must appear on all simple variables in **scanf** calls. If you were working with the preceding declarations, then **scanf** would act as follows:

Call	Notes
scanf("%d", &day);	Input int value to day
scanf("%c",&character);	Input char value to character
scanf("%lf",&salary);	Input double value to salary

Whenever you use **printf** or **scanf** in a file, you should include this line at the beginning of the file:

```
#include <stdio.h>
```

This statement tells the compiler to read a file named **stdio.h** and place its contents in your file before compiling it. Although your current compiler may not require this statement, it is good practice to use it. The chapter on the preprocessor covers the **#include** command in more detail.

Be sure to check all **scanf** calls for the address operator on simple variables. Omitting it may cause your program to malfunction.

#DEFINE

C uses the **#define** command to assign a name to a constant value using the form

```
#define LABEL value
```

The label may be in upper, lower, or mixed case. Wherever the label appears in your program, C will substitute the value given for it. For example, if you code

```
#define FEBRUARY 2
```

and then write

```
month = FEBRUARY;
```

C will interpret this statement as if you had written

```
month = 2;
```

Using **#define** for names of constants makes your program more readable and maintainable. By convention, the label portion of a **#define** command is in upper case characters. The chapter on the preprocessor deals with the many other uses of **#define**.

Do not use a variable name as the label in a **#define** command because the value of the label will be used wherever the variable occurs. For example,

```
#define months 12
int months;
```

will produce a compiler error because the compiler will interpret **int months;** as

```
int 12;
```

SAMPLE PROGRAMS

The two programs presented below demonstrate some of the basic operations described in this chapter. Try inputting, compiling, and running them.

Example 2.1

```
#define OFFSET 32.           /* Zero degree offset */
#define SCALE (5./9.)        /* scale factor for degrees */

#include <stdio.h>
#include <stdlib.h>

void main()
/* Converts Fahrenheit to Celsius */
{
    double celsius;          /* Temperature in Celsius */
    double fahrenheit;       /* Temperature in Fahrenheit */

    /* Input a temperature */
    printf("\n Input a temperature in Fahrenheit: ");
    scanf("%lf", &fahrenheit);

    /* Convert it */
    celsius = (fahrenheit - OFFSET) * SCALE;
    printf("\n Temperature in Celsius is %lf", celsius);

    exit(0);
}
```

Example 2.2

```
#include <stdio.h>
#include <stdlib.h>

void main()                    /* Nicomachus's game */
{
    int remainder_3;           /* Remainder of division by 3 */
    int remainder_5;           /* Remainder of division by 5 */
    int remainder_7;           /* Remainder of division by 7 */
    int answer;                /* Answer */

    printf("\n Think of a number between 1 and 100");
    printf("\n What is the remainder when your number is divided by 3? ");
    scanf("%d", &remainder_3);
    printf("\n What is remainder when divided by 5? ");
    scanf("%d", &remainder_5);
    printf("\n What is remainder when divided by 7? ");
    scanf("%d", &remainder_7);

    answer = 70 * remainder_3 + 21 * remainder_5 + 15 * remainder_7;
    answer = answer % 105;
    printf("\n Your number was %d", answer);
    printf("\n If you don't agree, check your arithmetic");

    exit(0);
}
```

Example 2.1 converts a temperature in Fahrenheit to its equivalent in Celsius. Note that the constant **SCALE** is specified as a division and is actually computed by the compiler. Using this procedure is much clearer than using .55555555555555. Example 2.1 follows an arrangement similar to that of Example 1.1.

Example 2.2 is adapted from *101 BASIC Computer Games* by Digital Equipment Corporation (1975). It is based on a formula in *Arithmetica,* by Nicomachus, who died in 120 A.D. You are to think of a number between 1 and 100 and divide it by 3, 5, and 7. The program asks for the remainders and places them in **remainder_3**, **remainder_5**, and **remainder_7**. It then computes and prints out **answer**, using the formula which was created by Nicomachus.

SUMMARY

- Three data types for variables and constants are integer (**int**), floating point (**double**), and character (**char**).
- All variables must be declared before they are used. They may also be initialized in the declaration.
- C has the standard arithmetic operators +, −, *, and /.
- Assignment operators assign the value of an expression to a variable.
- The increment (++) and decrement (−−) operators change the value of a variable by one.
- Expressions are combinations of operators, constants, variables, and function calls.
- Precedence and associativity rules determine how an expression is interpreted.
- A statement is an expression followed by a semi-colon.
- A compound statement is enclosed by braces.
- A C program is free-form. The compiler ignores white space and comments enclosed within /* and */.
- The **printf** output function converts numeric variables from internal to external format.
- The **scanf** input function converts numeric variables from external to internal format.
- The **#define** command is a symbolic substitute for constants.

3
Control Flow

Like COBOL, C provides statements that control the flow of execution either by selecting alternative statements to execute (**if** and **switch**) or by repeating a series of statements (**while**, **do-while**, and **for**).

IF STATEMENT

The **if** statement works like the IF in COBOL and has the form

```
if (test-expression)
      statement
```

If the *test-expression* is true, the *statement* will be executed; otherwise it will be skipped. The test is usually a comparison of two values, using the relational and equality operators. C syntax requires the parentheses around the test expression. Compare the following examples:

```
COBOL
   IF MONTH EQUALS 1
       COMPUTE NUMBER-DAYS = 31.
```

C
```
   if (month == 1)
      number_days = 31;
```

If you want the **if** statement to do two statements, then you need to use a compound statement. The compound statement works like the END-IF statement following an IF statement in COBOL.

COBOL
```
   IF MONTH EQUALS 2
      COMPUTE NUMBER-DAYS = 28
      DISPLAY "THIS IS A SHORT MONTH"
   END-IF
```

C
```
   if (month == 2)
     {
     number_days = 28;
     printf("\n This is a short month");
     }
```

TEST EXPRESSION

The test expression of an **if** statement—or any other control statement—tests for the true or false value of an expression. In C, false has a numeric value of zero. Any non-zero value is considered to be true. The relational operators and the logical operators provide numeric results of zero for false and one for true.

RELATIONAL AND EQUALITY OPERATORS

C has the same relational and equality operators that COBOL has. Table 3.1 shows the symbolic equivalents for these relational and equality operators.

The following examples demonstrate how these operators work in C and in COBOL. Given the declarations

COBOL
```
   01  MONTH  PIC '99'  COMP.
   01  DAY    PIC '99'  COMP.
   01  YEAR   PIC '99'  COMP.
```

Table 3.1. Relational Operators

COBOL	C
GREATER THAN >	>
NOT GREATER THAN NOT >	<=
LESS THAN <	<
NOT LESS THAN NOT <	>=
EQUAL TO =	==
NOT =	!=

```
C
    int month;
    int day;
    int year;
```

the following expressions perform the same tests:

```
COBOL                            C

MONTH LESS THAN 1                month < 1
DAY GREATER THAN 31              day > 31
YEAR NOT LESS THAN 80            year >= 80
```

Unlike COBOL, C interprets the result of a relational operator as an arithmetic value that may be used in an expression. If the result is true, the value is 1. If the result is false, the value is 0. For example,

```
(month < 1) * 10
```

has the arithmetic value 0 or 10, depending on the result of the comparison. Use of this feature is not generally recommended.

Both COBOL and C have the same two binary logical operators: AND (&&) and OR (||). The result of a logical operator is a true or false value which is a numeric value of one or zero, respectively. The logical operators test whether the values to their left and to their right are false (zero) or true (nonzero). Table 3.2 gives the results of the operations.

Table 3.2. AND and OR operators.

&& (AND) Left side	Right side	Result
0	0	false 0
0	non-zero	false 0
non-zero	0	false 0
non-zero	non-zero	true 1

|| (OR) Left side	Right side	Result
0	0	false 0
0	non-zero	true 1
non-zero	0	true 1
non-zero	non-zero	true 1

Given the declarations in the preceding example statements, the following tests are equivalent:

```
COBOL:    IF MONTH LESS THAN 1 OR MONTH GREATER THAN 12
          IF DAY NOT LESS THAN 0 AND DAY NOT GREATER THAN 31

C:        if (month < 1 || month > 12)
          if (day >= 0 && day <= 31)
```

In C, you cannot code with shortened tests such as the COBOL expression

```
MONTH LESS THAN 1 OR GREATER THAN 12
```

If you are tempted to use the equivalent of this COBOL expression in C,

```
month < 1 || > 12   /* COMPILER ERROR */
```

the result will be an error message because the syntax is not legal.

The unary NOT operator, !, logically negates the expression that follows. That is, it reverses the logical sense of the value following it.

```
! (NOT)
```

Expression   *Value*

```
! month > 12                    same as month <= 12

!0                              true 1
!5                              false 0
```

The logical and relational operators fit into the precedence scheme shown in Table 3.3

Table 3.3.   Precedence of operators.

!	logical negation
−	unary minus
*	multiplication
/	division
%	modulus
+	addition
−	subtraction
<	less than
<=	less than or equal to
>	greater than
>=	greater than or equal to
==	equality
!=	inequality
&&	logical AND
||	logical OR
=	assignment

TEST EXPRESSION EXPLORED

Recall that the result of an assignment operator has a value. One of the most common mistakes programmers make in C is to use the assignment operator rather than the equality operator in a test expression. The first example shown in this chapter was

```
if (month == 1)
    number_days = 31;
```

If you coded

```
if (month = 1)
    number_days = 31;
```

then **month** would be set to the value 1. The test would always be true, and **number_days** would always be set to 31.

Sometimes you can take advantage of the fact that the test expression in an **if** statement actually tests for a zero or a non-zero value by using a variable to hold only a true or false value. For example, suppose you code

```
#define TRUE 1
#define FALSE 0
int done_flag = FALSE;
```

Then you may use

```
if (done_flag)
```

instead of

```
if (done_flag == TRUE)
```

This is common practice when dealing with variables that contain only true and false values, that is, with *boolean variables* or *flags*. On the other hand, the fact that the condition is simply a numeric value explains why some programs do not work, as shown in the example assignment at the beginning of this section.

The testing of **done_flag** corresponds roughly to the COBOL statements

CONTROL FLOW **35**

```
01 DONE-FLAG PIC X VALUE 'F'.
   88 DONE-TRUE VALUE 'T'.
   88 DONE-FALSE VALUE 'F'.
...
IF DONE-TRUE
   ...
```

IF-ELSE AND COMPOUND IF

Another form of the **if** statement, **if-else**, works like the COBOL IF-ELSE and uses the syntax

```
if (condition)
        statement-if-true
else
        statement-if-false
```

Figure 3.1 illustrates the flow of this syntax. Compare the following examples of **if-else** statements.

```
COBOL:
        IF MONTH EQUALS 2
            COMPUTE SHORT-MONTH = 1
        ELSE
            COMPUTE SHORT-MONTH = 0
        END-IF
```

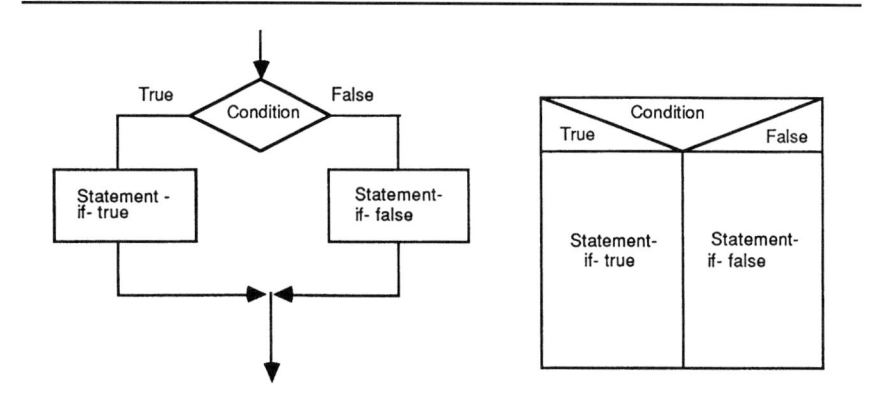

Figure 3.1.   Flow control of the **if-else** statement.

36   C FOR COBOL PROGRAMMERS

C:
```
    if (month == 2)
            short_month = 1;
    else
            short_month = 0;
```

Just as in COBOL, **if** statements in C can be nested. The following examples of nesting in both languages compute the number of days in each month.

COBOL:

```
IF MONTH EQUALS 2
   IF LEAP-YEAR EQUALS 0
       COMPUTE LAST-DAY = 29
   ELSE
       COMPUTE LAST-DAY = 28
   END-IF
ELSE
   IF MONTH EQUALS 1 OR MONTH EQUALS 3 OR MONTH EQUALS
       5 OR MONTH EQUALS 7 OR MONTH EQUALS 8 OR MONTH
       EQUALS 10 OR MONTH EQUALS 12
       COMPUTE LAST-DAY = 31
   ELSE
       IF MONTH EQUALS 4 OR MONTH EQUALS 6 OR MONTH
           EQUALS 9 OR MONTH EQUALS 11
           COMPUTE LAST-DAY = 30
       ELSE
           COMPUTE LAST-DAY = 0
       END-IF
   END-IF
END-IF
```

C:

```
if (month == 2)
   {
   if (leap_year == 0)
       last_day = 29;
   else
       last_day = 28;
   }
```

```
else
   if (month == 1 || month == 3 || month == 5 ||
       month == 7 || month == 8 || month == 10 ||
       month == 12)
      last_day = 31;
   else
      {
      if (month == 4 || month == 6 || month == 9 ||
          month == 11)
         last_day = 30;
      else
         last_day = 0;
      }
 }
```

Although the braces are not needed in the second part of the C example, they help clarify its logical flow. Overbracing does not affect the execution speed of a program and often makes the program easier to understand.

If you do not use braces, the compiler assumes that an **else** clause pairs with the most recent unpaired **if**. This can cause logic problems, as you may already have found in COBOL. I strongly suggest using braces with nested **if** statements to avoid problems like the following:

```
if (year % 4 == 0)
        if (day > 29)
                valid = FALSE;
    else if (day > 28)
                valid = FALSE;
```

Remember that indentation is ignored by the compiler. The **else** is thus matched to the second **if**. The effect is the same as if the code were

```
if (year % 4 == 0)
       {
       if (day > 29)
                valid = FALSE;
       else if (day > 28)
                valid = FALSE;
       }
```

WHILE STATEMENT

The **while** statement repeats a statement as long as a given condition is true. Something inside the loop must cause the condition to become false or the loop will continue endlessly. The **break** statement may be used to exit a loop prematurely, before the condition becomes false. The syntax for **while** statements, illustrated in Figure 3.2, is

```
while (test-expression)
    statement
```

Although its name is quite different, the **while** statement in C works like the PERFORM UNTIL command in COBOL. The test-expression is checked before the statement in the body is executed. Note, however, that the *statement* is executed if the *test-expression* is true; conversely, the PERFORM is executed if the UNTIL test is false. If the test-expression is false the first time, the body of a **while** statement will not be executed at all.

The body of the loop of a **while** statement is typically a compound statement enclosed by braces. I suggest using braces even around a single statement for consistency.

COBOL:

```
    COMPUTE COUNT = 0.
    COMPUTE SUM = 0.
    PERFORM UNTIL COUNT IS NOT LESS THAN 12
        ADD COUNT TO SUM
    END-PERFORM
```

C:

```
    count = 0;
    sum = 0;
    while (count < 12)
        {
        sum += count;
        }
```

CONTROL FLOW   39

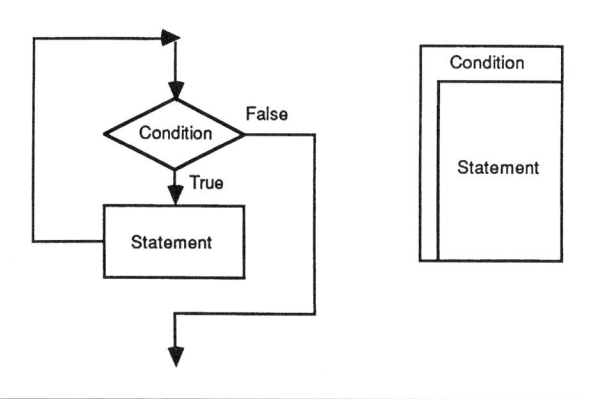

Figure 3.2.   Flow control of the **while** statement.

A common error that occurs when writing loop constructs is typing an extraneous semicolon. If the loop above were written as

```
count = 0;
sum = 0;
while (count < 12);
    {
    sum += count;
    }
```

the **while** loop will continue endlessly. The body of the loop in this case is the null statement, (;).

DO-WHILE STATEMENT

A **while** loop will never be executed if the test-expression is false the first time it is tested. In contrast, the **do-while** statement creates a loop that will be executed at least once before checking the test- expression. To create a COBOL equivalent to **do-while**, set the UNTIL test in a PERFORM so that it is false the initial time. Or use PERFORM UNTIL with the TEST AFTER option. The syntax for the **do-while** statement, depicted in Figure 3.3, is

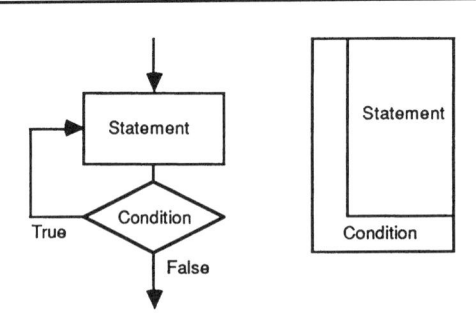

Figure 3.3. Flow control of **do-while** statements.

```
do
    statement
while (test-expression);
```

The semicolon after the test-expression is required. Equivalent COBOL and C codes appear in the following examples.

COBOL:

```
COMPUTE COUNT = 15.
COMPUTE SUM = 0.
PERFORM UNTIL COUNT IS NOT LESS THAN 12 WITH TEST AFTER
    ADD COUNT TO SUM
END-PERFORM
```

C:

```
count = 15;
sum = 0;
do
    {
    sum += count;
    }
    while (count < 12);
```

In both these examples, the value of **sum** is 15 and the value of **count** is not tested until after the loop is executed.

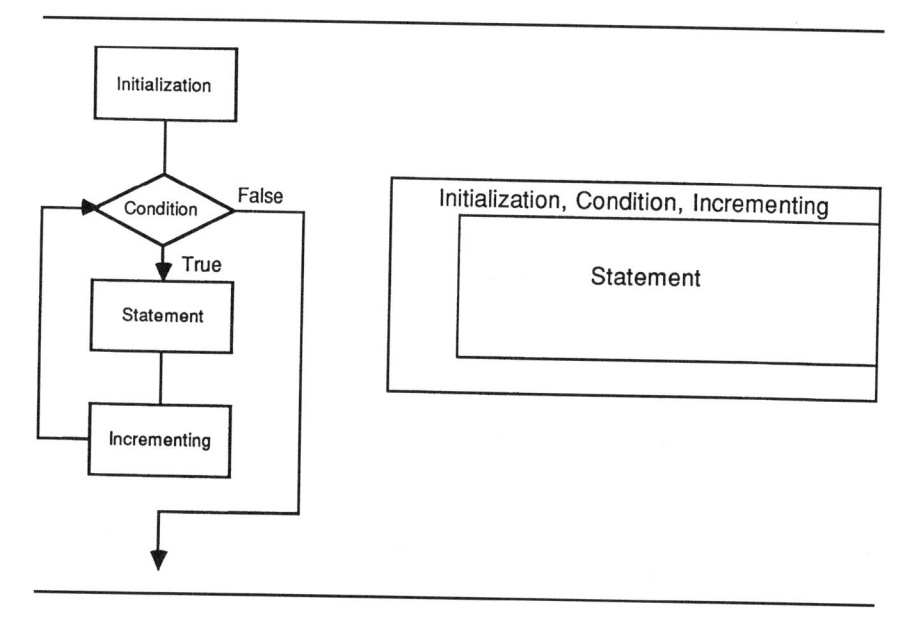

Figure 3.4. Control flow of the **for** statement.

FOR STATEMENT

The VARYING option of the PERFORM command is usually used for subscripting through tables. The **for** statement in C is typically used for indexing through arrays, which are C's equivalent of tables. Arrays will be covered in Chapter 5. The syntax of the **for** statement is

```
for ( initial-expression; test-expression; increment-expression)
    statement
```

Figure 3.4 shows how the control of the for statement operates. Equivalent codes in COBOL and C given below illustrate how the **for** statement works.

```
COBOL:

COMPUTE COUNT = 0.
PERFORM VARYING COUNT FROM 1 BY 1 UNTIL COUNT NOT LESS THAN 12
    ADD COUNT TO SUM
END-PERFORM
```

42 C FOR COBOL PROGRAMMERS

```
C:
   sum = 0;
   for (count = 1; count <= 12; count++)
       {
       sum += count;
       }
```

You may eliminate any of the expressions in the **for** control statement. For example, you may see

```
for (;;)
    {
    /* Body of loop */
    }
```

The preceding loop executes forever, since there is no ending test. It is the equivalent of the **while** loop

```
while (1)
    {
    /* Body of loop */
    }
```

Your must enter a break statement somewhere in these loops to exit them.

BREAK STATEMENT

You may terminate a loop before the test-expression is false by using a **break** statement. A **break** statement causes the statement following the loop to be executed. The **break** statement operates like a NEXT SENTENCE statement in COBOL. However, **break** statements must occur inside a loop, whereas NEXT SENTENCE statements may appear in a separate IF. For example, the following loop will terminate when **sum** is greater than 30.

```
sum = 0;
for (count = 1; count < 12; count++)
    {
```

```
    sum += count;
    if (sum > 30)
        break;
    }
```

You could achieve the same effect by adding the condition to the test-expression for the loop. Compare these examples in COBOL and C:

```
COBOL:
    COMPUTE COUNT = 0.
    PERFORM VARYING COUNT FROM 1 BY 1 UNTIL COUNT NOT
        LESS THAN 12 OR SUM GREATER THAN 30
        ADD COUNT TO SUM
    END-PERFORM

C:
    sum = 0;
    for (count = 1; count <= 12 && sum <= 30; count++)
        {
        sum += count;
        }
```

If the termination conditions for a loop are more complicated, it is sometimes easier to employ a **break** statement. Some programmers consider the **break** statement equivalent to a **goto**. However, because a **break** goes to a well-defined place—the next statement after the loop—it does not share many of the disadvantages of the **goto** statement.

SWITCH STATEMENT

If you are testing the value of an integer expression multiple times, as with a nested if, using the **switch** construct instead will make the code clearer. The **switch** statement works like COBOL's EVALUATE statement and uses the following syntax:

```
switch( integer-test-expression )
    {
```

```
case integer-constant:
   statements
   ....
default:
   statements
   }
```

The **switch** construct evaluates the *integer-test-expression* and compares the result to each constant value following the **case** key word. If there is a match, then the next statement executed is that following the label. An optional **default** label may be included in the **switch**. If the value tested does not match a **case** label, then the next statement executed is the one following the **default** label. The following equivalent codes in COBOL and C demonstrate the use of **switch**.

COBOL:

```
    EVALUATE MONTH
    WHERE 1 COMPUTE NUMBER-DAYS = 31
    WHERE 2 COMPUTE NUMBER-DAYS = 28
    WHERE 3 COMPUTE NUMBER-DAYS = 31
    WHERE 4 COMPUTE NUMBER-DAYS = 30
    WHERE 5 COMPUTE NUMBER-DAYS = 31
    WHERE 6 COMPUTE NUMBER-DAYS = 30
    WHERE 7 COMPUTE NUMBER-DAYS = 31
    WHERE 8 COMPUTE NUMBER-DAYS = 31
    WHERE 9 COMPUTE NUMBER-DAYS = 30
    WHERE 10 COMPUTE NUMBER-DAYS = 31
    WHERE 11 COMPUTE NUMBER-DAYS = 30
    WHERE 12 COMPUTE NUMBER-DAYS = 31
    WHERE OTHER COMPUTE NUMBER-DAYS = 0
    END-EVALUATE
```

C:

```
    switch(month)
        {
    case 1:
        number_days = 31;
        break;
    case 2:
        number_days = 28;
```

```
        break;
    case 3:
        number_days = 31;
        break;
    case 4:
        number_days = 30;
        break;
    case 5:
        number_days = 31;
        break;
    case 6:
        number_days = 30;
        break;
    case 7:
        number_days = 31;
        break;
    case 8:
        number_days = 31;
        break;
    case 9:
        number_days = 30;
        break;
    case 10:
        number_days = 31;
        break;
    case 11:
        number_days = 30;
        break;
    case 12:
        number_days = 31;
        break;
    default:
        number_days = 0;
    }
```

Note the additional break statements that end each **case**. If you do not include a **break** statement, the statements are simply executed in order. The **case** label does not separate out a sequence of statements to be executed, but rather shows where the first statement will be executed. The **switch** acts like a controlled **goto**, (similar to the old COBOL GOTO DEPENDING ON). Figure 3.5 shows the flow of this statement.

This concept may seem odd at first, but the underlying reason is that you may only specify a single constant using the case label. There is no way to specify multiple values. To shorten the preceding case statement, you may code it as:

```
switch(month)
    {
case 1:
case 3:
case 5:
case 7:
case 8:
case 10:
case 12:
    number_days = 31;
    break;
case 2:
    number_days = 28;
    break;
case 4:
case 6:
case 9:
case 11:
    number_days = 30;
    break;
default:
    number_days = 0;
    }
```

SAMPLE PROGRAMS

This section presents some example programs using the control flow statements. These programs reappear in several forms throughout this book to show you how to approach the same problem in different ways.

Date Check

Example 3.1 asks the user for a month, day, and year. It then checks to see if the date is valid. The program requires only two digits for the year, and assumes that users will input a year

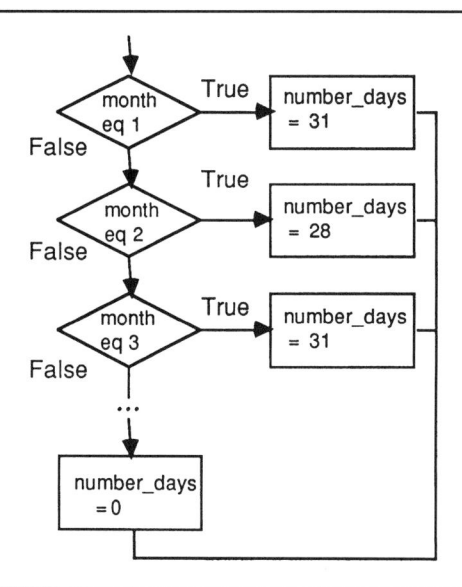

Figure 3.5. Switch statement example control flow.

between 1901 and 2000. As an exercise, modify Example 3.1 so that it works for dates beyond this range.

The program inputs the date into **month**, **day**, and **year**. It then checks whether **day** is less than 1. Next, the program performs multiple tests on **month** to determine the maximum number of days in the month specified. If **year** is evenly divisible by 4, the program can recognize that it is a leap year, and will test February for 29 rather than 28 days.

Note that you need not enclose in braces the statement belonging to each **else**. The code shown below without these braces would execute in exactly the same way.

```
else if ((month == JAN) || (month == MAR) ||
    (month == MAY) || (month == JUL) || (month == AUG)
    || (month == OCT) || (month == DEC))
        {
        /* Month is a 31 day month */
        if (day > 31)
                valid = FALSE;
        }
```

Example 3.1

```c
#include <stdio.h>
#include <stdlib.h>
#define TRUE 1
#define FALSE 0

/* Months of the year */
#define JAN 1
#define FEB 2
#define MAR 3
#define APR 4
#define MAY 5
#define JUN 6
#define JUL 7
#define AUG 8
#define SEP 9
#define OCT 10
#define NOV 11
#define DEC 12

void main()
/* This program inputs a date and checks for its validity */
    {
    int month;                  /* Month to check */
    int day;                    /* Day to check */
    int year;                   /* Year to check */
    int valid;                  /* Flag for valid date */

    /* Input the date */
    printf("\n This program checks for a valid date");
```

```c
    printf("\n Enter the month: ");
    scanf("%d", &month);
    printf("\n Enter the day: ");
    scanf("%d", &day);
    printf("\n Enter the year: ");
    scanf("%d", &year);

    /* Assume date is good until proven otherwise */
    valid = TRUE;

    /* Check the low end of the day value */
    if (day <= 0)
        valid = FALSE;

    /* Check for February */
    if (month == FEB)
    {
        /* Month is February, check on leap year */
        if (year % 4 == 0)
        {
            if (day > 29)
                valid = FALSE;
        }
        else if (day > 28)
            valid = FALSE;
    }
    else
    {
        if ((month == JAN) || (month == MAR) || (month == MAY) ||
            (month == JUL) || (month == AUG) || (month == OCT)
```

49

```c
        || (month == DEC))
    {
        /* Month is a 31 day month */
        if (day > 31)
            valid = FALSE;
    }
    else
    {
        if ((month == APR) || (month == JUN) || (month == SEP)
            || (month == NOV))
        {
            /* Month is a 30 day month */
            if (day > 30)
                valid = FALSE;
        }
        else
            /* Month was not one of the twelve */
            valid = FALSE;
    }

    /* Print the result */
    if (valid)
        printf("\n Day is valid");
    else
        printf("\n Day is invalid");
    exit(0);
}
```

CONTROL FLOW

```
else if ((month == APR) || (month == JUN) ||
    (month == SEP) || (month == NOV))
        {
        /* Month is a 30 day month */
        if (day > 30)
                valid = FALSE;
        }
else
        /* Month was not one of the twelve */
        valid = FALSE;
```

Example 3.2 program performs the same tasks as Example 3.1, but uses the **switch** statement.

Averaging Program

Example 3.3 is a useful program that sums a series of numbers and determines their average. The program inputs numbers until a zero value is entered, and then computes and outputs the average. The values of **sum** and **count** are set to 0, and **done**, the flag that controls the loop, is set to **TRUE**. The program repeatedly asks for a number from the user, and places the value in **number**. When **number** is 0.0, the value of **done** is set to **FALSE**, the loop terminates, and the average is computed.

A Guessing Program

This program asks the user in Example 3.4 to input values for minutes and seconds, and to guess and input a number within a range for the computer. The values for minutes and seconds are combined to get **answer**. The program loop compares the user's guess to **answer** and repeats until **done** is set **TRUE**, that is, until the user gives up by guessing a zero or negative number or the guess is correct.

Example 3.2

```
#include <stdio.h>
#include <stdlib.h>

#define TRUE  1
#define FALSE 0

#define JAN 1
#define FEB 2
#define MAR 3
#define APR 4
#define MAY 5
#define JUN 6
#define JUL 7
#define AUG 8
#define SEP 9
#define OCT 10
#define NOV 11
#define DEC 12

void main()
/* This program inputs a date and checks for its validity */
{
    int month;          /* Month to check */
    int day;            /* Day to check */
    int year;           /* Year to check */
    int valid;          /* Flag for valid date */
```

```
/* Input the date */
printf("\n This program checks for a valid date");
printf("\n Enter the month: ");
scanf("%d", &month);
printf("\n Enter the day: ");
scanf("%d", &day);
printf("\n Enter the year: ");
scanf("%d", &year);

/* Assume date is good until proven otherwise */
valid = TRUE;

/* Check the low end of the day value */
if (day <= 0)
        valid = FALSE;

switch(month)
    {
    case FEB:
            /* Month is February, check on leap year */
            if (year % 4 == 0)
                {
                if (day > 29)
                        valid = FALSE;
                }
            else if (day > 28)
                    valid = FALSE;
            break;
    case JAN:
    case MAR:
```

```
        case MAY:
        case JUL:
        case AUG:
        case OCT:
        case DEC:
                /* Month is a 31 day month */
                if (day > 31)
                        valid = FALSE;
                break;
        case APR:
        case JUN:
        case SEP:
        case NOV:
                /* Month is a 30 day month */
                if (day > 30)
                        valid = FALSE;
                break;
        default:
                /* Month was not one of the twelve */
                valid = FALSE;
        }

        /* Print the result */
        if (valid)
                printf("\n Day is valid");
        else
                printf("\n Day is invalid");

        exit(0);
}
```

Example 3.3

```
#include <stdio.h>
#include <stdlib.h>

#define TRUE 1
#define FALSE 0

void main()
/* This program averages the input values until a 0 is entered */
{
    int count;              /* How many numbers */
    double sum;             /* Running sum */
    double number;          /* Input number */
    double average;         /* Computed average */
    int done;               /* Loop termination flag */

    /* Initialize values */
    sum = 0.0;
    count = 0;
    done = FALSE;

    /* Get the input values */
    while (!done)
    {
        printf("\n Input a number to be averaged (0 to exit): ");
        scanf("%lf", &number);
        if (number == 0.0)
            done = TRUE;
```

```
    else
        {
        /* Add to sum and increment count */
        sum = sum + number;
        count = count + 1;
        }

/* Compute the average */
if (count > 0)
    average = sum / count;
else
    average = 0.0;

/* Output the results */
printf("\n Sum of %d numbers is %lf", count, sum);
printf("\n Average of these numbers is %lf ", average);

exit(0);
}
```

Example 3.4

```
#define FALSE 0
#define TRUE 1
#define MAXIMUM_NUMBER 200
#include <stdio.h>
#include <stdlib.h>

void main()
/* Guessing game */
{
    int done;       /* When done with guessing */
    int answer;     /* The computer's answer */
    int guess;      /* The user's guess */
    int minutes;    /* Time in minutes */
    int seconds;    /* Time in seconds */

    /* Initialize--get a number */
    done = FALSE;

    /* Get some numbers to make up a guess */
    printf("\n How many minutes past the hour is it? ");
    scanf("%d", &minutes);
    printf("\n How many seconds past the minute is it ?");
    scanf("%d", &seconds);
    answer = (minutes * seconds + seconds) % MAXIMUM_NUMBER + 1;

    printf(" \n I'm thinking of a number between 1 and %d",
        MAXIMUM_NUMBER);
    printf(" \n You can enter 0 or a negative number to give up");
```

```
/* Loop until correct guess or guess less than 1 */
while (!done)
    {
    printf(" \n What is your guess: ");
    scanf("%d", &guess);

    if (guess < 1)
        {
        /* User is giving up */
        printf(" \n You giving up? ");
        printf(" \n The answer was %d", answer);
        done = TRUE;
        }
    else if (guess > MAXIMUM_NUMBER)
        /* Guess was too big */
        printf(" \n That's too too big");
    else if (guess == answer)
        {
        /* Guess was correct */
        done = TRUE;
        printf(" \n That's it--good guessing");
        }
    else if (guess < answer)
        /* Guess was too small */
        printf(" \n Too low");
    else if (guess > answer)
        /* Guess was too big */
        printf(" \n Too big");
    } /* End of while loop on done */

exit(0);
}
```

SUMMARY

- The **if** statement executes a statement if a condition is true.
- The **if-else** executes one of two statements, depending on whether a condition is true or false.
- The **while** loop executes a statement repeatedly while a condition is true.
- The **do-while** routine executes a statement repeatedly until a condition is false. The statement will be executed at least once.
- The **for** statement is a generalization of the **while** loop, combining an initialization part, a test part, and an increment part.
- The **break** statement exits a **for** or **while** loop prematurely.
- The **switch** statement goes to a **case** label or a **default** label based on the value of an expression, and acts like a **goto** statement. It acts like a selection when used with the **break** statement.
- Relational and equality operators compare two values and produce a true (one) or false (zero) result.
- Logical operators combine true (nonzero) and false (zero) values, and produce a true (one) or false (zero) result.

4
Functions

Functions in C are used for the same purpose as subprograms in COBOL. In addition, they may be called from within an expression, and the return value may be used in the evaluation of that expression. One basic philosophical design difference between C and COBOL is that C programs tend to consist of many small functions that operate on data passed to them. In contrast, COBOL programs usually consist of paragraphs that PERFORM various operations on data in the DATA DIVISION that is common to all of them. Though COBOL uses subprograms frequently, C employs them to an even greater extent.

FUNCTION DEFINITION

A C function has many features in common with a COBOL subprogram. Functions may accept a number of passed parameters and return a value. The parameters a C function receives are copies of the arguments that are passed to it. Unlike a COBOL subprogram, a C function cannot change the value of those arguments in the function that called it. However, C functions can return values of a type other than an integer, whereas COBOL subprograms cannot.

The syntax for a C function is

```
return-type function-name (parameters)
   {
   declarations of variables
   executable statements
   }
```

The *return-type* declares the data type that the function will return. We will explore the return-type later in this chapter. The *parameters* act like the LINKAGE section in COBOL, giving the names the function will use for the arguments that are passed to it.

The body of the function acts like a miniprogram. The declarations come first (as does the COBOL DATA DIVISION), followed by the executable statements (as in the PROCEDURE DIVISION). All variables used in the function must be declared. The variables declared inside a function are known only to that function. We will examine external variables—those declared outside a function—later in this chapter.

The **return** statement acts similar to setting the RETURN-CODE and using GOBACK. Its syntax is simply

```
return expression;
```

The **return** statement need not come at the end of the function; it may appear anywhere within the function. A function may contain multiple **return** statements. Whichever **return** is executed first will end the function execution. If you forget to include a **return** statement, the closing brace acts as an implicit **return** statement. The function will execute as if you had included a **return** with no explicit value.

The following abbreviated example compares the C function to the COBOL function, showing the full test of input values.

```
COBOL:

Calling program

01 MONTH COMP PIC 99.
01 DAY   COMP PIC 99.
01 YEAR  COMP PIC 99.
```

```
CALL 'CHECK-DATE' USING MONTH DAY YEAR.
 IF RETURN-CODE = 0
    ...
```

Subprogram

```
IDENTIFICATION DIVISION.
    ...
ENVIRONMENT DIVISION.
    ...
DATA DIVISION.
LINKAGE SECTION.

01 MY-MONTH COMP PIC 99.
01 MY-DAY   COMP PIC 99.
01 MY-YEAR  COMP PIC 99.

PROCEDURE DIVISION USING MY-MONTH MY-DAY MY-YEAR

IF MY-MONTH < 1 OR MY-MONTH > 12
    COMPUTE RETURN-CODE = 16
    GOBACK
ELSE
    ...
END-IF
```

C:

Calling program

```
int month, day, year;
int ret_code;
ret_code = check_date(month, day, year);
if (ret_code == 0)
        ...
```

Called function

```
int check_date(int my_month, int my_day, int my_year)
    {
    int return_value;
    if (my_month < 1 || my_month > 12)
```

```
        {
        return_value = 16;
        return return_value;
        }
    ....
    }
```

Alternatively, we could test the return value of the function directly. This option is typically used when the function does not need the value again.

```
if (check_date(my_month, my_day, my_year) == 0)
    ...

int check_date(int my_month, int my_day, int my_year)
    {
    int return_value;
    if (my_month < 1 || my_month > 12)
        {
        return_value = 16;
        return return_value;
        }
    ....
    }
```

The return value may also be specified directly after the **return** statement.

```
int check_date(int my_month, int my_day, int my_year)
    {
    if (my_month < 1 || my_month > 12)
        {
        return 16;
        }
    ....
    }
```

I generally prefer having only one **return** statement in each function. Though some authorities disagree with this position, I find that limiting each function to a single **return** makes it easier to trace what the function is returning. You should employ whatever convention feels comfortable or follow your company's standard on the use of **returns**.

FUNCTION NAMES

To name functions, follow the same rules as for naming variables and use meaningful function names. Be aware that you should not use any of the reserved function names in the C library, listed in Appendix B.

If you define two functions with the same name, the linker will give you a "DUPLICATE NAME XXXX" or other similar error message. Unfortunately, some linkers use only the first six characters of the function name, without regard for upper or lower case. Thus, **check_date** and **CHECK_TIME** may represent the same name to your linker, even though you consider them as two different functions.*

FUNCTION PROTOTYPES AND PARAMETER CHECKING

The function prototype is a useful addition to the C language that gives the compiler information as to what number and types of parameters a function expects. Using this information, the compiler can check to be sure you have called the function properly. A function prototype looks like the header of a function that terminates with a semi-colon.

```
int check_date(int my_month, int my_day, int my_year);
```

Typically, programmers put this declaration at the top of the source file. If the preceding prototype appears there, the compiler checks every time you call **check_date** to be sure that you have called it with three integer parameters. If you call it with

---

*Although the examples in this book use long function names, within each program there is no duplication of their first six characters. If your linker has this limitation, you can use macros (see chapter on Preprocessor) to rename functions without changing your code.

```
check_date(month, day);
```

or

```
check_date();
```

the compiler will warn that you did not specify the right number of parameters.

If such a prototype is not in the source file, the compiler will not issue a warning. When you call the function incorrectly, any parameters whose corresponding arguments have not been passed will have garbage values.

Although using prototypes will save programmers some grief, the compiler is not perfect. If you call the function **check_date** with

```
check_date(day, month, year);
```

the compiler will not issue a warning because you are passing three **int** arguments. However, the function will not work logically as you expected as the order is not correct.

If a function has no parameters, use the key word **void** in the parameter list to denote this.

While you may specify the prototype with no parameter names as

```
int check_date(int , int , int );
```

you will typically include them so that a user can readily see what the meanings of the parameters are.

Call by Value

In contrast with COBOL, changing the values of parameters in C will not change the values of the arguments in the calling function. This protocol is named *call by value*, meaning that the value of the argument is copied to the parameter. If you call a function with constants rather than variables, the value of the constant is copied to the parameter. So you can call **check_date** with

```
check_date(1, 3, 88);
check_date(5, 12, 92);
```

You may also specify an expression such as

```
check_date (month, day + 3, year - 1);
```

as the argument in calling function. The expression is evaluated and the result is passed to the function.

Call by Reference

An alternative to call by value is *call by reference*. Call by reference is the way the subprograms work in COBOL, and is covered in detail in Chapter 8. Call by reference requires the address operator **&** on simple variables, and is most commonly found with the **scanf** function. The **&** operator actually passes the address of the variable. Once the input value is translated to its internal machine representation, **scanf** puts it into this address. For example, in

```
scanf("%d%d%d", &day, &month, &year);
```

scanf will return values from the keyboard input and place them into **day**, **month**, and **year**.

If you leave off the address operator on a parameter to be passed by reference, your program will run either incorrectly or not at all. The value passed will be the value of the variable, not its address.

Return Values

A function can return values other than **int**. The value type is specified by placing the data type before the name of the function. In COBOL, you may pass an argument whose value is provided by a function. In C, you can pass this value back as the return value for the function. A function that returns something other than an integer requires a prototype for that function so that the return value can be obtained properly. For example:

```
double compute_weekly_pay(int hours_worked, double
        hourly_rate); /* Prototype */
```

```
double compute_weekly_pay(int hours_worked, double
    hourly_rate)
    {
    double weekly_pay;
    weekly_pay = hours_worked * hourly_rate;
    return weekly_pay;
    }
```

You may only return one value, or more specifically, the value of one data type, from a function. If you need to return multiple values, use call by reference.

void Return Type

When a function need not return a value, use the data type **void**. This data type is mostly used as a programmer's aid. Since you need not use the return value of a function in the calling program, you can simply ignore any function declared as returning an **int**. Declaring a function as returning **void** simply makes the compiler check to ensure that you do not attempt to use that return value as

```
int function_that_returns_value()
    {
    ...
    return 1;
    }

void function_that_does_not_return_value()
    {
    ...
    return;
    }

my_function()
    {
    int i;

    function_that_returns_value(); /* Okay to ignore it */
```

```
    i = function_that_does_not_return_value();
                                /* Compiler error */
    ...
}
```

Implicit Function Calls

If you use a name followed by a list enclosed in parentheses in the executable part of a function, C assumes that the name is a function you want to call. If there is no prototype for that function, C assumes that the function returns an integer. If you later declare that the function returns something other than an integer, the compiler will signal an error.

Because it is such a good idea to include function prototypes for all functions your program uses, some compilers give warnings if they do not find a prototype when you call a function. The only reasonable exception to this rule is if all your functions return only integer values and you do not want the compiler to check the parameter types for you. The lint programs available from several sources can perform the parameter/argument checking for you if you do not use prototypes.

Library Functions

A complete listing of the C library, which includes over a hundred functions that perform various operations, is included in Appendix B. Many commercial libraries exist that have functions for creating user interfaces with both textual and graphic windows, for painting graphical pictures, for communicating over modems, and for many other purposes. To save time, you may want to investigate and perhaps purchase these libraries. You can also create your own libraries.

A SAMPLE C PROGRAM

In COBOL, the first executed line of code is the first line in the PROCEDURE DIVISION. In C, the first line executed from the programmer's perspective is the first line in the **main** function.

In each C program there must be one—and only one—function named **main**. This function is called by the startup code, which is performed when your executable program is loaded and started by the operating system.

The main function can call other functions, each of which may, in turn, call other functions. Whereas in COBOL you might have a mixture of PERFORMS and CALLS, in C you would have a set of function calls.

Example 4.1, a rewrite of Example 1.2, uses a function call to check the salary.

Depending on the design, functions such as in Example 4.2 may be written to return minimum and maximum salaries for an employee class.

MAIN AND EXIT

As noted in the preceding section, **main** is the name for the first function executed as the program runs. When a program starts, compiler supplied startup code is executed which then calls this function. The operating system passes two values to **main**. Chapter 11 discusses the use of these parameters, which are similar to PROCEDURE DIVISION USING.

Like STOP RUN, **exit** ends the execution of a program. The **exit** function may be called from anywhere in a program, but is normally called only from the function **main**. As in the case of **return**, it is best to have only one **exit** call in your entire program. If you forget to put one in, C assumes the closing brace of the function **main** represents a call to **exit**. You may declare the value **main** returns as either an **int** or a **void**.

The value passed to **exit** is returned to the operating system just like the RETURN-CODE. Many systems have a provision for checking the value an executed program returns. This value may be tested in a batch, an exec, or a shell file to control what program is run next. Check your operating systems manual for further details.

VARIABLE STORAGE CLASSES

In COBOL, all variables in the DATA DIVISION are stored in memory and are accessible to all paragraphs in the PROCEDURE

Example 4.1

```
#include <stdio.h>
#include <stdlib.h>
#define TRUE 1
#define FALSE 0

int salary_in_range (int employee_class_comp, double employee_salary_comp);

void main()
   {
   /* Declarations */

   double employee_salary_comp;
   int employee_class_comp;
   int salary_ok;
   /* Executable */
   employee_class_comp = 1;
   while (employee_class_comp != 0)
      {
      printf("enter class\n");
      scanf("%d", &employee_class_comp);
      printf("enter salary\n");
      scanf("%lf", &employee_salary_comp);
      salary_ok = salary_in_range (employee_class_comp,
                    employee_salary_comp);
```

```c
        if (!salary_ok)
            printf("salary out of range\n");
    }
    exit(0);
}

int salary_in_range (int employee_class_comp, double employee_salary_comp)
{
    int return_value;
    return_value = TRUE;
    if (employee_class_comp == 1)
    {
        if (employee_salary_comp < 10000.00 ||
            employee_salary_comp > 1000000.00)
        {
            return_value = FALSE;
        }
    }
    if (employee_class_comp == 2)
    {
        if (employee_salary_comp < 100000.00 ||
            employee_salary_comp > 10000000.00)
        {
            return_value = FALSE;
        }
    }
```

```
if (employee_class_comp == 3)
    {
    if (employee_salary_comp < 1000000.00 ||
        employee_salary_comp > 10000000.00)
        {
        return_value = FALSE;
        }
    }
return return_value;
}
```

Example 4.2

```
#define BIG_HONCHO 3
#define MEDIUM_HONCHO 2
#define LITTLE_HONCHO 1
#define TRUE 1
#define FALSE 0

double minimum_salary_for_employee_class(int class)
{
    double minimum_salary;
    switch(class)
    {
        case BIG_HONCHO:
            minimum_salary = 1000000;
            break;
        case MEDIUM_HONCHO:
            minimum_salary = 100000;
            break;
        case LITTLE_HONCHO:
            minimum_salary = 10000;
            break;
        default:
            minimum_salary = -1;
            break;
    }
```

```
    return minimum_salary;
}

double maximum_salary_for_employee_class(int class)
{
    double maximum_salary;
    switch(class)
    {
    case BIG_HONCHO:
        maximum_salary = 10000000;
        break;
    case MEDIUM_HONCHO:
        maximum_salary = 1000000;
        break;
    case LITTLE_HONCHO:
        maximum_salary = 100000;
        break;
    default:
        maximum_salary = -1;
        break;
    }
    return maximum_salary;
}

double maximum_salary_for_employee_class(int class);
double minimum_salary_for_employee_class(int class);
```

```
int salary_in_range (int employee_class_comp,
                     double employee_salary_comp)
{
        int return_value;
        return_value = FALSE;
        if (employee_salary_comp >=
                minimum_salary_for_employee_class(employee_class_comp)
                && employee_salary_comp <=
                maximum_salary_for_employee_class(employee_class_comp)
                return_value = TRUE;
        return return_value;
}
```

DIVISION the entire time the program is executing. In C, some variables, called *local variables*, may be accessible only to a single function. Variables accessible to multiple functions are called *external variables*.

Local Variables—Auto and Static

In C, certain local variables called **static** are stored in memory the entire time a program is executing. Other local variables, called **automatic** or **auto**, are allocated space in memory only when a function is executing. The default storage class for variables inside a function is automatic. If an automatic variable is not initialized, its content is whatever was previously in the storage location. This value is sometimes called a garbage value. If you initialize an automatic variable with a specific value, every time the function is executed it will be reinitialized with that value.

To make a variable static, the word **static** must precede the declaration. If the programmer assigns an initialization value, the variable is initialized once when the program is loaded. **Static** variables with no initialization value are set to 0. **Static** variables are used to remember values between calls to the function. For example,

```
a_function()
    {
    int automatic_variable = 3;
    static int static_variable;
    ....
    }
```

External Variables

External or global variables are declared **outside** of functions and are accessible to all functions in much the same way that all DATA DIVISION variables are accessible to all paragraphs. For example,

```
int outside;
one_function()
```

78 C FOR COBOL PROGRAMMERS

```
    {
    outside = 5;
    ...
    }
another_function()
    {
    outside = 10;
    ...
    }
```

The variable **outside** has been declared external to **one_function** and to **another_function**, so it is accessible to both. The assignment statements will change the variable's value.

Let us rewrite the **check_date** subprogram from Chapter 3 as a paragraph in COBOL and then as a function in C using external variables. Note the effort required to pass values to functions using external variables.

COBOL Calling Program

```
01 MONTH COMP PIC 99.
01 DAY   COMP PIC 99.
01 YEAR  COMP PIC 99.

01 CHECK-MONTH COMP PIC 99.
01 CHECK-DAY COMP PIC 99.
01 CHECK-YEAR COMP PIC 99.
01 CHECK-RETURN-VALUE COMP PIC 99.

COMPUTE CHECK-MONTH = MONTH.
COMPUTE CHECK-DAY = DAY.
COMPUTE CHECK-YEAR = YEAR.
PERFORM CHECK-DATE.
IF CHECK-RETURN-VALUE = 0
        ...

CHECK-DATE.
    IF CHECK-MONTH < 1 OR CHECK-MONTH > 12
        COMPUTE CHECK-RETURN-VALUE = 16
    ELSE
```

```
    ...
    END-IF
```

C Calling Program

```
int check_month;
int check_day;
int check_year;
int check_return_value;

calling_function
    {
    int month, day, year;
    ...
    check_month = month;
    check_day = day;
    check_year = year;
    check_date();
    if (check_return_value == 0)
    ...
```

Called Function

```
int check_date()
    {
    if (check_month < 1 || check_month > 12)
        {
        check_return_value = 16;
        }
    ....
    }
```

Using the parameter list to pass all the values that a function needs makes your programs more modular and more maintainable. If the operation of a function depends only on its input parameters rather than on global variables, then the function is much easier to debug and maintain. As a beginning programmer in C, you may carry over from COBOL the programming habit of making all variables in a program accessible from everywhere within that program. However, the sooner you break that habit, the more readily you will benefit from C. In general, external variables should be avoided in C because programs that employ them are more difficult to maintain.

Externals and Multiple Source Files

A C program may be made up of multiple source files compiled separately and then linked together to form an executable program. A variable declared externally in one source file is not accessible to the other source files unless it is also declared in them. To do this, use the key word **extern**.

Source file "one"

```
int outside;
one_function()
    {
    outside = 4;
    }
```

Source file "two"

```
extern int outside;
another_function()
    {
    outside = 5;
    }
```

In source file "one," the external variable **outside** is declared. All the functions following this declaration can access its value. In source file "two," which is to be linked with source file "one," an **extern** declaration is made for **outside**. The reference to **outside** in **another_function** refers to that **extern** declaration. When the two source files are linked together, the reference in **another_function** will be set to the variable **outside** in source file "one."

In technical terms, the declaration of **outside** in source file "one" is the definition of **outside**. The **extern** declaration in source file "two" is a reference to **outside**. The linker will connect the reference to **outside** to the definition of **outside** when the files are linked.*

If the **calling_function** and **check_date** in the preceding example appeared in separate source files, then they would look like

Calling program

```
int check_month;     /* Definitions */
int check_day;
```

---

*Some linkers will link together multiple definitions that appear in separate source files as if one is the definition and the others are references. The ANSI standard requires only one definition.

```
int check_year;
int check_return_value;

calling_function
    {
    int month, day, year;
    ...
    check_month = month;
    check_day = day;
    check_year = year;
    check_date();
    if (check_return_value == 0)
    ...
    ...
```

Called function

```
extern int check_month;         /* References */
extern int check_day;
extern int check_year;
extern int check_return_value;

int check_date()
    {
    if (check_month < 1 || check_month > 12)
        {
        check_return_value = 16;
        }
    ....
    }
```

SAMPLE PROGRAMS

Examples 4.3, 4.4, and 4.5 illustrate the use of functions. They follow the same logic as the sample programs in Chapter 3.

Date Check

The function in Example 4.3 checks dates by receiving values for **month**, **day**, and **year** and returning a value of **TRUE** or **FALSE**.

Because the function returns a value, it is more flexible than

Example 4.3

```
#define JAN 1
#define FEB 2
#define MAR 3
#define APR 4
#define MAY 5
#define JUN 6
#define JUL 7
#define AUG 8
#define SEP 9
#define OCT 10
#define NOV 11
#define DEC 12
#define TRUE 1
#define FALSE 0

int date_check(int month, int day, int year)
            /* returns TRUE if valid */
            /* FALSE if not valid */
{
    int valid;              /* Flag for valid date */

    /* Assume date is good until proven otherwise */
    valid = TRUE;

    if (day <= 0)
        valid = FALSE;
```

```
if (month == FEB)
        /* Month is February, check for leap year */
    {
    if (year % 4 == 0)
            if (day > 29)
                    valid = FALSE;
        else
            if (day > 28)
                    valid = FALSE;
    }
else if ((month == JAN) || (month == MAR) || (month == MAY)
    || (month == JUL) || (month == AUG) || (month == OCT)
    || (month == DEC))
    {
    /* Month is a 31 day month */
    if (day > 31)
            valid = FALSE;
    }
else if ((month == APR) || (month == JUN) || (month == SEP)
    || (month == NOV))
    {
    /* Month is a 30 day month */
    if (day > 30)
            valid = FALSE;
    }
else valid = FALSE;

return valid;
}
```

Example 4.4

```
#include <stdio.h>
#include <stdlib.h>

int date_check(int month, int day, int year);

void main()
/* Checks a date for validity */
{
    int month;                /* Month to check */
    int day;                  /* Day to check */
    int year;                 /* Year to check */
    int valid;                /* Valid date flag */

    /* Input the date */
    printf("\n This program checks for a valid date");
    printf("\n Enter the month: ");
    scanf("%d", &month);
    printf("\n Enter the day: ");
    scanf("%d", &day);
    printf("\n Enter the year: ");
    scanf("%d", &year);
    printf("\n Date is %d/%d/%d", month, day, year);
```

```
/* Check the date and print the result */
valid = date_check(month, day, year);
if (valid)
         printf("\n Date is valid");
else
         printf("\n date is invalid");
exit(0);
}
```

Example 4.5

```
#include <stdio.h>
#include <stdlib.h>

#define TRUE 1
#define FALSE 0

#define RESET_AVERAGE 0
#define ADD_TO_AVERAGE 1
#define COMPUTE_AVERAGE 2

double compute_average(int what_to_do, int number);

void main()
/* Computes the average of input numbers */
{
    int done;                    /* Flag for done with input */
    int number;                  /* Input number */
    double average;              /* For result */

    done = FALSE;
    compute_average(RESET_AVERAGE, 0);
    printf("\n This program averages numbers till a zero is input");

    while (!done)
    {
        printf("\n Input a number, 0 to end ");
```

```c
            scanf("%d", &number);
            /* If number is 0, then exit */
            if (number == 0)
                    done = TRUE;
            else
                    average = compute_average(ADD_TO_AVERAGE, number);
    }

    average = compute_average(COMPUTE_AVERAGE, 0);
    printf("\n Average is %lf", average);

    exit(0);
}

double compute_average(int what_to_do, int number)
{
    static int count;
    static double sum;
    double average = 0.0;
    switch(what_to_do)
    {
    case RESET_AVERAGE:
            sum = 0.0;
            count = 0;
            break;
    case ADD_TO_AVERAGE:
            sum = sum + number;
```

```
            count = count + 1;
            break;
    case COMPUTE_AVERAGE:
            if (count != 0)
                average = sum / count;
            else
                average = 0.0;
            break;
    }
    return average;
}
```

if it printed out the result. If the date is invalid, the caller of the function can decide what to do: print a message, for example, or ask for another date. Assume that the preceding **date_check** function is called by the **main** function shown in Example 4.4. Note that you could change what occurs in response to invalid dates without changing the **date_check** function.

Averaging Program

Example 4.5 is a function that computes averages. It takes two parameters: one to tell it what to do and the other to set the value. The function has two **static** variables that retain their values between calls to the function.

SUMMARY

- A function is the basic program module in C. It may be passed values as parameters and return a value.
- The parameters passed when a function is called should agree in type, number, and order with the parameters in the function definition.
- Variables declared within a function are only available to that function.
- In a given function, automatic local variables are allocated memory space and optionally initialized every time the function is executed. Static variables are allocated memory space and initialized at program startup.
- External variables are available to all functions in a program.

5
Arrays

A table in COBOL is a variable whose parts are referenced with an index. The variable OCCURS a number of times. An index between parentheses specifies the part of the variable to which we are currently referring. In C, a table is called an *array*. Arrays are used not only for tables of values, but also for strings of characters, such as PIC X(20).

DECLARATION AND USE OF ARRAYS

C arrays differ from COBOL tables in several respects, as we shall shortly see. An array declaration takes the form

```
data_type variable_name[size];
```

The index or subscript in C starts with the value 0, not the value 1 as in COBOL. The last element is the index *size* −1, not the value of the OCCURS.

To compare the two languages, let's take a simple example. Suppose our company had three classes of employees as in previous examples. However, now they are simply designated by the values 1, 2, and 3. We want to develop a table that will keep track of the total salaries for the employees in each class. In COBOL, this might look like

```
01 SOME_TABLE.

   05 TOTAL_SALARY COMP-2  PIC 9(10)V99  OCCURS 3 TIMES.
```

To reference an individual element in TOTAL_SALARY, index it with a value in parentheses. The valid elements are

```
TOTAL_SALARY(1)
TOTAL_SALARY(2)
TOTAL_SALARY(3)
```

If you want to clear all the elements out of TOTAL_SALARY, code

```
PERFORM VARYING CLASS_INDEX FROM 1 BY 1 UNTIL CLASS_INDEX > 3
  MOVE 0 TO TOTAL_SALARY(CLASS_INDEX)
END-PERFORM.
```

In C, you code this as

```
double total_salary[3];
```

The elements of **total_salary** are

```
total_salary[0]
total_salary[1]
total_salary[2]
```

Each element acts like a simple variable of type **double**. To zero out the elements in **total_salary**, code

```
for (class_index = 0; class_index < 3; class_index += 1)
    {
    total_salary[class_index] = 0.0;
    }
```

Like many forms of COBOL, C provides no subscript (index) checking. If you go beyond the end of the table, you will write to or read from other variables, or perhaps code. For that purpose, as well as for maintenance considerations, arrays are usually declared using a **#define**. The declaration for the preceding example would be coded as

```
#define SIZE_TOTAL_SALARY 3
double total_salary[SIZE_TOTAL_SALARY];

for (class_index = 0; class_index < SIZE_TOTAL_SALARY;
    class_index += 1);
    {
    total_salary[class_index] = 0.0;
    }
```

Initialization

To initialize a table in COBOL, you use REDEFINE. Suppose you had a table of values of MINIMUM_SALARY for each class.

```
01 SOME_TABLE.
    05 MINIMUM_SALARY  COMP-2 PIC 9(10)V99  OCCURS 3
           TIMES.

01 ANOTHER_TABLE REDEFINES SOME_TABLE.
    05  FILLER COMP-2 PIC 9(6) VALUE 10000.
    05  FILLER COMP-2 PIC 9(6) VALUE 100000.
    05  FILLER COMP-2 PIC 9(6) VALUE 1000000.
```

You could then test a variable called CLASS_LEVEL, containing the value of the class, using

```
IF CLASS_LEVEL GREATER THAN OR EQUAL TO 1 AND LESS THAN OR
        EQUAL TO 3
    IF SALARY LESS THAN MINIMUM_SALARY(CLASS_LEVEL)
       ...
    END-IF
END-IF
```

In C, the initialization of an array takes place in the same statement as the declaration. The syntax is

94 C FOR COBOL PROGRAMMERS

```
data_type variable_name[size] = { values... };
```

For example, to declare and initialize a minimum salary table, code

```
double minimum_salary[3] = {10000., 100000., 1000000.};
```

Note that braces surround the list of initializers and commas separate them.* To perform the C equivalent of the COBOL test, write

```
if (class_level >= 1 && class_level <= 3)
    {
    if (salary < minimum_salary[class_level-1];
        {
        /* Do appropriate action */
        }
    }
```

Note the subtraction of 1 in the index expression to set the index back to 0. The table could have been written with a dummy first element to eliminate the subtraction.

```
double minimum_salary[4] = {0.0, 10000., 100000., 1000000.};
```

When you declare an array, you must include its size. You may do so explicitly as above, or you may let the compiler determine the size if you include an initialization list. The first declaration could have been coded as

```
double minimum_salary[] = {10000., 100000., 1000000.};
```

In this case, the compiler would count the number of initializers and set the size of the array to 3. You cannot simply declare an array as

```
double minimum_salary[];
```

---

*ANSI C compilers are required to support the initialization of automatic arrays. However, many compilers that support most ANSI features do not support this one. If your compiler does not, make the array **static**.)

except as a function parameter, which will be shown later in this chapter.*

If you declare an array in this manner, you can determine the number of elements it contains by using the **sizeof** operator. This operator gives the size of memory required by a data type or variable. For this array, the number of elements would be **sizeof(minimum_salary)/sizeof(int)**. You can code a **#define** statement such as

```
#define SIZE_MINIMUM_SALARY (sizeof(minimum_salary)\
    sizeof(double))
```

Sample Functions

Example 4.2 in the previous chapter returned the minimum salary for a class using a **switch** statement. Example 5.1 uses an array and assumes the classes run from 1 to 3.

Example 5.1

```
double minimum_salary_for_employee_class(int class)
        {
        static double minimum_salary_table[3] =
                        {1000000., 100000., 10000.};
        double minimum_salary;

        minimum_salary = 0.0;
        if (class >= 1 && class <= 3)
                minimum_salary = minimum_salary_table
                [class - 1];
        return minimum_salary;
        }
```

This alternative function makes no assumptions about the values of the classes. The salary table can be kept in any order as long as the class table is kept in matching order.

If your program deals only with a few levels, the **switch** method is probably preferable. With many choices, the two-array

---

*This form can be used as the declaration of an external reference, but it is seldom used in that way.

method is more efficient. Chapter 7 presents an alternative to the two-array method that keeps the levels and salarys typographically closer together.

TRANSITIONING TO C ARRAYS

In transforming code from an existing COBOL program to a C program, you are faced with a decision on using subscripts. If you want to make a direct transformation, it is sometimes easier to use subscripts starting from 1 rather than 0. In that case, you need to declare the array to be one greater than the largest subscript you will use. For the case of the three employee levels, you might use

```
double total_salary[4];
```

The first element, total_salary[0], would not be used in this event. You may choose to code things in what is perhaps a more familiar way. For example,

```
for (class_index = 1; class_index <= 3; class_index += 1)
    {
    total_salary[class_index] = 0.0;
    }
```

It is generally better to start fresh code with the intention to use the first element, the 0 subscript.

Array Restrictions

You cannot move an array as a whole. For example, if you have the two arrays

```
double maximum_salary[3];
double salary[3];
```

you *cannot* code

```
maximum_salary = salary;
```

You must move each element in the array individually. For example

Example 5.2

```
#define BIG_HONCHO 1
#define MEDIUM_HONCHO 2
#define LITTLE_HONCHO 3

double minimum_salary_for_employee_level(int in_class)
{
    static double minimum_salary[3] =
                    {1000000., 100000., 10000.};

    static int class[3] =
                    {BIG_HONCHO, MEDIUM_HONCHO, LITTLE_HONCHO};

    double salary;
    int class_index;

    salary = 0.0;
    for (class_index = 0; class_index < 3; class_index ++)
    {
        if (in_class == class[class_index])
        {
            salary = minimum_salary[class_index];
            break;
        }
    }
    return salary;
}
```

```
int array_index;
for (array_index = 0; array_index < 3; array_index++)
    {
    maximum_salary[array_index] = salary[array_index];
    }
```

The name of an array by itself represents its address in memory where the array is stored. Trying to assign the name of one array to the name of another is like trying to assign one constant to another. The compiler will not let you.

Arrays and Functions

You can pass an array to a function, but when you do so, the entire array is *not* passed to the function. The function merely receives the starting address of the array. Any references inside the function will retrieve or affect the values in the array which is passed. This works as a call by reference. To declare the parameter as an array, use the array name followed by square brackets with no value for the size between them.*

Example 5.3 illustrates a function that will zero out the values in an array that is passed.

Example 5.3

```
void zero_double_array(double array[], int size)
    {
    int index;
    for (index = 0; index < size; index += 1)
        {
        array[index] = 0.0;
        }
    return;
    }
```

You could use this function in a calling routine such as Example 5.4.

---

*The array notation for a function parameter may also be coded using pointer notation, which is described in Chapter 8.

Example 5.4

```
void zero_double_array(double array[], int size);
void main()
    {
    double salary[3];
    zero_double_array(salary, 3);
    }
```

Each element in **salary** is set to 0.0. The function that is called needs to know the size of the array as a separate parameter. The array itself does not contain that information.

Note that you need not declare the size of the array in the function header. At this point you are not laying out in memory an array of a particular size. You are simply indicating to the function that it will be receiving an array name, which is in reality an address. The array whose name is passed will have been declared with a constant size in the calling routine.

Example 5.5 presents another use of the array function. Suppose you want to pass back the values in an entire table of minimum salaries. The function itself cannot do that as a return value. However, the caller can create an array, pass it to the function, and the function can then fill in the table, as follows.

This function would be called by the program shown in Example 5.6.

Example 5.5

```
#define SIZE_MINIMUM_SALARY_TABLE 3

void get_minimum_salary_table(double minimum_salary[])
{
    static double minimum_salary_table[SIZE_MINIMUM_SALARY_TABLE] =
                    {1000000., 100000., 10000.};
    int level_index;

    for (level_index = 0; level_index < SIZE_MINIMUM_SALARY_TABLE ;
                level_index += 1)
    {
        minimum_salary[level_index] =
                    minimum_salary_table[level_index];
    }
    return ;
}
```

Example 5.6

```
#define SIZE_MINIMUM_SALARY_TABLE 3

void get_minimum_salary_table(double minimum_salary[]);
void main()
    {
    double minimum_salary[SIZE_MINIMUM_SALARY_TABLE];
    get_minimum_salary_table(minimum_salary);
    }
```

Note that it is the caller's responsibility to ensure that the array passed to the function is large enough to hold the result. The function does not know what size the array is; it only knows where the array starts.

You may see functions with headers such as

```
void get_minimum_salary_table(double * minimum_salary)
```

Although this header has a slightly different connotation than the preceding header, it basically means the same thing—the function expects the name of an array, an address.

Sample Averaging Program

Example 5.7 is a different approach to the averaging program shown in Example 4.6. The main program in Example 5.7 has an array called **numbers**. The input routine **input_array** stores the values to be averaged in the **numbers** array. The **numbers** array is then passed to the averaging routine **average_array** to compute the average. In both calling sequences, the size of the array—either the actual size or the number of elements that have input values—is passed as a parameter.

The advantage of this approach is that once the values are in the array, you may call other functions to perform operations on it, such as finding the lowest or highest value. The disadvantage is that there is a memory limitation on how big **numbers** can be

Example 5.7

```c
#include <stdio.h>
#include <stdlib.h>
#define TRUE 1
#define FALSE 0

double average_array(int array[], int size);
int input_array(int array[], int max_size);

double average_array(int array[], int size)
/* Computes average of values in an array */
{
    double sum;                    /* To keep the sum */
    double result;                 /* The answer */
    int index;                     /* Index for array */

    /* Initialize sum */
    sum = 0.0;

    /* Compute the total */
    for (index = 0; index < size; index++)
    {
        sum = sum + array[index];
    }
```

```
    /* Compute the average */
    if (size > 0)
        result = sum / size;
    else
        result = 0.0;

    return result;
}

int input_array(int array[], int max_size)
/* Returns number of values input */
{
    int done;                   /* Flag when input is done */
    int count;                  /* Number of values */

    done = FALSE;
    count = 0;

    /* Input numbers until maximum count or zero value is entered */
    while (!done)
    {
        printf("\n Enter a number");
        scanf("%d", &array[count]);
        if (array[count] == 0)
            done = TRUE;
        else
```

103

```
        {
        count++;
        if (count == max_size)
                done = TRUE;
        }
    }
    return count;
}

#define SIZE 50          /* Maximum number of values to average */

void main()
/* Averages up to SIZE numbers */
{
    int numbers[SIZE];       /* Values */
    int count;               /* Number of values */
    double result;           /* Average */

    printf("\n This program averages up to 50 numbers");

    /* Input numbers, average them, and print result */
    count = input_array(numbers, SIZE);
    result = average_array(numbers, count);
    printf("\n Average is %lf", result);

    exit(0);
}
```

and thus how many values you can average. In contrast, the functions in Example 4.6 have no limit on the number of values they may accept.

Strings

One of the most difficult transitions for programmers coming to C from any other computer language is the way in which C forms strings. A COBOL variable declared as:

```
01 A_STRING PIC X(5).
```

declares that A_STRING contains 5 characters. The variable itself can be used in MOVE statements, comparisons, and so forth.

In C, a string or set of characters is not a basic part of the language. A few features of the C compiler support the notation of strings, but not to the same extent as other languages. A string in C is an array of characters that has a zero value in it. Consider a simple example.

```
static char a_string[5] = {'A', 'B', 'C', 'D', '\0'};
```

This statement declares that a_string is an array of characters and initializes it. The fifth character ('\0') does not represent the ASCII value for zero, but rather the binary value of 0—a character with all its bits set to 0 and a numeric value of 0. Called the NUL character, it shows where the end of the string is located.

Functions and Strings

As you have already seen, you cannot simply assign one array to another. For instance, if your program contains the preceding declaration and

```
char another_string[5];
```

you may not code

```
another_string = a_string;
```

To move one string to another, you must either code it directly or call a function. The standard library includes a function called **strcpy**, which stands for string copy. This function copies all the characters in one array to another. Its header is*

```
void strcpy(char destination[], char source[]);
```

To copy strings, you would call

```
strcpy(another_string, a_string);
```

Note that the function is not told how many characters are in the source string. The NUL character at the end of the string designates the end of the string and indicates when to stop copying. To see how to code this function if you did it yourself, consider Example 5.8.

Example 5.8

```
void strcpy(char destination[], char source[])
        {
        int done;
        int index;

        done = 0;
        index = 0;
        while (!done)
                {
                destination[index] = source[index];
                if (source[index] == '\0')
                        done = 1;
                index += 1;
                }

        return;
        }
```

---

*The actual definition,

```
char * strcpy(char * destination, char * source);
```

has been simplified for the purposes of this chapter.

ARRAYS

The function copies all characters up to and including the NUL character. If the source array passed to it does not include the NUL character, the function will keep going through memory until it finds one.

String Length

The length of a string is not dependent on the size of the array, but instead is determined by the position of the terminating NUL character. If the declared array were

```
static char a_string[10] = {'A', 'B', 'C', 'D', '\0'};
```

only the first five characters would be initialized. Although the array is ten bytes long, the string ends at the NUL.

C provides a function that returns the length of a string. Its header is

```
int strlen(char string[]);
```

This function may be implemented as shown in Example 5.9.

Example 5.9

```
int strlen(char string[])
    {
    int length;

    length = 0;
    while (string[length] != '\0')
        {
        length += 1;
        }
    return length;
    }
```

Note that the function does not count the terminating character, but instead returns four because there are only four characters before NUL. It will return four regardless of the declared length of **a_string**.

A variation of the string copy function is **strncpy()**, which copies up to a specified number of characters, but terminates if it reaches the NUL character first.* The syntax for **strncpy()** is

```
void strncpy(char destination[], char source[], int number);
```

Suppose you had declared the following:

```
char a_destination[4];
static char a_source[5] = {'A', 'B', 'C', 'D','\0'};
```

If you simply copied the arrays as

```
strcpy(a_destination, a_source);
```

then five characters would be copied. Since **a_destination** has only four bytes, the fifth character would be copied to the byte following **a_destination** and would overwrite some other variable. You could use strncpy to do the copying as

```
strncpy(a_destination, a_source, 4);
```

This instruction copies only four characters from **a_source** to **a_destination**, because it reaches the size before the NUL character. The NUL character is not copied, so there is no overwriting of another variable. As a result, **a_destination** gets four characters, but does not contain a string because it has no NUL character. If you then called

```
strlen(a_destination);
```

it would keep going until it found a NUL byte.

Other String Functions

The standard C library contains many string functions that provide for comparison of strings, character or string searches within strings, and other similar operations. These functions are docu-

---

*This actually returns a char *, but it has been simplified for this explanation.

mented as requiring **char*** arguments; that is, the names of **char** arrays. Several of these functions return the address of one of the strings passed to them. For example, **strcpy** actually returns the address of the destination string. Though this may seem redundant, it is useful for increasing program efficiency.*

The library includes two useful functions for comparing and concatenating strings. These are **strcmp** and **strcat**. The prototype for **strcmp**,

```
int strcmp(char first_string[], char second_string[]);
```

compares two strings. If **first_string** is less than **second_string**, the function returns a value less than 0. If they are equal, it returns 0. Otherwise it returns a value greater than 0.

The prototype for **strcat**,

```
strcat(char destination[], char to_be_cated[]);
```

concatenates the **to_be_cated** string at the end of the **destination** string.

String Literals

String literals in C are sets of characters enclosed in double quotation marks. Each string literal represents an array of characters terminated by a NUL character. The string literal is used in two places in C. The first is in the initialization of a character array. If you declare

```
static char a_string[5] = "ABCD";
```

---

*The reason is that this redundancy allows you to nest calls to the function. For example, you may code either
```
char still_another_string[5];
strcpy(another_string, a_string);
strcpy(still_another_string, another_string);
```
or
```
   strcpy(still_another_string, strcpy(another_string,
a_string));
```

it is the same as declaring the characters individually as in the prior declaration. Four characters and a NUL character are placed into a_string. The braces are no longer needed, since the string represents an array initialization.*

Because the compiler can determine the size of an array if there is an initialization list, character arrays are frequently initialized as

```
static char a_string[] = "ABCD";
```

The compiler includes the NUL character when calculating the size of the string constant.

The second place string literals appear is in the executable portion of the code. In this context, they work as string constants. The string characters are placed in an unnamed array and the address of that array is substituted for the string. For example, with **strcpy**, you might code:

```
strcpy(another_string, "Yes");
```

The compiler puts the string "Yes" in an unnamed array that is four characters long and passes **strcpy** the address of that array.

You should not use a string constant as a destination. If you coded

```
strcpy("Yes", another_string);
```

the contents of the string constant would be overwritten.

A string literal may be carried over to a new line in one of two ways. First, the line can end with a backslash (\) immediately followed by the new-line character (carriage return). The string then continues in the first column of the next line. In the second method,

---

*You may also initialize the array with exactly as many characters in the string as the size of the array.

```
static char a_string[5] = "ABCDE";
```

In this case, no NUL character is placed in the array and thus **a_string** is not a string.

two string literals next to each other or separated only by white space are concatenated. For example, the first approach gives

```
"This is a long \
string"
```

Here **"string"** must begin in the first column or else there will be extra spaces in the string constant. Using implicit concatenation produces

```
"This is a long "
"string"
```

Both of these strings have the same value of

```
"This is a long string"
```

Input and Output

Several input and output functions operate using strings. Both **printf** and **scanf** have a format specifier for strings ("**%s**"). The corresponding value passed is the address of a character array. Thus

```
char a_string[] = "A STRING";
printf("This is a string %s", a_string);
```

prints out

```
This is a string A STRING
```

If you are inputting a string, you must pass **scanf** an address in which to put the string. Since the name of an array is an address, you do not need to attach the address operator **&** to the name.

```
char a_string[20];
scanf("%s", a_string);
```

When as a user inputs **a_string**, **scanf** stops when any white-space character—a space, carriage-return, or tab—is input. Thus an input string must consist of a contiguous set of characters. Just like the other string functions, **scanf** receives only an address. It does not know how big the array is. If a user inputs more characters than the size of **a_string**, the extras will go into memory following **a_string**, overwriting other variables.

Arrays of Character Arrays

If you needed an array of strings in your COBOL program, you might use something similar to

```
01 EMPLOYEE-CLASS-TITLE-ENTRIES
       05 FILLER PIC X(15) VALUE 'BIG HONCHO'.
       05 FILLER PIC X(15) VALUE 'MEDIUM HONCHO'.
       05 FILLER PIC X(15) VALUE 'SMALL HONCHO'.
01 EMPLOYEE-CLASS-TITLE-TABLE REDEFINES EMPLOYEE-
   CLASS-TITLE-ENTRIES
       05 EMPLOYEE-TITLE PIC X(15) OCCURS 3 TIMES.
```

One way to do this in C is to make an array of arrays, such as

```
char class_names[3][20] = {
    "Little Honcho", "Medium Honcho", "Big Honcho"};
```

To use one of the strings, use a single index. For example,

```
printf("\n First class is %s", class_names[0]);
```

would print as

```
First class is Little Honcho
```

A call to a string function such as

```
strlen(class_names[1])
```

would yield a value of 13, the length of "Medium Honcho". Example 5.10 illustrates a function that puts a string containing a name into an array that is passed.

Example 5.10

```
#include <string.h>
#define FALSE 0
#define TRUE 1

int get_class_name(char class_name[], int class)
{
    char class_names[3][20] =
        {"Little Honcho", "Medium Honcho", "Big Honcho"};
    int return_value;

    if (class < 0 || class > 2)
    {
        strcpy(class_name, "Invalid Class");
        return_value = FALSE;
    }
    else
    {
        strcpy(class_name, class_names[class]);
        return_value = TRUE;
    }
    return return_value;
}
```

113

SUMMARY

- An array is a group of variables with a single name.
- An element of an array is referenced using the array name and a subscript.
- Passing the name of an array to a function permits the function to change the values in the array.
- A string is an array of characters that contains a terminating NUL byte.
- The C library provides a number of functions that operate on strings, including **strcpy** and **strncpy** to copy strings, **strlen** to determine the length of a string, **strcmp** to compare two strings, and **strcat** to concatenate a string.

6

Input and Output Functions

COBOL has the DISPLAY and ACCEPT commands to read and write data to the terminal. It also offers the READ and WRITE commands to communicate with the world outside the computer's central processor. Though C does not have these commands, it does provide a standard set of functions to perform input and output. In this chapter, you will learn to use these functions to communicate with the human executing your program or with I/O redirection. The functions for reading and writing to disk files will be covered in Chapter 10.

FORMATTED OUTPUT

The standard C output function **printf** works like DISPLAY with the option of some PICTURE type formats. It outputs to the file **stdout**, which is by default the terminal screen. What **printf** outputs are strings of characters. **printf** converts internal machine representation of numbers to characters for output. The format of **printf** is

printf(*format,zero-or-more-values*);

This format controls what will be output. Characters other than specifiers that appear in the *format* will be output just as they appear. Specifiers are sets of characters that begin with the percent sign (%). A specifier tells **printf** that a corresponding value will also be passed in the call and how to convert that value.

Nonprinting characters that control how the output will appear on the screen may also be passed to **printf**. The most common of these is the new-line character, **\n**, which forces the next character to begin in the first column of the next line. Subsequent calls to **printf** simply continue to print characters on a line starting where the previous **printf** left off. If you do not use any new-line characters, the output will start on a new line when it reaches the end of a terminal line. The underscores in the examples below show where the next character to be output would be placed.

Call to printf	Output on screen
printf("Output line");	Output line_
printf("\n First line\n" "Second line\n");	First line Second line _
printf("These two"); printf("together");	These twotogether_

The four format type specifiers introduced so far are: **%d**, **%lf**, **%c** and **%s**. These correspond respectively to the data types **int**, **double**, **char**, and strings or arrays of **char**.* Sample output from these specifiers appears below.

Statements	Output
int day= 1; printf("\n Day is %d", day);	Day is 1
double salary = 12000.30; printf("\n Salary is %lf", salary);	Salary is 12000.300000

---

*The format letter **d** stands for decimal integer and **lf** for long float. The term long float is an obsolete synonym for **double**. However, the format specifier is not.

INPUT AND OUTPUT FUNCTIONS

```
printf("\n 1 + 4 is %d", 1+4);        1 + 4 is 5

printf("\n A is %c", 'a');            A is a

printf("\n A is %d", 'a');            A is 97

 char string[] = "abc";
 printf("\n String is %s", string);   String is abc


 printf("\n String is %S", "Constant");
```

In the fourth and fifth examples above, the value output is the ASCII value of the letter 'a'. The **%c** specifier prints this as the character, the **%d** prints it as a decimal value. C has a wide variety of data types, each of which requires its own particular format specifier. A detailed listing of specifiers appears in Appendix B.

If you forget to put a variable after the format and have included a format specifier, your output will contain a garbage value. Similarly, if the data type specified in the format does not agree with the data type of the value you pass, you will see a garbage value. The output format is determined by the specifier, not by the data type of the value passed. Table 6.1 lists some of the possible errors. Unfortunately, neither the compiler nor most lint programs check for these errors.

You can print out multiple values with a single **printf** call. For instance,

```
int month = 5;
int day = 1;
int year = 78;
 printf("Date is %d/%d/%d", month, day, year);
```

outputs

```
Date is 5/1/78
```

Just be sure that the number and types of values agree with the number and types of the format specifiers.

You should get into the habit of placing the line **"#include**

118 C FOR COBOL PROGRAMMERS

Table 6.1   Sample output errors due to conflicting format specifiers.

Statements	Output
int day = 1; printf("Day is %lf",day);	Day is ?
double salary = 12000.30; printf("Salary is %d",salary);	Salary is ?
printf("Day is %d");	Day is ?
printf("Salary is %d",12000.30);	Salary is ?
printf("String is %s");	String is ?

<stdio.h>" at the beginning of every file in which input or output functions are called. Your compiler may not require it to run the program correctly, but some compilers do.

FORMAT SPECIFIERS

There are several options you can use with format specifiers. These options work in a manner similar to the PICTURE clause. The most common options specify a width to be printed out and specify the number of decimal digits for float values.

A number between % and the format letter gives the width to be printed. If the number of characters required to print the value is smaller than this width, additional spaces will be printed to the value's left. These additional spaces may be added to the value's right (called left justification) by prefacing the number with a hyphen (-). If the number of characters is larger than the width value, **printf** will use as many characters as necessary to print the value. Placing a 0 immediately after the % makes that the fill letter, rather than a space.

For **double** values, a period and another number may follow the width value. This second number tells how many digits following the decimal point to print. If you do not specify this precision, **printf** will print six digits.

For strings, a period followed by another number gives the maximum number of characters to output.

To demonstrate some of the options format specifiers offer,

sample output of an integer value 12, a double value of 12.5, and a string value of "Hello" appear in Table 6.2. The length is the number of characters that **printf** will output. The underscore indicates where the next character will print. A %% is an escape sequence to print the character %.

Table 6.2.   Output for sample format specifiers

Specifier	Printout	Length in Characters
%d	12_	2
%4d	12_	4
%-4d	12 _	4
%lf	12.500000_	9
%10lf	12.500000 _	10
%10.2lf	12.50_	10
%-10.2lf	12.50 _	10
%s	Hello_	5
%10s	Hello_	10
%10.3s	Hel_	10
%%	%_	1

FORMATTED INPUT

In COBOL, ACCEPT reads values from the keyboard and places them in variables. The corresponding function in C for input is **scanf**, which reads the **stdin** file. This file defaults to the keyboard and converts the characters received from it into internal machine representation. The format for **scanf** is

scanf(*format,&variable*);

For example,

```
int class;
double salary;
char name[10];
scanf("%d", &class);
scanf("%lf", &salary);
scanf("%s", name);
```

For numbers, **scanf** reads the input until it reaches a character that could not possibly be part of the number. Suppose that for the functions above you typed the information in the first column of Table 6.3. The results are shown in the rightmost two columns of the table.

Table 6.3. Results of input with scanf

Keyed in	Input Function	Result	Next Character Read
1345.45	scanf("%d", &class);	class is 1345	.
1345.45	scanf("%lf", &salary);	salary is 1345.45	space
1345.45	scanf("%s", name);	name is "1345.45"	space

Be sure to attach the the address operator **&** to all simple variable names you pass to **scanf**. You do not need to add **&** to the name of an array because the name of an array is an address. If you do not use the address operator, the value of the variable will be passed to **scanf**. When **scanf** converts the input value, it will place it at the address given by that value. For example,

```
int number = 5;
scanf("%d", number);
```

will read a value from the keyboard and place it at address 5. That may cause either an addressing exception or failure of the program.

You may input or output multiple items with a single **scanf** or **printf**. Be sure that the number and types agree. The program examples in this text do not use **scanf** in this fashion. However, assuming

```
scanf("%s%lf%d",name, &salary,&class);
```

and the input given in Table 6.4, consider the possible pitfalls of this approach.

In the first line, the spaces separate the input values. In the second line, the commas input as part of the string will cause a

Table 6.4. Results of input using scanf with multiple format specifier.

Input	Name	Salary	Class	Return Value
George 12000.45 1	George	12000.45	1	3
George,12000.45,1	George,12000.45,1	not set	not set	1
George Jones	George	not set	not set	1
George 12000.45,1	George	12000.45	not set	1
George 12000.45 1	George	12000.45	1	3

problem because **name** is only ten characters long. Eighteen characters (seventeen input plus a terminating null) cannot be placed into it, so other data items will be overwritten.

In the third example, the values of salary and class are not set. The value of "J" cannot be part of a **double** number, so the scanning stops there. With the fourth example, the scanning stops at the comma, which cannot be part of an **int** number.

As the fifth example shows, **scanf** does not work on a line-per-line basis. White space—new lines, tabs, etc.—are all treated the same way; they act as terminators for the input of numbers and strings. Leading white space characters are ignored when translating the input (except in the case of the **%c** specifier).

As Table 6.4 shows, **scanf** returns a value you can test—the number of items converted.

You may include a width with the **%c** specifier to read a string that contains embedded spaces. For example, this code works as shown in Table 6.5.

```
int name[21];
scanf("%20c", name);
```

Table 6.5.

Input	Name	strlen of Name
George Jones	George Jones	20

You can use a value for the width with the format specifiers (especially the **%c** specifier) to read data records written in COBOL format, as we shall see in Chapter 10. Additional specifiers and features of **scanf** are listed in Appendix B.

String Conversion

A useful function that converts from strings to internal format is **sscanf**. It works like **scanf**, but instead of reading from the keyboard, **sscanf** scans an array of characters passed to it. One form is

```
sscanf(char array[], format, &variable);
```

You can read an array of characters from **stdin** by using the **gets** function, which requires only the name of an array.*

```
gets(char array[]);
```

These two functions could be used together as

```
char input_array[100];
gets(input_array);
sscanf(input_array, "%lf", &salary);
```

Suppose the input is "12.3XXX". In that event, **gets** will put a NUL- terminated string into **input_array**; **sscanf** will scan this array for a **double**, put the value 12.3 into **salary**, and return a 1. The extra characters in the input value will have been read from the keyboard, but will not be translated. The next time **gets** is called, it will start with the next line. This combination makes it easy to input a single value per line.

CHARACTER INPUT AND OUTPUT

The two functions for reading characters from the standard input and writing them to the standard output are **getchar** and **putchar**.

The function **getchar** returns characters typed on the key-

---

*A "safer" version of this function, **fgets**, is covered in Chapter 10.

board. If you type an end-of-file character (Control-D on UNIX, Control-Z on MS-DOS), **getchar** returns the value defined as **EOF** in **stdio.h**, usually a negative one.

The function **putchar** puts the character it is passed on the screen. The terminal may not necessarily display the character if it is part of a control sequence that performs operations such as positioning the cursor or changing character attributes. Note that **putchar** requires a character, not a string. The expression **putchar('A');** outputs the character A to the screen, but **putchar("A");** will give a compile error or output a garbage character to the screen.

The program in Example 6.1 copies keyboard input to the screen, looping until the character **getchar** returns is the end-of-file value. If you run this program and type in the letters "abc" followed by a carriage return, you will see a second line on the screen that reads "abc". The **getchar** function echoes the input character to the screen, so **getchar** produces the first line. However, **getchar** does not return any characters to the calling program until a carriage return (i.e., a new line) is entered. Because **getchar** stores the characters in its own buffer until the new line is entered, the user may backspace over errors in typing.

When it reads the carriage return, **getchar** returns each character, following the sequence in which the characters were entered for each successive call. Then **putchar** produces the second line of output, outputting each character returned by **getchar**.

STANDARD REDIRECTED INPUT AND OUTPUT

C assumes that the standard input device is the terminal keyboard and the standard output device is the terminal screen. Output from **printf** and **putchar** goes to the screen. Input from **scanf** and **getchar** comes from the keyboard.

On UNIX and MS-DOS systems, you can redirect the input and output when you execute the program.* To redirect, simply use the redirect input (<) and redirect output (>) symbols. These will cause the input to be read from the specified file and the output to be written to the specified file as

---

*On some other systems, you can set the SYSIN and SYSOUT definitions to obtain this same effect.

program-name < input-file > output-file

Using redirection and assuming the name of the program in Example 6.1 is *copyfile*, you may copy any file by executing it as

copyfile < *infile* > *outfile*

SAMPLE FUNCTIONS

The following sample functions demonstrate formatting operations.

Print Date

The function **print_date** in Example 6.2 prints the date in a standard fashion, as 02/01/94.

Example 6.2

```
#include <stdio.h>
void print_date(int month, int day, int year)
        {
        printf("%02d/%02d/%02d", month, day, year);
        }
```

The variation of this function in Example 6.3 prints the date with the month in characters, as FEB 1, 1994.

Example 6.3

```
#include <stdio.h>
void print_date(int month, int day, int year)
        {
        static char month_abbreviations[12][4] = {
                  "JAN", "FEB", "MAR", "APR", "MAY", "JUN",
                  "JUL", "AUG", "SEP", "OCT", "NOV", "DEC"
                  };
 printf("%s %d,19%d",
     month_abbreviations[month - 1], day, year);
        }
```

Example 6.1

```
#include <stdio.h>
#define TRUE 1
#define FALSE 0

void main()
/* copies input to output */
{
    int c;                          /* Current character */
    int eof;                        /* End of file flag */

    /* Initialize end of file */
    eof = FALSE;

    /* Output character till end of file */
    do
        {
        c = getchar();
        if (c == EOF)
                        eof = TRUE;
            else        putchar(c);
        }
    while (!eof);

    return;
}
```

SUMMARY

- Input and output in C are provided by library functions.
- The **printf** function provides formatted output to the standard output device, usually the terminal screen.
- The **scanf** function provides formatted input from the standard input device, usually the keyboard.
- The **getchar** and **putchar** functions read and write one character at a time.
- Using the redirection operators < and > on the command line switches input and output to files other than the keyboard and the screen.

7

Structures

Because you have used many records in COBOL, you are already aware that every time you break up an 01 level into sublevels, you create a record with a hierarchical set of fields. You can design the same sort of hierarchy in C; however, it is usually built from the lowest level outward.

COMPARISON BETWEEN COBOL AND C FIELDS

If you have two breakdowns that are the same, you may use a COPY BOOK to copy an external file into your source code. For example, if you use dates frequently, you may have a file called *date.src* that contains:

```
05 MONTH PIC XX  COMP.
05 DAY   PIC XX  COMP.
05 YEAR  PIC XX  COMP.
```

In your program, using

```
01 A_DATE  COPY DATE.SRC
```

would produce the same result as writing

127

```
01 A_DATE.
   05 MONTH PIC XX  COMP.
   05 DAY   PIC XX  COMP.
   05 YEAR  PIC XX  COMP.
```

Now you could use the COPYBOOK again as

```
01 ANOTHER_DATE COPY DATE.SRC.
```

and obtain the equivalent of

```
01 ANOTHER_DATE.
   05 MONTH PIC XX  COMP.
   05 DAY   PIC XX  COMP.
   05 YEAR  PIC XX  COMP.
```

If both declarations using the COPYBOOK appear in the same program, you must reference them using a fully qualified name such as

```
MONTH OF ANOTHER_DATE
YEAR OF DATE
```

Many COBOL programmers wish to avoid using fully qualified names, so instead of making a COPY BOOK, you may use a structure similar to

```
01 A_DATE.
   05 A_MONTH PIC XX  COMP.
   05 A_DAY   PIC XX  COMP.
   05 A_YEAR  PIC XX  COMP.
01 ANOTHER_DATE.
   05 AN_MONTH PIC XX  COMP.
   05 AN_DAY   PIC XX  COMP.
   05 AN_YEAR  PIC XX  COMP.
```

We shall see later that this approach actually complicates coding in C. You can move an entire level from one variable to another in COBOL by simply coding

```
MOVE A_DATE TO ANOTHER_DATE.
```

STRUCTURES

Of course, you cannot perform any arithmetic on a 01 level that has sublevels. A statement such as

```
ADD 1 to A_DATE
```

makes no sense, and the compiler will issue a message to that effect.

TEMPLATES

In C, the coding of a variable that has a hierarchy is split into two parts.* The first part names a breakdown of fields, and the second part declares a variable with that breakdown. In C terms, the first part describes a template with a tag-type and the names of the members, and the second part declares a variable of that tag-type. The template does not reserve any storage. The result is similar to COPYBOOK, but it is achieved in a manner better supported by C.

The syntax for coding the template is

```
struct tag-type
    {
    /* Declarations of members
    };
```

A variable using that template is declared as

```
struct tag-type variable-name;
```

For example, a structure containing a date may be coded as

```
struct s_date
        {
        int month;
        int day;
        int year;
        };
struct s_date a_date;
```

---

*Although both parts may be incorporated into a single statement, its usefulness in that form is much more limited.

The name of the tag-type is **s_date**. The prefix **s_** is simply a convention I use for tag-type names. To get to a member, or field, of a structure, you must use a fully qualified name. The member operator (.) separates the overall name from the member name. The fields in **a_date** are:

```
a_date.month
a_date.day
a_date.year
```

Each fully qualified name is a variable of the type that the member is declared to be. For example,

```
a_date.month = 12;
if (a_date.day > 1 || a_date.day < 12)
```

Just as in COBOL, you cannot perform arithmetic operations on a variable that is a component of a structure.

```
a_date = a_date + 1;
```

is not legal. However, you can move a structure as a whole into another structure of the same tag-type.

```
struct s_date another_date;
another_date = a_date;
```

moves all the values of **a_date** into **another_date**. The members of **another_date** are:

```
another_date.month
another_date.day
another_date.year
```

The members of a structure need not be simply **ints** or **doubles**. They can also be arrays. For example,

```
struct s_date_external
   {
   char c_month[3];
   char c_day[3];
```

STRUCTURES 131

```
    char c_year[3];
    };
struct s_date a_date_external;
```

The members of **a_date_external** are:

```
a_date_external.c_month
a_date_external.c_day
a_date_external.c_year
```

Because each of these is an array (in this case, a **char** array), you can use the index operator on them. The three elements in the second member are

```
a_date_external.c_day[0]
a_date_external.c_day[1]
a_date_external.c_day[2]
```

Example 7.1 is a program that demonstrates structure usage. It has a simple day test, rather than the more complex on in previous examples to emphasize the structure members.

Example 7.1

```
#include <stdio.h>
#include <stdlib.h>

#define GOOD 0
#define BAD 1

struct s_date
    {
    int month;
    int day;
    int year;
    };

void main()
        {
        struct s_date in_date;
        int ret_value;
```

```
        /* Now convert each external to internal */
        printf("\n Month: ");
        scanf("%d", &in_date.month);
        printf("\n Day: ");
        scanf("%d", &in_date.day);
        printf("\n Year: ");
        scanf("%d", &in_date.year);

        /* Now print out the date */

        printf("%d/%d/%d", in_date.month, in_date.day,
            in_date.year);

        ret_value = GOOD;
        if (in_date.month < 1 || in_date.month > 12)
                {
                ret_value = BAD;
                printf("\n Bad month %d", in_date.month);
                }
           if (in_date.day < 1 || in_date.day > 31)
                {
                ret_value = BAD;
                printf("\n Bad day %d", in_date.day);
                }
           if (in_date.year < 60 || in_date.year > 95)
                {
                ret_value = BAD;
                printf("\n Bad year %d", in_date.year);
                }
        exit(ret_value);
        }
```

In early versions of C, the member names in each tag-type had to be unique. You will still see remnants of this requirement in some of the library functions that use structures, such as the time functions. Members need not have unique names because the compiler knows which tag-type a variable is declared to be and uses the corresponding member type. The second template could be declared as

```
struct s_date_external
```

STRUCTURES

```
    {
    char month[3];
    char day[3];
    char year[3];
    };
struct s_date_external a_date_external;
```

and the members (all of which are **char** arrays) would be

```
a_date_external.month
a_date_external.day
a_date_external.year
```

The compiler will only allow assignment of two structures of the same tag-type.* Even though **a_date_external** as declared here and **a_date** as declared previously both have three members with the same names, they are not of the same tag–type. Therefore the compiler will *not* allow:

```
a_date_external = a_date;
```

Note that whenever you see structure templates used, you will know that the members have exactly the same names. In our COBOL example, the coder could have used level 5 names of MM or DATE_HIRED_MONTH or DH_MONTH.

A structure template must be declared before it is used. Typically, the templates are put in a header file included at the top of each source file that needs them. The templates in a hierarchy should be declared in order, from the innermost to the outermost.

Initializing Structures

Structures are initialized using the same syntax as arrays. The values in the list initialize each member in order. For example,

---

*Compilers will treat as equivalent any structures of the same member order and types, regardless of the names of the members. Though this feature is useful for advanced applications in certain programs, it is not recommended for general use.

```
struct s_date my_date = {1, 2, 3}:
```

initializes **my_date.month** to 1, **my_date.day** to 2, and **my_date.year** to 3.

Functions and Structures

Functions in C can receive and return not only simple variables, but also structures. A primary reason for creating structure templates is to be able to code functions that operate on the members of the structure.

A structure is passed like a normal variable with call by value. A function can be declared in such a way that it returns the values in a structure of a particular type.

```
void print_date(struct s_date date);
```

declares that **print_date** will receive the values in a structure of **s_date** type.

```
struct s_date input_date(void);
```

declares that **input_date** will return all the values in a structure of **s_date** type. Using the same logic employed in Example 7.1, the code could be rewritten as shown in Example 7.2. The only difference is that **print_date** contains calls to **sprintf** to convert the members of the structure with the internal form back to external form.

This function delineation is useful in that one function converts from external format to internal format, and the other converts from internal format to external format. A similar application appears in Example 10.4.

Consider the following COBOL equivalent of Example 7.2.

```
01 DATE.
    05 MONTH COMP PIC XX.
    05 DAY   COMP PIC XX.
    05 YEAR  COMP PIC xx.
    ...
CALL INPUT_DATE USING DATE.
```

Example 7.2

```
#include <stdio.h>
#include <stdlib.h>

struct s_date
    {
    int month;
    int day;
    int year;
    };

#define GOOD 0
#define BAD 1

struct s_date input_date(void);
void print_date(struct s_date date);
int check_date(struct s_date date);

void main()
    {
    struct s_date in_date;
    int ret_value;

    in_date = input_date();
    print_date(in_date);
```

135

```c
        ret_value = check_date(in_date);
        exit(ret_value);
    }

struct s_date input_date(void)
{
    struct s_date ret_date;

    printf("\n Month: ");
    scanf("%d",&ret_date.month);
    printf("\n Day: ");
    scanf("%d",&ret_date.day);
    printf("\n Year: ");
    scanf("%d",&ret_date.year);

    return ret_date;
}

void print_date(struct s_date in_date)
{
    printf("%d/%d/%d", in_date.month,
                      in_date.day,in_date.year);
    return;
}

int check_date(struct s_date in_date)
{
```

136

```
int ret_value;
ret_value = GOOD;
if (in_date.month < 1 || in_date.month > 12)
   {
   ret_value = BAD;
   printf("\n Bad month %d", in_date.month);
   }
if (in_date.day < 1 || in_date.day > 31)
   {
   ret_value = BAD;
   printf("\n Bad day %d", in_date.day);
   }
if (in_date.year < 60 || in_date.year > 95)
   {
   ret_value = BAD;
   printf("\n Bad year %d", in_date.year);
   }
return ret_value;
}
```

```
CALL PRINT_DATE USING DATE.
CALL CHECK_DATE USING DATE.
```

PRINT_DATE would contain

```
LINKAGE SECTION.

01 WORK_DATE.
   05 MONTH COMP PIC 99.
   05 DAY   COMP PIC 99.
   05 YEAR  COMP PIC 99.

INPUT-OUTPUT SECTION.

01 PRINT_OUT.
   02 MONTH PIC 99.
   02 FILLER PIC X VALUE '/'.
   02 DAY PIC 99.
   02 FILLER PIC X VALUE '/'.
   02 YEAR PIC 99.

PROCEDURE DIVISION USING WORK_DATE.

    MOVE MONTH OF WORK_DATE TO MONTH OF PRINT_OUT.
    MOVE DAY OF WORK_DATE TO DAY OF PRINT_OUT.
    MOVE YEAR OF WORK_DATE TO YEAR OF PRINT_OUT.
```

Alternatively, the last three statements might be coded as

```
MOVE CORRESPONDING WORK_DATE TO PRINT_OUT.
```

Hierarchies

COBOL records typically have several levels. The way to achieve this in C is to build structure templates with a structure as a member. This bottom-up record building is the reverse of typical COBOL design. For example, given the **s_date** template

```
struct s_date
   {
   int month;
   int day;
```

```
   int year;
   };
```

you can construct an **s_employee** template and declare a variable in that template as follows.

```
struct s_employee
   {
   char name[40];
   struct s_date date_hired;
   struct s_date date_last_raise;
   };
struct s_employee employee;
```

The members of employee are

member	data type
employee.name	array of char
employee.date_hired	struct s_date
employee.date_last_raise	struct s_date

The members of the latter two variables are

```
employee.date_hired.month
employee.date_hired.day
employee.date_hired.year
employee.date_last_raise.month
employee.date_last_raise.day
employee.date_last_raise.year
```

Since **date_last_raise** and **date_hired** are of the same tag-type, you can assign them to one another.

```
employee.date_hired = employee.date_last_raise;
```

You may assign the return value of **input_date()** to either, as shown in

```
employee.date_hired = input_date();
employee.date_last_raise = input_date();
```

Or you may pass either to **print_date()**. An equivalent COBOL record is

```
01 EMPLOYEE.
   05 NAME PIC X(40).
   05 DATE_HIRED.
         10  MONTH COMP PIC 99.
         10  DAY COMP PIC 99.
         10  YEAR COMP PIC 99.
   05 DATE_LAST_RAISE.
         10  MONTH COMP PIC 99.
         10  DAY COMP PIC 99.
         10  YEAR COMP PIC 99.
```

with the following references:

```
YEAR OF DATE_LAST_RAISE OF EMPLOYEE
MONTH OF DATE_HIRED OF EMPLOYEE
```

Packages

One useful tool that you can create with C is a package of functions that all operate on a particular structure tag-type. Object-oriented programming is based on this concept. A date is a very typical example of an object. Any breakdown for which you have created a COPYBOOK or that you frequently cut and paste from another source is a candidate for a structure, which then becomes the basis for a set of functions.

Since this chapter has focused on applications dealing with dates, let us consider other useful functions to perform involving dates. You may want to determine the last day of the month for a particular date. Example 7.3 shows how to accomplish this by passing a function and returning the values in a structure.

Example 7.3

```
struct s_date /* This should be in a header file */
        {
        int month;
        int day;
```

```
        int year;
        };

struct s_date last_date_of_month(struct s_date  in_date)
        {
        static int days_in_month[12] =
                {31,28,31,30,31,30,31,31,30,31,30,31};
        struct s_date ret_date;

        ret_date = in_date;
        if (ret_date.month != 2)
                {
                ret_date.day = days_in_month[ret_date.month -  1];
                }
        else
                {
                if (ret_date.year % 4 == 0)
                        ret_date.day = 29;
                 else
                        ret_date.day = 28;
                }

        return ret_date;
        }
```

Now let's consider an example using this function. The record and code might resemble

```
struct s_employee
   {
   char name[40];
   struct s_date date_hired;
   struct s_date date_first_paycheck;
   };
struct s_employee employee;

employee.date_first_paycheck =
   last_date_of_month(employee.date_hired);
```

This structure simply sets **date_first_paycheck** to the end of the month. For those who may complain that names of members have to be fully qualified, please note that by using functions that operate on dates, we have avoided the need for a second member operator. The internal members of date have been hidden from the program that uses dates. As a basic rule of thumb, no more than one member operator should appear in code. Each declared structure template should have associated functions that operate on it. Try to design your structures so that you do not use more than one member operator.

UNIONS

Members of structures do not overlap. Each member has its own memory location. In contrast, union members share the same memory space, just as the terms in REDEFINES. The declaration of a union looks like the declaration for a structure.

```
union template-name {
       declarations of members
       } ;
union template-name name-of-union-variable ;
```

or

```
union {
       declarations of members
       } name-of-union-variable ;
```

Consider the example union

```
union example_union_template {
       int int_number;
       double double_number;
       };
union example_union_template example_union;
```

The two members are

```
example_union.int_number      int
example_union.double_number   double
```

Unions are rarely used in C. Pointers, described in Chapter 8, are used with much greater frequency and serve the same purpose as unions.

EXAMPLE FUNCTIONS

Example 7.4 is a function that keeps employee classes and salaries in the same structure for easier program maintenance. Of course, we could also have included the maximum salary for each class in this structure.

The COBOL equivalent of this table is

```
01 SOME_TABLE.
    05 SALARY_TABLE OCCURS 3 TIMES.
        10 MINIMUM_SALARY COMP-2.
        10 LEVEL COMP.

01 ANOTHER_TABLE REDEFINES SOME_TABLE.
    05 SALARY_TABLE_1.
        10 FILLER COMP-2 VALUE 10000000.
        10 FILLER COMP VALUE 1
    05 SALARY_TABLE_2.
        10 FILLER COMP-2 VALUE 1000000.
        10 FILLER COMP VALUE 2
    05 SALARY_TABLE_3.
        10 FILLER COMP-2 VALUE 100000.
        10 FILLER COMP VALUE 3
```

Alternatively, we may want the routine to return a structure containing the minimum and maximum salaries for each employee class, as shown in Example 7.5.

EXAMPLE PROGRAM

Using these structures and the function from Example 7.5, we may rewrite Example 1.1 to yield the program in Example 7.6.

Example 7.4

```
#define BIG_HONCHO 1
#define MEDIUM_HONCHO 2
#define LITTLE_HONCHO 3

double minimum_salary_for_employee_class(int in_class)
{
    #define SIZE_SALARY_TABLE 3
    struct s_salary_table
    {
        double minimum_salary;
        int class;
    };
    struct s_salary_table salary_table[SIZE_SALARY_TABLE] =
    {
        {1000000., BIG_HONCHO},
        { 100000., MEDIUM_HONCHO},
        { 10000., LITTLE_HONCHO}
    };
    double ret_value;
    int class_index;

    ret_value = -1;
    for (class_index = 0; class_index < SIZE_SALARY_TABLE; class_index ++)
    {
```

```
        if (in_class == salary_table[class_index].class)
            {
            ret_value = salary_table[class_index].minimum_salary;
            break;
            }
        }
    return ret_value;
    }
```

Example 7.5

```
struct s_salary_range
    {
    int class;
    double minimum; double maximum;
    };

#define BIG_HONCHO 1
#define MEDIUM_HONCHO 2
#define LITTLE_HONCHO 3

#define SIZE_SALARY_TABLE 3

struct s_salary_range salary_table[SIZE_SALARY_TABLE] =
    {
    {BIG_HONCHO,    1000000.,10000000.},
    {MEDIUM_HONCHO,  100000., 1000000.},
    {LITTLE_HONCHO,   10000.,  100000.},
    };

struct s_salary_range salary_range_for_employee_class(int class)
    {
    double minimum_salary;
    int index;
```

```
/* Default value for return if not found */
struct s_salary_range salary_range_ret = {0,0.0,1.0};

for (index = 0; index < SIZE_SALARY_TABLE; index++)
    {
    if (class == salary_table[index].class)
        {
        salary_range_ret = salary_table[index];
        break;
        }
    }
return salary_range_ret;
}
```

Example 7.6

```
#include <stdio.h>
#include <stdlib.h>

struct s_salary_range /* Should be in a header file */
    {
    int class;
    double minimum;
    double maximum;
    };
struct s_salary_range salary_range_for_employee_class(int class);

void main()
    {
    /* Declarations */
    double employee_salary_comp;
    int employee_class_comp;
    struct s_salary_range salary_range;
    /* Executable */

    employee_class_comp = 1;

    while (employee_class_comp != 0)
        {
```

```c
    printf("Enter class: ");
    scanf("%d", &employee_class_comp);
    printf("Enter salary: ");
    scanf("%lf", &employee_salary_comp);
    salary_range =
            salary_range_for_employee_class(employee_class_comp);
    if (employee_salary_comp < salary_range.minimum ||
            employee_salary_comp > salary_range.maximum)
        {
        printf("salary out of range\n");
        }
    }

exit(0);
}
```

149

SUMMARY

- A structure is a group of variables that need not be of matching data types.
- Each member of a structure acts as a variable of its type.
- Structures can be passed as parameters to functions, be returned from functions, and be assigned.
- A union is an overlapping set of variables. Changing any of these variables changes all of the others.

8

Pointers

Pointers are both the bane and the boon of C programmers. This chapter covers only one basic use for the pointer—passing parameters by reference to functions. Programmers converting from COBOL do not normally need to learn the other uses of pointers, such as accessing direct memory locations and speeding up programs.

INTRODUCTION

Consider the following basic example of pointers. Suppose we have the following declarations:

```
int a_number;
int another_number;
```

and a variable called **p_number**. Suppose that these variables are stored at locations 100, 200, and 300, respectively. The following table illustrates their location and contents.

Variable	Location	Contents
a_number	100	?
another_number	200	?
p_number	300	?

152   C FOR COBOL PROGRAMMERS

If we code*

```
a_number = 5;
p_number = a_number;        /* See footnote */
another_number = p_number;
```

then the values in the table become

Variable	Location	Contents
a_number	100	5
another_number	200	5
p_number	300	5

The address operator **&** gives the location of a variable, rather than its contents, so if we code

```
a_number = 5;
p_number = &a_number;
another_number = p_number;
```

then the table becomes

Variable	Location	Contents
a_number	100	5
another_number	200	100
p_number	300	100

Now suppose we want to access not what **p_number** contains, but rather the contents of the location corresponding to the value of **p_number**, that is, the actual contents of **a_number**. To do this we use the indirection operator (*). If we code

---

*This and the following assignments are not legal in ANSI C. They are used here simply as an illustration.

POINTERS **153**

```
a_number = 5;
p_number = &a_number;
another_number = *p_number;
```

then the values change to

Variable	Location	Contents
a_number	100	5
another_number	200	5
p_number	300	100

Since **p_number** contains 100, ***p_number** is interpreted as "go to location 100 and get the contents of that location," that is, the integer value 5. This is the meaning of indirection. Now suppose we have the following assignments, with the indirection operator applied on the left side of the assignment:

```
p_number = &a_number;
*p_number = 10;
```

The values become

Variable	Location	Contents
a_number	100	10
p_number	300	100

The first line places the address of **a_number** into **p_number**. The second line does not put 10 into **p_number**, but takes the contents of **p_number** (100) as an address, then places the 10 in that location. This is equivalent to saying simply **a_number = 10**.* In fact, if **p_number** contains the address of **a_number**, then you can use ***p_number** anywhere in the executable code that you would use a_number and the result will be exactly the same.

---

*In fact, ***&a_number = 10;** takes the address of **a_number**, then goes to that location and puts 10 in it.

We have thus far avoided describing the declaration of **p_number**. Only variables that are declared to hold addresses should be used to contain addresses. The declaration for a variable that contains addresses uses the same character as the indirection operator. The declaration

```
int *p_number;
```

states that **p_number** is a variable that contains addresses of **ints**, or, as it is more commonly called, a pointer to **int**.

Two assignments used in the first example in this chapter, **p_number = a_number** and **another_number = p_number**, are illegal if **p_number** is a pointer to **int**. Only the address of an **int** may be put into a pointer to **int**. On the other hand, you may use the indirection operator only if **p_number** is a pointer. You may not use the indirection operator with a simple **int** variable.

POINTERS AND DATA TYPES

The compiler requires you to declare the variable type stored at the address indicated by a pointer for two reasons. Suppose you have

```
int a_number;
int another_number;
int *p_number;
p_number = &a_number;

another_number = *p_number;
```

The compiler needs to know how many bytes to access at the location pointed to by **p_number** and how to treat the bytes at that address. Since **p_number** points to an **int**, *****p_number** tells the compiler to get whatever number of bytes corresponds to the size of that **int** from that address and treat those bytes as an integer. Likewise, with the assignment

```
*p_number = 3.3;
```

the compiler interprets the need to convert 3.3 to an **int** and stores the resulting value at the address indicated by **p_number**.

You can declare a pointer for any data type. The code

```
int integer_number = 4;
int double_number = 3.3;
double *p_double;
int *p_integer;
p_double = &double_number;
p_integer = &integer_number;
*p_double = *p_integer;
```

takes the value of **integer_number** (to which **p_integer** points), converts it to a **double**, and stores it at the address to which **p_double** points (that is, **double_number**).

The address of the data type must match the type of the pointer. If you reverse the assignments as follows,

```
p_double = &integer_number;
p_integer = &double_number;
*p_double = *p_integer;
```

then your compiler should issue a warning. ***p_integer** retrieves two bytes starting at the address of **double_number**. That value is computed to a **double**, and eight bytes are stored at the address of **integer_number**. Six bytes of memory following **integer_number** will be overwritten as a result.

FUNCTION PARAMETERS

The main use of pointers is to pass parameters by reference. Recall that the **scanf** function set required address operators to store converted strings in the addresses passed to it. Often you will want to write functions that return more than one value. One way to do this is to have the calling function pass the addresses of variables to the called function. The called function then places values at each of those addresses.

Example 5.2, repeated below, passed back the minimum salary for a particular employee level.

```
double minimum_salary_for_employee_level(level)
    {
    double minimum_salary;
    switch(level)
        {
```

```
    case BIG_HONCHO:
        minimum_salary = 1000000;
        break;
    case MEDIUM_HONCHO:
        minimum_salary = 100000;
        break;
    case LITTLE_HONCHO:
        minimum_salary = 10000;
        break;
    default:
        minimum_salary = -1;
        break;
        }
    return minimum_salary;
    }
```

Each time we called this function, the return value was checked to see if it was greater than 0. This test attributed too much meaning to the return value.

```
if (minimum_salary_for_employee_level(level) < 0)
    /* Level was bad */
```

Now let us assume that we want to obtain two return values: an indication of whether the level was bad and the actual value of the salary. Example 8.1 illustrates a function that accomplishes both tasks.

Example 8.1

```
#define BIG_HONCHO 1
#define MEDIUM_HONCHO 2
#define LITTLE_HONCHO 3
#define TRUE 1
#define FALSE 0

int minimum_salary_for_employee_level(int level, double *p_salary)
        {
        double minimum_salary;
        int ret_value;
```

```
        switch(level)
                {
        case BIG_HONCHO:
                minimum_salary = 1000000;
                ret_value = TRUE;
                break;
        case MEDIUM_HONCHO:
                minimum_salary = 100000;
                ret_value = TRUE;
                break;
        case LITTLE_HONCHO:
                minimum_salary = 10000;
                ret_value = TRUE;
                break;
        default:
                minimum_salary = -1;
                ret_value = FALSE;
                break;
                }
        *p_salary = minimum_salary;
        return ret_value;
        }
```

To call this function, use

```
double minimum_salary;
if (minimum_salary_for_employee_level(level, &minimum_salary))
     /* Level was bad */
```

With the function in Example 8.1, we cannot return both the minimum and maximum salaries for each level. However, if we use a second pointer, as shown in Example 8.2, it is possible to obtain both as return values.

Example 8.2

```
#define BIG_HONCHO 1
#define MEDIUM_HONCHO 2
#define LITTLE_HONCHO 3
#define TRUE 1
```

```c
#define FALSE 0

int salary_range_for_employee_level(int level,
      double *p_minimum, double *p_maximum)
   {
   double minimum_salary;
   double maximum_salary;
   int ret_value;

   /* Set as before */
   switch(level)
       {
   case BIG_HONCHO:
       minimum_salary = 1000000;
       maximum_salary = 10000000;
       ret_value = TRUE;
       break;
   case MEDIUM_HONCHO:
       minimum_salary = 100000;
       maximum_salary = 1000000;
       ret_value = TRUE;
       break;
   case LITTLE_HONCHO:
       minimum_salary = 10000;
       maximum_salary = 100000;
       ret_value = TRUE;
       break;
   default:
       minimum_salary = 0;
       maximum_salary = 1;
       ret_value = FALSE;
       break;
       }
   *p_minimum = minimum_salary;
   *p_maximum = maximum_salary;

   return ret_value;
   }
```

Note that many of the C library functions have parameters that are pointers. Many of the string functions expect **char** * values. The name of an array all by itself is its address. For example, recall from Chapter 5 that the prototype for **strcpy** is

```
char *strcpy(char * destination, char * source);
```

You can call it with

```
char out[20];
strcpy(out, "This is moved");
```

POINTERS AND STRUCTURES

Just as a pointer may point to any data type, such as **int** or **double**, it may also point to a structure. Consider the example date structure

```
struct s_date
    {
    int month;
    int day;
    int year;
    };
struct s_date a_date = {5, 3, 92};
struct s_date another_date;
p_date = &a_date;
another_date = *p_date;
```

The variable **a_date** is a structure of type **s_date**. The variable **p_date** is used to point to structures of type **s_date**. The first assignment sets the address of **a_date** into **p_date**. The expression ***p_date** now refers to the variable **a_date**. The second assignment moves all values in the structure to which **p_date** points (**a_date**) to **another_date**. This assignment is equivalent to **another_date = a_date;**

The first member in **a_date** is **a_date.month**, an **int**. The expression **(*p_date).month** also refers to the same member in **a_date**. The reasons for using parentheses in this expression have to do with the precedence of the operators. The member operator (.) has higher precedence than the indirection operator

(*). We want to perform the indirection first to get a structure of type **s_date**, and then take a member of that structure.

The use of pointers to structures is so common that there exists a special operator meaning "the member in the structure indicated by the pointer". This operator, –>, is the pointer-member operator. If **p_date** contains the address of **a_date**, then the following expressions refer to the same item:

```
(*p_date).month
p_date->month
a_date.month
```

Example 8.3 is a rewrite of Example 7.2 using pointers.

Example 8.3

```
#include <stdio.h>

struct s_date
       {
       int month;
       int day;
       int year;
       };

void input_date(struct s_date *p_date);
void print_date(struct s_date *p_date);

void main()
       {
       struct s_date in_date;
       input_date(&in_date);
       print_date(&in_date);
       }

void input_date(struct s_date *p_date)
       {
       struct s_date ret_date;
       printf("\n Month: ");
       scanf("%d",&ret_date.month);
       printf("\n Day: ");
```

```
              scanf("%d",&ret_date.day);
              printf("\n Year: ");
              scanf("%d",&ret_date.year);
              /* Put it into the structure whose address
                  was passed */
              *p_date = ret_date;
              return;
              }

    void print_date(struct s_date *p_date)
              {
              printf("%02d:%02d:%02d",p_date->month,
                      p_date->day, p_date->year);
              return;
              }
```

Alternatively, the **input_date** function could have read the values directly into the structure to which **p_date** points. Since **p_date->month** refers to an **int**, **&p_date->month** is the address of that **int**. Example 8.4 shows the code for this function.

Example 8.4

```
#include <stdio.h>
struct s_date  /* Template should be in header file */
          {
          int month;
          int day;
          int year;
          };

void input_date(struct s_date *p_date)
     {
     printf("\n Month: ");
     scanf("%d",&p_date->month);
     printf("\n Day: ");
     scanf("%d",&p_date->day);
     printf("\n Year: ");
     scanf("%d",&p_date->year);
     return;
     }
```

162 C FOR COBOL PROGRAMMERS

This version of the function may be a bit harder to absorb. You might want to use **p_date**, for example, because that is an address. Note, however, that it is the address of the entire structure. Bear in mind that **p_date->month** is an **int**, and the expression **&p_date->month** is the address of that **int**. Since **p_date->month** is the first member in the structure **p_date**, by coincidence its address will be the same as that of the whole structure. However, the addresses of **&p_date->day** and **&p_date->year** are *not* the same as that of **&p_date**.

POINTERS AND UNIONS

Suppose you had a data record that you wanted to read in two different ways. In COBOL, it might look like

```
01 MY_RECORD.
    05 RECORD_TYPE PIC 'X'.
    05 TYPE_ONE.
        10 FIRST_FIELD PIC 'XXXX'.
        10 SECOND_FIELD PIC 'XX'.
    05 TYPE_TWO REDEFINES TYPE_ONE.
        10 FIRST_FIELD COMP PIC 'XX'.
        10 SECOND_FIELD PIC 'XXXX'.
```

You could create a union in C to perform the same operation, but pointers are usually clearer. For example, the C structures equivalent to the preceding COBOL code are

```
struct s_my_record
    {
    char record_type;
    char remainder[60];
    };
struct s_type_one
    {
    char first_field[4];
    char second_field[2];
    };
struct s_type_two
    {
    char first_field[2];
    char second_field[4];
    };
```

POINTERS

To use these structures, assign a pointer to them. For example,

```
struct s_my_record my_record;
struct s_type_one *ptype_one;
struct s_type_two *ptype_two;

if (my_record.record_type == '1')
    {
    ptype_one = (struct s_type_one *) my_record.remainder;
    /* Now use references as ptype_one->first_field */
    }
else if (my_record.record_type == '2')
    {
    ptype_two = (struct s_type_one *) my_record.remainder;
    /* Now use references as ptype_two->first_field */
    }
```

By using pointers, you eliminate some of the extra levels of members that unions create.

POINTER ERRORS

The most frequent error programmers make with pointers is using them before assigning them a value. A **static** or external pointer has a default value of 0. Some compilers place a special value in address 0. If you change the value in that location when your program runs, you will get the error indication "Null pointer used".

An automatic pointer variable has a garbage value. There is no telling where it may point. Changing the location to which it points may or may not keep your program running. For example,

```
static int *pointer_zero;

function()
        {
        int *pointer_garbage;

        /* This will put the value 17 at memory location 0 */
        *pointer_zero = 17;

        /* This will put the value 29 at some memory location */
```

```
            *pointer_garbage = 29;
        }
```

Initialize all pointers.

Null Pointer

The **NULL** pointer is the pointer whose value is zero. Functions that return pointers to indicate an error or abnormal condition return this value. **NULL** is **#defined** in many of the standard header files, such as **stdio.h**.

VOID POINTERS

A **void** pointer is a pointer used as a general memory pointer (**void ***). You may assign it to and from a pointer to any other type without a cast, as you will see in Chapter 11. For now, suffice it to say that you cannot reference memory directly using a **void** pointer. Note that some input and output functions are documented to expect a **void** pointer. You can pass these functions the address of any data type. Of course, you will want to pass the address for the variable you wish to input.

EXAMPLE PROGRAM

Using pointers and Example 8.2, we may rewrite Example 1.1 as Example 8.5.

This program follows the same logic as Example 8.2. As an exercise you may wish to alter Example 8.5 to avoid receiving the extra error message before exiting the program.

SUMMARY

- A pointer is a variable that stores the addresses of other variables. It points to variables of a particular data type.
- Pointers are used for call by reference.
- Pointers to structures can be used in place of unions.

Example 8.5

```
#include <stdio.h>
#include <stdlib.h>

int salary_range_for_employee_level(int level,
                    double *p_minimum, double *p_maximum);

void main()
    {
    /* Declarations */

    double employee_salary_comp;
    int employee_class_comp;
    int ret_value;
    double minimum_salary;
    double maximum_salary;

    /* Executable */

    employee_class_comp = 1;

    while (employee_class_comp != 0)
        {
        printf("Enter class: ");
        scanf("%d", &employee_class_comp);
```

165

```
    printf("Enter salary: ");
    scanf("%lf", &employee_salary_comp);
    ret_value =
        salary_range_for_employee_level(employee_class_comp,
        &minimum_salary, &maximum_salary);
    if (ret_value)
        {
        if (employee_salary_comp < minimum_salary ||
            employee_salary_comp > maximum_salary)
            {
            printf("salary out of range\n");
            }
        }
    else
        printf("bad employee class\n");
    }
exit(0);
}
```

9
The Preprocessor and Other Data Types

The preprocessor translates your source code to a form that the compiler can accept. It can perform several operations, including reading in entire source files, converting symbols to their equivalents, and conditionally including code.

PREPROCESSOR COMMANDS

All preprocessor commands start with the **#** character. The **#** need not be in the first column, although it is typically placed there.

Preprocessor commands terminate with the end of the line, rather than with the semicolon that ends a normal C statement. If you need to continue the command to a new line, then an escape sequence (\ followed by a new-line character) must appear at the end of the line.

The preprocessor commands are executed before the compiler sees the source code. In fact, you could actually use the preprocessor to transform non-C text files if you wished.

The #define Statement

The **#define** preprocessor statement allows you to name a value. It works like the search and replace mechanism of a text editor.

Wherever the name assigned in a **#define** appears in your code, the compiler replaces it with the value you specify. The syntax for **#define** is

```
#define name value
```

For example, in

```
#define TRUE 1
#define FALSE 0
...
if (month < 1 || month > 12)
    valid = FALSE;
```

the value 0 replaces the characters FALSE, so the compiler actually sees

```
if (month < 1 || month > 12)
    valid = 0;
```

Do not include a semicolon on the **#define** line, because it will become part of the substitution string. In this example, it would be harmless, because the result of

```
#define FALSE 0;
```

would simply be an extra null statement,

```
if (month < 1 || month > 12)
    valid = 0;;
```

However, if you coded

```
if (valid == FALSE)
```

it would be translated as

```
if (valid == 0;)
```

which is a syntax error.

Once you assign a name with **#define**, you may use that name in another **#define**.

```
#define MINIMUM_YEARS 2
#define MAXIMUM_YEARS MINIMUM_YEARS + 10
```

A typical use for the **#define** statement is establishing the size of an array. All loops that refer to the array then use that name in the controlling test. This procedure avoids many problems that can arise from exceeding the bounds of an array.

```
#define SIZE_TABLE 10
int table[SIZE_TABLE];
for (i = 0; i < SIZE_TABLE; i++)
    {
    table[i] = ...
    }
```

Using **#define** statements also makes your code more readable and maintainable.

ANSI C reserves certain **#define** names for common uses. These names appear in Table 9.1. You may find some of them useful. For example, you may wish to use

```
printf("\n This program was compiled on %s at %s",
       __DATE__, __TIME__);
printf("\n Program logic error at line %d File %s",
       __LINE__, __FILE__);
```

The many other names defined by ANSI C appear in Appendix B.

You may place the starting character **#** in all preprocessor directives anywhere on the line. For instance, there can be white space between # and the name of the directive itself. Any of the spacings below are acceptable, but the first form is the preferred one for lines outside functions and the third for lines inside functions. Usually it is best to place all **#define** statements outside functions and at the beginning of the source file, so they are easy to spot.

```
#define TOKEN 1
#   define  TOKEN 1
    #define TOKEN 1
```

170 C FOR COBOL PROGRAMMERS

Table 9.1   Table of predefined Macro names

Macro Name	Meaning
__LINE__	line number of current source line (integer)
__FILE__	file name of source file (string)
__DATE__	translation date of source file (string)
__TIME__	time of translation (string)
__STDC__	the version number of the C standard (the integer value 1)

The #include Statement

The **#include** statement works like a COPYBOOK, reading a specified source file into the code to be compiled. The file read is typically a header file—one that contains **#defines** or function prototypes that generally appear at the head of a source file. By convention, the names of header files have the suffix ".h". The syntax for **#include** statement has two forms:

```
#include "filename"
#include <filename>
```

These two forms differ only in terms of where to search for the file. In the first form, the preprocessor assumes that the file is in the current directory. With the second form, the preprocessor looks for the file in a system–defined directory. The second form is typically used for files shared by many programs, such as the header files that come with the compiler library.

If you are creating a set of functions that other programs will use, you should also create a source file that contains prototypes for the functions and any **#define** statements or structure templates needed to use those functions. On a design level, this source file forms the interface specification between your functions and those who use them.

The C compiler uses the reserved **#include** file names listed in Table 9.2. Use these names to access the corresponding functions. You should not use any of these names for your own **#include** files.

Table 9.2. Reserved **#include** file names in C.

File Name	Purpose
assert.h	for program diagnostics
ctype.h	character typing functions
error.h	error values
float.h	ranges of floating point values
limits.h	limits of integer values
locale.h	setting the locale of a program
math.h	mathematical functions
setjmp.h	doing long jumps back through code
signal.h	setting functions to handle signals (exceptions)
stdarg.h	variable parameter lists
stddef.h	standard definitions
stdio.h	input and output
stdlib.h	miscellaneous functions
string.h	string functions
time.h	time functions

Conditional Compilation

Not all statements in a source file must always be compiled into executable code. For example, may you include certain statements only to help you debug your code. Once you have finished debugging, you may no longer want the statements to be executed. However, you may still want to retain them, just in case some program feature does not work right later. In other languages, you could "comment out" code, as in

```
/*
        printf("`\n Value of day is %d", day);
*/
```

Although you may do this in C, placing comments in code you are trying to eliminate will cause problems because comments do not nest. The conditional compilation or **#if** directives solve this problem, and also make your code more maintainable.

The **#if** directives are similar to if statements. If a given test is true, then the code following it is compiled. If the test is not true, then the compiler ignores the code. The **#endif** directive marks the end of the statements compiled if the test is true. The most common **#if** directive is **#ifdef**, which tests whether a particular name has been defined with a **#define** statement. For example,

```
#ifdef DEBUG
        printf("\n Value of day is %d", day);
#endif
```

If a **#define DEBUG** appears before the preceding code, then the **printf** call will be compiled. Otherwise, the compiler will ignore the **printf** call as if it were a comment. Most compilers also allow you to define a name on the command line that invokes the compiler, as in

```
cc -DDEBUG test.c
```

which defines **DEBUG** just as would a **#define DEBUG** in the source.

You may also add an **#else** directive between **#ifdef** and **#endif**. If a **#define** exists for the label, all lines between **#ifdef** and **#else** will be compiled. Otherwise, the lines from **#else** to **#endif** will be compiled.

Chapter 11 covers additional **#if** directives. Example 9.1 illustrates how to use the **#if** directives presented in this chapter to code a typical function with **#ifdef** statements.

ENUMERATION VARIABLES

Enumeration variable types work like "88" variables in COBOL, allowing you to use identifiers as values once you specify the list of names that constitute these values. To denote a type of enumerated variable, name the type and list the values a variable of that type may take. You may specify an enumerated variable in much the same way that you declare an ordinary variable, using the syntax*

---

*You can accomplish what both these statements do by coding:

enum *enum-type* {*names-of-values*} *enum-variable*;

but this format is seldom used, since it declares a variable at the same time.

Example 9.1

```
#define BIG_HONCHO 1
#define MEDIUM_HONCHO 2
#define LITTLE_HONCHO 3

double minimum_salary_for_employee_level(int in_class)
    {
    static double minimum_salary[3] =
            {1000000.,    100000.,      10000.};
    static int class[3] =
            {BIG_HONCHO, MEDIUM_HONCHO, LITTLE_HONCHO};

    double salary;
    int class_index;
#ifdef DEBUG
    printf("Minimum_salary_for_employee_level called\n");
    printf("In_class %d\n", in_class);
#endif
    salary = 0.0;
    for (class_index = 0; class_index < 3; class_index ++)
        {
#ifdef DEBUG_EXTENDED
        printf("Comparing to class_index %d", class_index);
#endif
        if (in_class == class[class_index])
            {
```

```
            salary = minimum_salary[class_index];
            break;
        }
    }
#ifdef DEBUG
    printf("Returning salary %lf", salary);
#endif
    return salary;
}
```

```
enum enum-type {names-of-values};
enum enum-type enum-variable;
```

Let us consider a common example of an enumerated variable, the days of the week. Example 9.2 shows how to code a function that checks whether a given day is a weekend day.

Enumerated variables tend to be self-documenting because you specify what values a variable can assume. However, you should be aware that the compiler treats an enumerated variable as an integer, so the variable may also take on values not included in the list. Thus you *can* compute expressions such as **day+3** or **day++**, even though such computations may not make any sense in the context of your program.

The compiler assigns integer values to the identifiers starting with 0. However, you can specify the integer value of an **enum** identifier by listing it in the declaration of the **enum** type, as shown in

```
enum eday { sunday=1, monday=4, tuesday=3, wednesday=7};
```

In the employee class problem discussed in preceding chapters, we could use the following enumeration instead of **#defines**.

```
enum e_class {LITTLE_HONCHO = 1, MEDIUM_HONCHO = 2,
    BIG_HONCHO = 3};
```

The compiler will check to ensure that you have not assigned the same value to two names.

TYPEDEF STATEMENT

The **typedef** statement provides a way of assigning a name to a particular data type. You may then use the name as a shorthand way to declare that particular type. To define a **typedef**, declare a variable of the type you want to define, then write a **typedef** statement, replacing the variable name with the name you want to use for that data-type. For example, to use a **typedef** for

Example 9.2

```
enum e_day { sunday, monday, tuesday, wednesday,
             thursday, friday, saturday};
        /* declares range of values for variables of enum type eday */

#define TRUE 1
#define FALSE 0

int weekend(day)
/* Returns true if day is weekend day, false otherwise */
enum e_day day;
{
    int ret;

    if (day == sunday || day == saturday)
        ret = TRUE;
    else
        ret = FALSE;

    return ret;
}
```

176

```
int variable;
```

write the code

```
typedef int COUNT;
```

You may then use this declaration as

```
COUNT x;
```

In the employee class problem, we could provide the following **typedef** for the class enumeration.

```
enum e_class {LITTLE_HONCHO = 1, MEDIUM_HONCHO = 2,
    BIG_HONCHO = 3};
typedef enum e_class CLASS;
```

and then use this typedef in the structure template as

```
struct e_employee
    {
    char name[50];
    CLASS class;
    double salary;
    };
```

The C language uses as **typedefs** the reserved names listed in Table 9.4. Thus you should not use these names in your **typedefs**. The most common reserved **typedef** is **size_t**, which represents units of storage, usually expressed in bytes. You may also use **typedef** for structures and arrays. For example,

```
typedef struct s_date DATE;
...
DATE a_date;
```

declares **a_date** as a structure for which **s_date** is the tag-type. This structure is useful if **DATE** is only passed to functions, and the user of those functions does not need to know the structure's internal details.

Table 9.4. Reserved names of **typedefs** in C.

Typedef	Defined in	Use
clock_t	time.h	time
div_t	stdlib.h	div()
fpos_t	stdio.h	file position
jmp_buf	setjmp.h	setjmp() / longjmp()
ldiv_t	stdlib.h	ldiv()
prtdiff_t	stddef.h	difference in two pointers
sig_atomic_t	signal.h	signals (exceptions)
size_t	stddef.h	result of sizeof
va_list	stdarg.h	variable parameter list

SUMMARY

- The **#define** directive specifies text to be replaced for a label in a source file.
- The **#include** directive specifies insertion of a source file's contents into your program's code before compilation.
- Conditional compilation directives allow the same source file to be compiled in various ways, depending on **#define** values and other testable values.
- Enumerated variables (**enum**) have a list of identifiers used as values.
- The **typedef** specifies a synonym for a data type.

10
File Input and Output

C uses functions to provide input and output to a file. These functions provide input and output in both internal and external format.

COBOL FILE I/O

Let us review reading a COBOL file before describing its equivalent in C. Example 10.1 is a simple COBOL program that performs file I/O.

Example 10.1

```
IDENTIFICATION DIVISION.

PROGRAM-ID.
   EXAMPROG.

*AUTHOR.
*   Kenneth Pugh
*DATE-WRITTEN.
*   January 29, 1992
```

```
ENVIRONMENT DIVISION.
INPUT-OUTPUT SECTION.
FILE-CONTROL.

    SELECT EMPLOYEE-FILE
        ASSIGN TO EFDAT.
    SELECT PRINT-FILE
        ASSIGN TO OUTDAT.

DATA DIVISON.

FILE SECTION.

FD EMPLOYEE-FILE
   RECORD CONTAINS 97 CHARACTERS
   BLOCK CONTAINS 0 RECORDS
   RECORDING MODE IS F.

01  EMPLOYEE-FILE-RECORD.
    05 NAME PIC X(40).
    05 ADDRESS.
       10 STREET PIC X(30).
       10 CITY PIC X(20).
       10 STATE PIC X(2).
       10 ZIP PIC 9(5).

FD PRINT-FILE
   RECORD CONTAINS 80 CHARACTERS
   BLOCK CONTAINS 0 RECORDS
   RECORDING MODE IS F.

01 PRINT-FILE-RECORD.
   05 NAME PIC X(40).
   05 FILLER PIC X(10) VALUE ' LIVES IN '
   05 STATE PIC X(2).

WORKING-STORAGE SECTION.

01 ALL-DONE PIC X VALUE 'N'.

PROCEDURE DIVISION.
```

```
OPEN OUTPUT PRINT-FILE.
OPEN INPUT EMPLOYEE-FILE.
PERFORM PROCESS-EMPLOYEE UNTIL ALL-DONE = 'Y'.
CLOSE PRINT-FILE.
CLOSE EMPLOYEE-FILE.

PROCESS-EMPLOYEE.

    READ EMPLOYEE-FILE
        AT END
            MOVE 'Y' TO ALL-DONE.
    MOVE CORRESPONDING EMPLOYEE-FILE-RECORD TO EMPLOYEE-LINE.
    WRITE PRINT-FILE.
```

If a program is to read a file in COBOL, you must insert several items into that program. In the FILE-CONTROL section, you must first designate the real file name assigned to the logical file name.

```
FILE-CONTROL.

    SELECT EMPLOYEE-FILE
        ASSIGN TO EFDAT.
```

Next, you must describe the file in the FILE SECTION.

```
FD EMPLOYEE-FILE

    RECORD CONTAINS 97 CHARACTERS
    BLOCK CONTAINS 0 RECORDS
    RECORDING MODE IS F.
```

Then you must open the file in the PROCEDURE DIVISION.

```
OPEN INPUT EMPLOYEE-FILE.
```

Now your program can read the file. If the FILE SECTION specifies a default record, then, when the program executes READ EMPLOYEE-FILE, the record will be read into that default record. Alternatively, the READ statement can include the Working Storage name

```
READ EMPLOYEE-FILE INTO EMPLOYEE-RECORD.
```

Most COBOL programs are set up for fixed-size records, which means that there are no end-of-record marks in the file. The AT END clause is true when all records have been read.

C FILE I/O

In C, functions perform the operations that open, read, and write a file. The **fopen** function returns a unique identifier, a pointer to type **FILE**, which is passed to the other functions to identify the file. When you open a file, you must also store the return value of **fopen** in a variable of this type. Thus the **fopen** function combines the features of FILE-CONTROL and OPEN INPUT.

The code to open the file named **efdat** is

```
FILE *employee_file;
employee_file = fopen("efdat","r");
```

A detailed description of **fopen** appears in Appendix B. A synopsis for **fopen** follows.

```
FILE *fopen(char * file_name, char * mode)
```

file_name is the name of the file to open, and **mode** is one of the following operations:

- **r**   for reading a text file,
- **w**   for writing a text file,
- **a**   for appending data to the end of a text file,
- **rb**   for reading a binary file,
- **wb** for writing a binary file,
- **ab**   for appending data to the end of a binary file.

The function returns **NULL** if the program is unable to open the file, or file pointer if the program is able to open file.

When you are done with a file, close it with **fclose** to ensure that characters written to the file, but not yet physically placed on the file, will be put there. If you do not call **fclose**, the **exit** function will call it for any open files. The syntax for **fclose** is simply

```
fclose(FILE *file_pointer);
```

so to close the example file previously opened, simply call

```
fclose(employee_file);
```

The characters in the file can be treated in one of two ways. The first is similar to the record oriented mode of COBOL, and uses the **fread** and **fwrite** functions. The synopsis for **fread** is

```
fread(void *address, size_t size_element,
      int count_elements, FILE *file_pointer)
```

In this function,

address	gives a location into which the characters should be read,
size_element	is the number of bytes in an element,
count_elements	is the number of elements to read,
file_pointer	represents the file where the characters to be read are stored.

This function returns the number of elements read. If an error or end-of-file occurred, this value will be less than **count_elements**.

The **fread** function presumes you are reading an array of records, so it includes both a size and a count. Most often, **count_elements** will be 1. The **sizeof** operator, which looks like a function call, gives the number of bytes in a variable or data type. In the case of a structure, this number of bytes includes any packing or filler bytes necessary for alignment on machine word boundaries.

184 C FOR COBOL PROGRAMMERS

You must describe the record you are reading with **fread** in the template of the structure whose address you pass to it. Implicitly, this template gives the same information as the FILE SECTION. The address of the variable must be passed to **fread** every time a record is, as in the second form of the READ statement. For example, the following code reads a single record into **employee_record**.

```
struct s_employee_record
    {
    char name[40];
    char other[57];
    };
struct s_employee_record employee_record;

fread(&employee_record, sizeof(employee_record), 1,
    employee_file);
```

Let us use all these functions in a program that reads an employee data file and prints the name of each employee. Example 10.1 reads **efdat**, an employee data file. The structure of the tag-type **s_employee** implicitly describes the layout of the data in **efdat**.

The synopsis of the write function, called **fwrite**, is

```
fwrite(void *address, size_t size_element,
    int count_elements, FILE *file_pointer)
```

where

>   **address**   gives the address from which to write the characters,
>
>   **size_element**   is the number of bytes in an element,
>
>   **count_elements**   is the number of elements to write,
>
>   **file_pointer**   represents the file to which the characters should be written.

This function are returns the number of elements written. If an error occurred, this value will be less than **count_elements**).

Like the **fread** function, **fwrite** presumes you are writing an array of records. Most often, **count_elements** will be 1.

Suppose you wanted to read a COBOL file with the following layout using a C program.

```
01 EMPLOYEE_PAYROLL.
    05 NAME PIC X(50).
    05 CLASS PIC 99.
    05 SALARY PIC 99999999V99.
```

The easiest way to do so is to define two structures. One structure will represent the file as it exists on the disk. The second structure will consist of the same fields expressed in internal format. This approach allows us to use the C arithmetic operators on the fields. The external format template is

```
struct s_employee_payroll_external
    {
    char name[50];
    char class[2];
    char salary[10];
    };
```

It matches exactly the layout of the COBOL record. The internal format template is

```
struct s_employee_payroll
    {
    char name[51];
    int class;
    double salary;
    };
```

Note that an additional character has been added to **name** in the internal format template, so that there is room for the terminating NUL. Example 10.2 is a payroll program utilizing these two structures. The templates for the two records are in **record.h**.

Example 10.1

```
#include <stdio.h>
#include <stdlib.h>
#define TRUE 1
#define FALSE 0

struct s_address
    {
    char street[30];
    char city[20];
    char state[2];
    char zip[5];
    };

struct s_employee
    {
    char name[40];
    struct s_address address;
    };

void main()
    {
    FILE *employee_file;
    struct s_employee employee_record;
    int count_read;
    int done;
```

```c
    employee_file = fopen("efdat","r");
    if (employee_file == NULL)
        {
        printf("\n Unable to open employee file efdat");
        exit(1);
        }
else
    {
    done = FALSE;
    while (!done)
        {
        count_read = fread(&employee_record, sizeof(employee_record),
                        1, employee_file);
        if (count_read == 1)
                printf("%40.40s lives in %2.2s",
                        employee_record.name, employee_record.address.state);
        else
                done = TRUE;
        }
    }
exit(0);
}
```

Example 10.2

```
#include <stdio.h>
#include <stdlib.h>
#include "record.h"
#define TRUE 1
#define FALSE 0
void main()
{
FILE *payroll_file;
struct s_employee_payroll payroll_external_record;
struct s_employee_payroll payroll_record;
int count_read;
int done;
payroll_file = fopen("payroll","r");
if (payroll_file == NULL)
    {
    printf("\n Unable to open payroll file ");
    exit(1);
    }
else
    {
    done = FALSE;
    while (!done)
        {
        count_read = fread(&payroll_external_record,
                sizeof(payroll_external_record), 1, payroll_file);
```

```c
        if (count_read == 1)
            {
            /* Convert to internal format */
            sscanf(payroll_external_record.name, "%50c",
                    payroll_record.name);
                    payroll_record.name[50]='\0';
            sscanf(payroll_external_record.class, "%2d",
                    &payroll_record.class);
            sscanf(payroll_external_record.salary, "%10lf",
                    &payroll_record.salary);
            /* Correct for decimal placement */
            payroll_record.salary /= 100.;
            /* Now call minimum_salary or other computations */
            printf("Name %50.50s Salary %10.2lf\n",
                    payroll_record.name, payroll_record.salary);
            if (payroll_record.class < 1 ||
                payroll_record.class > 3)
                printf(" ***** Error in class %d\n",
                        payroll_record.class);
            }
        else
            done = TRUE;
        }
    exit(0);
    }
```

189

File Positioning

The **fseek** function permits you to set the position in a file to which the next character will be read or from which it will be written. The **ftell** function returns the current position in a file, which you can pass to **fseek** if you wish to go back to that particular position in the file. The calls are

```
int fseek(FILE *file_pointer, long int offset, int mode);
```

where

    file_pointer   is the value returned by the **fopen** call,
    offset   is the the number of bytes to skip,
    mode   is how to use the offset:
        SEEK_SET   from beginning of file,
        SEEK_CUR   from current position,
        SEEK_END   from end of file.

and

```
long ftell(FILE *file_pointer)
```

where **file_pointer** is the value returned by the **fopen** call.

For the payroll file above, to get to the fifth record, you must position the file so the next read will occur there. You may accomplish this using a call such as

```
fseek(payroll_file,
    (long) 4 * sizeof(payroll_external_record), SEEK_SET);
```

Unlike COBOL, the standard library of C provides no indexing schemes. You can create your own or purchase prewritten libraries that have these features. Numerous such packages exist on the market, and they differ in speed, size of object code, number of files required for multiple indices, cost, and number of other languages supported. Some libraries support variable-length records as well as fixed-length records. Customer information at suppliers can help you decide which package is right for your particular application.

Formatted File Operations

To read characters from a file, use the **fscanf** function. This function works just like **scanf** with the addition of a parameter that specifies the file.

```
int fscanf(FILE *file_pointer, char *format, addresses...)
```

where

> **file_pointer** is returned by the **fopen** call,
> **format** is a character string,
> *addresses* specifies where to put the values read.

Without setting up a separate structure, you could use **fscanf** to read the payroll file above as follows:

```
fscanf(payroll_file,"%50c%2d%10lf",
    payroll_record.name,
    &payroll_record.class,
    &payroll_record.salary);
```

To write formatted output to a file, use **fprint**, which works just like **printf** with the addition of a file specifier.

```
int fprintf(FILE *file_pointer, char *format, values ..);
```

where

> **file_pointer**   is returned by the **fopen** call,
> **format**   is a character string,
> *values*   specifies values to output.

BINARY FILES VERSUS TEXT FILES

Slight differences exist between text and binary files that affect the manner in which you must treat them. Text files may contain carriage-return/new-line character combinations that are translated to a single new-line character on input. Conversely, new-lines in output are translated to a pair of characters. A text file may also contain an END_OF_FILE character (control-Z in MS-DOS).

A binary file has no END_OF_FILE character representation. The operating system keeps a count of how many bytes are in a file. When this number of bytes has been read, the read routine will report an **EOF**. There is no special treatment for any characters.

You may specify that a file be read or written in binary mode by using **b** in the call to **fopen**.

CHARACTER FUNCTIONS

The function **fgetc** reads one character at a time. The syntax for **fgetc** is

```
int fgetc(FILE *file_pointer);
```

The value that **fgetc()** returns is either a character or the value **EOF**. The assigned value of **EOF** in a **#define** is usually –1, so the return value of **fgetc** should also be an integer. If you specify **stdin** as the **file_pointer**, **fgetc** will read input from the keyboard unless you have redirected input.

The output function corresponding to **fgetc** is **fputc**; the syntax for **fputc**, which outputs one character at a time, is

```
int fputc(int character, FILE *file_pointer)
```

If for some reason **fputc** is unable to output a character (perhaps the disk is full or you have closed the file), then it returns **EOF** as its value.

You can read or write a line to a file using **fgets** or **fputs**, respectively. Each returns a pointer to the buffer read or written if the operation was successful. If the operation was not successful, each returns the **NULL** pointer. The synopsis for **fgets** is

```
char *fgets(char *buffer, int size, FILE *file_pointer)
```

where

buffer	is the address to read into,
size	is the maximum number of characters to read,
file_pointer	is the value returned by the **fopen** call.

The synopsis for **fputs** is

```
char *fputs(char *buffer, FILE *file_pointer)
```

where

buffer	is the address to write from,
size	is the maximum number of characters to write,
file_pointer	is the value returned by the **fopen** call.

PREOPENED FILES

Three file pointers point to files already opened when your **main** program starts execution. These files are **stdin**, **stdout**, and **stderr** which are the standard input, standard output and standard error files. The standard error file is usually set to the terminal screen. Any functions introduced in this chapter will work with these files simply by using one of these values as the file pointer. For example,

```
fprintf(stdout,"Hi");
```

will print to the standard output. If you specify **stdin** as the **file_pointer** for an input function, the function will read from the keyboard unless you have redirected input.

Example Functions

Example 10.3 is a program containing a function that copies a file one character at a time. The program uses the binary mode on the open to make it more general.

Example 10.4 is a program using a more general approach to the employee file reading program. It contains two functions that read and write particular employee records in a file.

Example 10.3

```
#include <stdio.h>
#define TRUE 1
#define FALSE 0
copy_file(char *filename_in, char * filename_out)
    {
    int result = TRUE;
    FILE *file_in;
    FILE *file_out;
    int done;
    int character;

    file_in = fopen(filename_in, "rb");
    if (file_in == NULL)
        {
        result = FALSE;
        }
    else
        {
        file_out = fopen(filename_out, "wb");
        if (file_out == NULL)
            {
            result = FALSE;
            }
        else
            {
            done = FALSE;
```

```
            while (!done)
               {
               character = fgetc(file_in);
               if (character == EOF)
                  done = TRUE;
               else
                  {
                  if (fputc(character, file_out) == EOF)
                     {
                     result = FALSE;
                     done = TRUE;
                     }
                  }
               }
            return result;
            }
         void main()
            {
            int result;
            result = copy_file("IN", "OUT");
            if (result)
               printf("Good copy\n");
            else
               printf("Bad copy\n");
            }
```

Example 10.4

```
#include <stdio.h>
#include "record.h"
#include <stdlib.h>
#define TRUE 1
#define FALSE 0
int read_employee_record(FILE *payroll_file, int record_number,
            struct s_employee_payroll *payroll_record);
int write_employee_record(FILE *payroll_file, int record_number,
            struct s_employee_payroll *payroll_record);

void main()
    {
    /* Give everyone a ten percent raise */
    FILE *payroll_file;
    struct s_employee_payroll payroll_record;
    int record_number;
    int done;

    payroll_file = fopen("payroll","r+");

    if (payroll_file == NULL)
        {
        printf("\n Unable to open payroll file ");
        exit(1);
        }
```

```
    else
        {
        done = FALSE;
        record_number = 0;
        while (!done)
            {
            if (read_employee_record(payroll_file, record_number,
                    &payroll_record))
                {
                printf("Record Name %50.50s old pay %10.21f",
                        payroll_record.name, payroll_record.salary);
                payroll_record.salary *= 1.10;
                printf(" new pay %10.21f\n", payroll_record.salary);
                if (write_employee_record(payroll_file, record_number,
                        &payroll_record) != TRUE)
                    {
                    printf("Error in rewriting record %d", record_number);
                    }
                record_number++;
                }
            else
                done = TRUE;
            } /* end of while */
        }
    fclose(payroll_file);
    exit(0);
    }
```

197

```
int read_employee_record(FILE *payroll_file, int record_number,
        struct s_employee_payroll *payroll_record)
    {
    int count_read;
    int result;
    struct s_employee_payroll_external payroll_external_record;

    if (fseek(payroll_file, (long) record_number *
              sizeof(payroll_external_record), SEEK_SET) != 0)
        result = FALSE;
    else
        {
        count_read = fread(&payroll_external_record,
                sizeof(payroll_external_record), 1, payroll_file);
        if (count_read == 1)
            {
            /* Convert to internal format */
            sscanf(payroll_external_record.name, "%50c",
                    payroll_record->name);
                    payroll_record->name[50]='\0';
            sscanf(payroll_external_record.class, "%2d",
                    &payroll_record->class);
            sscanf(payroll_external_record.salary, "%10lf",
                    &payroll_record->salary);
            /* Correct for decimal placement */
            payroll_record->salary /= 100.;
```

```c
            result = TRUE;
            }
        else
            result = FALSE;
        }
    return result;
    }

int write_employee_record(FILE *payroll_file, int record_number,
    struct s_employee_payroll *payroll_record)
    {
    int count_write;
    int result;
    struct s_employee_payroll_external payroll_external_record;

    if (fseek(payroll_file, (long) record_number *
            sizeof(payroll_external_record), SEEK_SET) != 0)
        result = FALSE;
    else
        {
        /* Convert to internal format */

        sprintf(payroll_external_record.name, "%50.50s",
                payroll_record->name);
        sprintf(payroll_external_record.class, "%2d",
                payroll_record->class);
        /* Correct for decimal placement */
```

```
        sprintf(payroll_external_record.salary, "%10.01f",
                payroll_record->salary * 100.);

        count_write = fwrite(&payroll_external_record,
                sizeof(payroll_external_record), 1, payroll_file);
        if (count_write == 1)
                result = TRUE;
        else
                result = FALSE;
        }
return result;
}
```

SUMMARY

The C library has the following built-in input and output functions:

fopen   to open a file for reading, writing, or appending
fclose   to close a file
fread   to read a block of data from a file
fwrite   to write a block of data to a file
fseek   to position a file for reading or writing
fscanf   to read formatted data from a file
fprintf to write formatted data to a file
fgetc   to read a character from a file
fputc   to write a character to a file
fgets   to read a string from a file
fputs   to write a string to a file

11

The Rest of the Story

The aspects of C covered thus far in this book represent those that most closely match features found in COBOL. This chapter presents other more advanced features of C for purposes of recognition only. Use of these features by beginning C programmers is not recommended.

VARIABLES AND FUNCTIONS

Variables may be declared in several places in a program. Functions may be defined in single or multiple source files.

Scope of Names

You may declare variables at any point after an opening brace in a compound statement. Following such an opening brace, any variable declared by a given name outside the compound statement is no longer accessible by that same name from within. References to that name will refer to the variable declared within the compound statement.

There are four scopes for a variable—block, function, file, and program. A variable declared within a block or function is known only within the block or function. A variable declared external to functions is known within the file in which it appears, from the point of its appearance to the end of the file. A variable declared as external in one source file and declared as **extern** in other files has program scope, as was shown in Chapter 4.

Redeclaring a variable is invalid in only two places. First, you may not redeclare a function parameter in the outermost block that begins the function. Otherwise you cannot access the value passed to the function. Second, you cannot redeclare a variable name in the same block where you declared it originally.

Static Externals and Functions

You may need to use an external variable to communicate between two functions. However, you do not want the name of this external variable to conflict with other external variables. To make an external name known only within a single source file, begin the variable declaration with the key word **static**. This use of **static** overloads the meaning of the term, so that in this instance it really means "private"—an external variable known only to a single source file.

You may also use the key word **static** to preface a function in a given source file. The name of that function will then be known only within that particular source file. Suppose you create a source file containing a package of functions that all require certain common functions. If these common functions are not designed to be called by any functions other than those in the package, using the key word **static** will ensure that the common functions are known only within that single source file.

DATA TYPES AND CONSTANTS

So far, this text has covered only the basic data types. C has many more types and operators, including bitwise operators.

Data Types

The data types available in C provide a range of storage alternatives. For instance, **short ints** use less storage space than or the same amount as regular **ints**; long **ints** use more than or the same amount as regular **ints**. Likewise, **floats** use less space than **doubles**; **long doubles** use the same space as or more than **doubles**.*

In unsigned integers, the bit normally used as the sign bit is used as another value bit. Only positive numbers are stored in unsigned **ints**. All arithmetic is done modulo the largest number plus one that can be represented in the unsigned **int**. The outline of data types is shown in Table 11.1.

Numeric Constants

The arithmetic constants corresponding to some of these data types consist of a suffix applied to the constant of the standard types **int** or **double**. The suffixes appear in Table 11.2.

Character Constants

To represent nonprintable characters in character constants and strings, use the set of escape sequences shown in Table 11.3. These sequences may be used as single characters (enclosed in single quotes) or in strings (enclosed in double quotes).

You can also represent characters using their octal or hexadecimal values. These values are represented by

Octal

```
\n or \nn or \nnn    where  n is a digit from 0 to 7;
```

Hexadecimal

```
\xn or \xnn or \xnnn  where  n is a hexadecimal
                      digit (0 to 9 and
                      A to F or a to f).
```

For example,

```
'\033'    escape character (decimal 27)
'\032'    control-Z (decimal 26)
```

---

*Formerly, a **double** was known as a **long float**, a term that is now obsolete, though you may see it in older programs.

Table 11.1. Data types in C.

Data Type	Can Also Use	Minimum Range of Values*	Typical Size
int	signed int	−32767 to 32767	2 or 4 bytes
short int	short	−32767 to 32767	2 bytes
	signed short		
	signed short int		
long int	long	−2147483647 to 2147483647	4 bytes
	signed long		
	signed long int		
float		10E-37 to 10E37	4 bytes
		6 decimal digits	
double		10E-37 to 10E37	8 bytes
		10 decimal digits	
long double		10E-37 to 10E37	8 to 16 bytes
		10 decimal digits	
unsigned int	unsigned	0 to 65535	2 or 4 bytes
unsigned short int	unsigned short	0 to 65535	2 bytes
unsigned long int	unsigned long	0 to 4294967295	4 bytes
char		−127 to +127 or 0 to 255	1 byte
unsigned char		0 to 255	1 byte
signed char		−127 to 127	1 byte

*Although **double** and **long double** appear equivalent here, **doubles** usually have 10 decimal digits with 1E-37 to 1E37 in the exponent, whereas **long doubles** may have 16 or more decimal digits of precision and range from 1E-300 to 1E300. The formal description of C specifies −32767, −2147483647, and −127 as the lowest negative numbers represented by **ints**, **longs**, and **signed chars**, respectively. These are the limits for computers that represent numbers using ones complement. Most computers use twos complement representation and have limits of −32768, −214783448, and −128, respectively.

Table 11.2. Suffixes applied to **int** and **double** to form arithmetic constants.

Suffix	Type	Example
U (or **u**)	unsigned int	4455U
L (or **l**)	long int	32456L
UL (or **LU**)	unsigned long int	324567UL
F (or **f**)	float	3.2F or 3.2E5F
L (or **l**)	long double	3.2L or 3.1E5L

Table 11.3. Escape sequences for nonprintable characters.

Sequence	Meaning
\a	alert (bell)
\b	back-space
\t	tab (horizontal)
\n	new-line
\v	vertical tab
\f	form-feed
\r	carriage-return
\"	quote (in a string)
\'	single quote (as a character constant)
\?	question mark
\\	backslash (the character itself)

CONVERSION

If the data types on either side of an operator disagree, one is converted to the type of the other before the operation is performed. A **char** or a **short int** is converted to an **int** value before it is used in an expression. Whether sign extension occurs on regular chars depends on the system. For all other types, values of a lower data type on the list that follows are converted to the higher data type.*

---

*Most compilers automatically convert floats to doubles so arithmetic is performed in double precision.

long double   Highest
double
float
unsigned long int
long int
unsigned int
int   Lowest

When you assign a value, that value may not fit in the variable to which it is assigned. In that case, the value assigned is based on the conventions in Table 11.4.

Table 11.4.   Conversions for assignment operator.

Left-hand type	Expression type	Conversion
double or **float**	**long double**	round off or truncate, depending on compiler
float	**double**	round off or truncate, depending on compiler
long or **int** or **char**	**long double** or **double** or **float**	truncate fractional part if integer cannot fit; result is undefined
int	**long**	high order bits eliminated*
char	**int**	high order bits eliminated*

*The result is undefined, but most compilers simply eliminate the high order bits.

Register Types

There are four types of storage in C. Three have already been described—automatic (**auto**), **static** (always allocated), and external. The fourth type, **register**, is a variation of **auto**.

The **register** storage class is a suggestion to the compiler to place the variable in a machine register. If the compiler is able to do this, the code will execute faster. A **register** variable acts just like an automatic variable, except that you cannot take the address of a register variable.

Type Modifiers

ANSI C provides for two type modifiers that help programmers write more efficient and bug-free programs. The **const** modifier (for constant) declares that a particular variable will not be altered during program execution.

The **volatile** modifier declares that the contents of a variable may be altered in ways not readily apparent to the compiler. This prevents the compiler from optimizing code that it deems useless, but which in reality is not.

Bit Pattern Constants

Two common forms of representation are hexadecimal and octal notation. Octal constants begin with the digit 0 and are followed by digits from 0 to 7. Hexadecimal constants begin with the prefix 0X or 0x, and are followed by digits 0 to 9 and letters A to F or a to f for the hexadecimal digits 10 to 15. A bit pattern can be represented either way.

```
Bit pattern                          1001011011010110

Octal representation       0113326   1  001  011  011  010  110
                                     1   1    3    3    2    6

Hexadecimal representation  0x96D6   1001     0101  1101  0110
                                      9        6     D     6
```

You can print out integers in hex or octal representation by using %**x** or %**o** as the format specifier. You can also read in integers in hex or octal using %**x** or %**o**.

Bitwise Operators

Several bitwise operators in C operate on the individual bits of integers. These operators include logical and shift operators used to turn on and off bits within a single integer. Table 11.5 lists the symbols that represent these operators and the operations they perform.

There are two shift operators—the left shift (<<) and the right shift (>>). The left shift moves the bits to the left and sets the rightmost (low-order) bit to zero. The leftmost (high-order) bit shifted out is thrown away.

The right shift moves bits to the right. The lower-order bits shifted out are thrown away. Depending on the compiler and the computer, one of two things will occur with the high-order bit of a signed value, the sign bit. It may be set to zero, just as on the left shift, in what is termed a logical shift. Alternatively, in what is termed an arithmetic shift, the value of the high-order bit may remain what it was. These two kinds of shifts differ only if the high-order bit equals one. Unsigned integers do not have a sign bit, so right shifts for them are always logical shifts.

Table 11.6 presents sample expressions using the bitwise operators and the values they yield. There are also shorthand assignment operators for |, &, <<, and >>. These are |=, &=, <<=, and >>=.

Table 11.5.   Bitwise operators and their purposes.

Operator	Operation
|	Bitwise OR
&	Bitwise AND
<<	Bitwise left shift
>>	Bitwise right shift
~	Bitwise negation (one's complement)

Conditional Operator

The conditional operator can be used in normal coding but is mainly used to create macros. This operator has the syntax

Table 11.6. Sample values obtained using bitwise operators.

Expression	Value
1 | 2	3
0xFF & 0x0F	0x0F
0x33 | 0xCC	0xFF
0X0F << 2	0x3C
0x1C >> 1	0X0E
~x03	0XFFFC (assuming 2 byte ints)

```
condition ? true-expression : false-expression
```

If the condition is true, then the value of the conditional expression is the true expression. Otherwise, it is the value of the false expression. For example,

```
day > 7 ? 5 : 3
```

has the value 5 if day is greater than 7, or the value 3 if it is not.

Comma Operator

The comma operator evaluates two expressions into one. It is used in places where the syntax only allows a single expression. The value of the comma operator is the value of the right-hand expression in the format.

```
left-expression , right-expression
```

For example, a **for** loop might start with

```
for (i=0, j < MAXIMUM; i < j; i++, j--)
```

Logical AND/OR

If the left-hand side of a logical operator is sufficient to determine the truth or falseness of the entire operation, then the right-hand side is not evaluated. For the AND (&&) operator, if the left-hand side is false (zero value), then the right-hand side is not evaluated. For the OR (||) operator, if the left-hand side is TRUE, then the right-hand side is not evaluated.

Cast Operator

The cast operator, a set of parentheses enclosing a data type, converts an expression from one type to another using the syntax

```
(data_type) expression
```

An example is

```
int i, j;
double d;
i = (int) d + j;
```

where **d** is converted to an **int** value and the addition is an integer addition.

A cast may be used to convert a pointer from one type to another. For example,

```
int *pi;
double *pd;
pi = (int *) pd;
```

Precedence and Associativity

Now that all operators have been introduced, a full precedence chart is given in Table 11.7. Note that the order of some of these operators is tricky. For example, **a & 0xF == 0x7** is interpreted as **a & (0xF == 0x7)**.

The order of evaluation is not specified, except that it is right to left for the comma, conditional, logical OR and logical AND.

CONTROL FLOW

The goto Statement

Devotees of structured programming reel with horror whenever someone mentions the GOTO statement. Though most of the jus-

Table 11.7. Precedence and associativity of operators.

Operator	Use	Associativity
()	function call	left to right
[]	array element	
->	pointer to structure member	
.	member of structure	
!	logical negation	right to left
~	one's complement	
++	increment	
--	decrement	
-	unary minus	
+	unary plus	
(type)	cast	
*	indirection (pointer)	
&	address	
sizeof	size of object	
*	multiplication	left to right
/	division	
%	modulus	
+	addition	left to right
-	subtraction	
<<	left shift	left to right
>>	right shift	
<	less than	left to right
<=	less than or equal to	
>	greater than	
>=	greater than or equal to	
==	equality	left to right
!=	inequality	
&	bitwise AND	left to right
^	bitwise XOR	left to right
|	bitwise OR	left to right
&&	logical AND	left to right

Table 11.7. Continued

Operator	Associativity	Order of evaluation
||	logical OR	left to right
? :	conditional	right to left
=	assignment	right to left
op=	shorthand assignment	
,	comma	left to right

tification for using a **goto** has disappeared with the advent of modern control statements. In a few instances I feel it is clearer to use a **goto** than to employ complex test-expressions. None of the programs in this book use the **goto**, but for those who may wish to use it, the syntax is:

```
goto label;

label:
    statement
```

The continue Statement

The **continue** statement skips to the end of a **for**, **while**, or **do-while** loop and performs the test without executing the intermediate instructions. With the **for** loop, the increment-expression is executed before the test is evaluated. Generally, you can eliminate the need for a **continue** simply by rearranging the code slightly, so its use is not too common. For that reason, you may find the following example somewhat contrived.

```
days = 0;
for (day = 0; day < 31; day++)
    {
    if (day > 3)
        continue;
    days += day;
    }
```

This loop will be executed 31 times, but the **continue** statement will cause the addition to be skipped once **day** is greater than 3. Only the values of **day** for 0, 1, 2, and 3 will be added to **days**.

POINTERS

Pointers appear in many parts of C programs. For instance, the **main** function receives arguments, one of which is an array of pointers. Allocated memory also requires pointers.

Pointers and Allocated Memory

The compiler provides all the storage types described so far in this text (automatic, external, and static). Storage is either allocated only while you are in a function (automatic) or during the entire program execution (external and static). A compromise between these two positions is memory that can remain allocated after a function is exited, but that may not be needed during the full program execution. This type of memory is called allocated storage.

The C library provides several routines that allocate storage. The most common of these, **malloc**, returns a pointer to the first byte of a block of memory; **malloc** requires the **stdlib.h** file. Its calling sequence is

```
void *malloc(size_t size)
/* Allocates a block of memory */
/* size is the number of bytes to allocate */
        /* Returns pointer to block, if available */
        /*         NULL if not available */
```

The type **size_t** is a **typedef** that is the equivalent of an integer. The corresponding routine to deallocate memory is **free**. The **free** routine receives an address that *must* come from an allocation function such as **malloc**. If the address is anything else, the program will not behave correctly. The calling sequence for **free** is

```
void free(void *pointer);
```

Pointer Arithmetic

C allows you to perform addition and subtraction on pointers. Although these look like integer operations, they act somewhat differently. They are based on the size of the pointer's object. You can add an integer value to a pointer or subtract one from it. Suppose each **int** is two bytes long and you have

```
int i=6;         i is at address 100
int *p_int=&i;   p_int is declared and initialized to 100.
```

then

Expression	Value
p_int	100
p_int + 1	100 + 1 * (sizeof int) = 102
p_int + 2	100 + 2 * (sizeof int) = 104
p_int - 2	100 - 2 * (sizeof int) = 96

You cannot add two pointers. However, you can subtract one pointer from another when they point to the same type of object. The difference between two pointers is an integer that represents the difference in the number of objects, not the absolute memory difference. Pointer subtraction is meaningful only if both pointers point to elements in the same array. Using pointer arithmetic, you can quickly index through arrays. This topic is covered in greater detail in many general texts on programming in C.

Strings and Pointers

As discussed in Chapter 5, a string is an array of characters stored as a constant. The name of an array is an address. Likewise, the string constant itself is an address. This address can be assigned to a pointer or passed to a function. For example,

```
char *p_chr="ABCDE";
```

sets up in memory an array of six **chars** and initializes the value of the pointer **p_chr** to the address of the array.

Arrays of Pointers

Pointers are variables, just like any others, so you may create an array of pointers, as in

```
char *strings[10];
```

This is an array of ten pointers, each of which points to characters or strings of characters. An array of character pointers is typically coded in a routine, as shown in Example 11.1.

Example 11.1

```
#include <stdio.h>
#define NUMBER_MESSAGES 3

void print_error(int error_number)
/* prints the error message corresponding to error_number   */
    {
    static char *error_messages[NUMBER_MESSAGES]
        {
        "No error ", /* Error number zero is null */
        "Bad file name",
        "Nonexistent file",
        };

    if (error_number >= 0 && error_number <
        NUMBER_MESSAGES)
        printf("\n%s\n",
            error_messages[error_number]);
    else
        printf("\n UNKNOWN ERROR MESSAGE \n");
    return;
    }
```

The Arguments argc and argv

Two arguments are passed to the function called **main** when the program begins. They represent whatever you typed on the command line to the operating system when you executed the program. These arguments are conventionally named **argc** and **argv**. **argc** shows how many words, or strings of characters separated by spaces, there are on the command line. **argv** is an array of pointers to these words. The first element in **argv** usually points to the name of the program. If you use these arguments, your **main** function could resemble

```
#define FALSE 0
#define TRUE 1
static int debug;                    /* Debug flag */

void main(int argc, char *argv[])
        {
        debug=FALSE;
        if (argc>1)
                {
                /* Test to see if debug should be set */
                if (toupper(*argv[1])=='D')
                        debug=TRUE;
                ...
```

The characters in the strings may or may not be converted to lower case, depending on your operating system, so if you are testing for a specific character, use **toupper** as shown above.

By convention, options on the command line are passed when preceded by a hyphen. Filenames are passed with no hyphen. So the test portion of the preceding code might resemble

```
                for (i=1; i < argc; i++)
                        {
                        if (*argv[i] == '-')
                                /* check for option */
                                {
                                if (toupper(argv[i][1]) == 'D')
                                        debug=TRUE;
                                ...
```

For example, if you executed this program as

```
test -R -D
```

then the values of **argc** and **argv** would be:

Expression	Value
argc	3
argv[0]	"test"*
argv[1]	"-R"
argv[2]	"-D"

*Some systems cannot set the value of the expression **argv[0]** and will instead set it to point to a **NULL** string ("").

ADDITIONAL PREPROCESSER STATEMENTS

The preprocessor has other statements in addition to **#define**, **#include**, and **#ifdef**.

#define with Tokens

You can include replacement tokens with **#define** statements. The tokens act like textual parameters. Wherever the token name appears in the replacement string, the value used in code will replace that token in the string.

```
#define name(tokens) string-with-tokens
```

For example,

```
#define check_month(month)    (month < 1 || month > 12)

if (check_month(my_month))
    ....
```

gets translated to

```
if ((my_month < 1 || my_month > 12))
```

This form of **#define** permits you to convert what looks like function calls to in-line code.

Conditional Compilation Directives

You can "undefine" a name assigned in a **#define** by using the **#undef** command. This command removes the definition from the preprocessor.

The **#if** tests whether an expression is true or false. If the expression is true, the code from the test to the next **#endif** (or **#else**) is compiled. You can nest conditional compilations by using the **#elif** directive, which acts like **else if**.

You can also test in an **#if** to see whether a name has been assigned in a **#define** by using **defined(***name***)**. This directive returns a true or false value, depending on whether *name* does or does not appear in a **#define**. You can use this value in an expression, such as:

```
#if defined(NAME)                         does same as #ifdef
                                          NAME

#if defined(NAME_A)&&defined(NAME_B)      code is compiled
                                          only if both NAME_A
                                          and NAME_B are
                                          defined.
```

Quoting and Token Concatenation

Two operators available only in the preprocessor directives are the quote operator and the token concatenator.

The quote operator puts quotes around a given set of characters. If you had **#define STRING(string) #string**, then **STRING(abc)** would compile as if you had written **"abc"**. The token concatenator takes two sets of characters and concatenates them. It operates on unquoted strings. For example,

```
#define VAR_NUMBER(number) var##number

int VAR_NUMBER(3)
is compiled as if it were int var3.
```

Other Directives

The typical programmer will seldom use the other preprocessor directives. They are included here for completeness.

The **#line** directive sets the compiler line counter to a new value, and is used in computer-generated C programs.

The **#error** directive forces the compiler to issue an error message. In conditional compilation, you may use this directive as a flag if an odd case comes up, in much the same way as you would use an error message in the **default** of a **switch**.

The **#pragma** directive is a compiler-specific directive that commands the compiler to perform operations not included in standard C.

The null directive (**#**) is permitted, but has no effect.

SUMMARY

- Variations exist on integer and floating point data types. Their purpose is to contain smaller or larger numbers than fit in the standard sizes for these types of values.
- Unsigned integers contain only positive integer values.
- The **register** storage type, a variation of the automatic type, helps produce more efficient code.
- The storage type modifiers **const** and **volatile** describe the ways in which variables may be used.
- Bitwise operators treat integers as collections of bits, so that individual bits can be manipulated.
- **Static** externals are known only in the source file in which they are declared.
- Functions are known throughout an entire linked program unless they are declared **static**.

Appendix A

Comparison of COBOL and C

COBOL AND C EQUIVALENTS

Consult the Table of Contents or Index for the page number where a detailed description of each C statement listed below appears.

COBOL	C Equivalent
Commands	
ACCEPT	getchar(), scanf()
AT END	EOF
CALL	function
CLOSE	fclose()
COMP	int
COMP-2	double
COMPUTE	= (assignment)
DEPENDING ON	switch
ELSE	else
END-IF, END-PERFORM	compound statement
EVALUATE	switch
END	exit()

COBOL	C Equivalent
FILE	file pointer
FOR	for
GOTO	goto
IF	if
INDEXED	[ ] (arrays)
INITIAL	initializers
OCCURS	[ ] in array declaration
OPEN	fopen()
READ	read()
REDEFINES	unio
REWIND	fseek()
SPACE	' ' (character constant)
PICTURE X()	char [ ] (array)
PICTURE ...	format control
PERFORM VARYING	for
PERFORM ... UNTIL	while
PERFORM ... UNTIL TEST AFTER	do-while
RECORD	struct
STOP RUN	exit()
WRITE	fwrite()

Operators

LESS THAN	<
GREATER THAN	>
EQUAL TO	==
AND	&&
OR	||
NOT	!
+ – * /	+ – * /

Appendix B
Function Listing

The C library provides a number of useful functions. Many of the operations these functions provide are performed by statements in COBOL. The library includes functions in the areas shown in Table B.1. The function descriptions in Table B.2 are adapted from the ANSI C standard. For the page number where the detailed description of each of these functions appears, consult the Table of Contents or Index.

Table B.1. Operations performed by functions in C.

Mathematical Functions
    Trigonometric
        Regular
        Arc
        Hyperbolic
    Exponential
    Floating Point Breakdown
    Miscellaneous
Input/Output
    File Manipulations
    File Errors

Table B.1. *Continued*

- File Buffering
- File Positioning
- Formatted I/O
- Character I/O
- String I/O
- Direct I/O

General Utility
- String to Number Conversion
- Random Numbers
- Memory Management
- Sorting and Searching
- Integer Breakdown

String Handling
- Copying
- Concatenation
- Comparison
- Search
- Miscellaneous
- Memory Functions

Date and Time
- Timing
- Time Conversion

Character Handling
- Character Conversion
- Character Testing

Program Environment

Diagnostic

Nonlocal Jumps

Signal Handling

Variable Arguments

LIBRARY NAMES

All library function names, **typedefs**, and **#define** names are reserved. You may not create a function with the same name as one in the library. Consult the Table of Contents or Index for the page number where a detailed description of these functions appears.

Table B.2. Library functions summary in alphabetical order.

Name	Use
abort	forces an abnormal termination of a program
abs	returns absolute value of an integer
acos	returns arc cosine
asctime	converts a time structure into a string
asin	returns arc sine
atan	returns arc tan
atan2	returns arc tangent
atexit	sets a function to be called on program termination
atof	converts a string to a double
atoi	converts a string to an integer
atol	converts a string to a long
bsearch	searches an array of objects for a match
calloc	allocates memory for number of objects
ceil	returns smallest integer (ceiling)
clearerr	clears end-of-file and error indicators for a file
clock	returns processor time used
cos	returns cosine
cosh	returns hyperbolic cosine
ctime	converts calendar time to string with local time
difftime	computes difference between two calendar times
div	computes quotient and remainder of an integer division
exit	exits a program
exp	returns exponential
fabs	returns absolute value of double
fclose	closes a file
feof	tests if file is at end-of-file

Table B.2. *Continued*

Name	Use
ferror	tests if file has error indicator set
fflush	flushes the output buffers of a file
fgetc	gets a character from a file
fgetpos	gets the current position in a file for use by **fsetpos**
fgets	gets a string of characters from a file
floor	returns largest integer (floor)
fmod	returns remainder of double divided by double
fopen	opens a file
fprintf	formatted output to a file
fputc	puts a character to a file
fputs	puts a string of characters to a file
fread	reads a number of bytes from a file
free	frees allocated memory
freopen	reopens a file
frexp	breaks double into fraction and power of 2
fscanf	formatted input from a file
fseek	sets the current position of a file by character count
fsetpos	sets the current position of a file from previous **fsetpos**
ftell	gets the current position of a file in characters
fwrite	writes a number of bytes to a file
getc	gets a character from a file
getchar	gets a character from the standard input
getenv	gets a value from the program environment
gets	gets a string of characters from the standard input
gmtime	converts calendar time to string with Greenwich Mean Time
isalnum	tests for alphabetic/numeric character
isalpha	tests for alphabetic character
iscntrl	tests for control character
isdigit	tests for digit
isgraph	tests for graphic character
islower	tests for lower case character

FUNCTION LISTING

Table B.2. *Continued*

Name	Use
isprint	tests for printable character
ispunct	tests for punctuation character
isspace	tests for white-space character
isupper	tests for upper case character
isxdigit	tests for hexadecimal digit
labs	returns absolute value of a long
ldexp	multiplies double by power of 2
ldiv	computes quotient and remainder of a long division
localtime	converts calendar time to a time structure with local time
log	returns natural logarithm
log10	returns logarithm base 10
longjmp	returns execution to point where setjmp was called
malloc	allocates memory for a given size
memchr	finds character in memory
memcmp	compares two areas of memory
memcpy	copies a number of bytes to another location
memmove	moves a number of bytes to another location and checks for overlap
memset	sets memory to a value
mktime	converts a string into a calender time
modf	breaks double into integer and fraction
perror	write a file error to the standard output
pow	returns double raised to a power
printf	formatted output to standard output
putc	puts a character to a file
putchar	puts a character to the standard output
puts	puts a string of characters to the standard output
qsort	sorts an array of objects for a match
raise	raises a signal to be handled
rand	returns a random number
realloc	changes the size of allocated memory
remove	removes a file from the system

Table B.2. *Continued*

Name	Use
rename	renames a file on the system
rewind	sets the current position in a file to zero
scanf	formatted input from standard input
setbuf	sets a buffer for a file
setjmp	sets up return for longjmp
setlocale	selects program environment
setvbuf	sets the type of buffering for a file
signal	sets up handling for system signals
sin	returns sine
sinh	returns hyperbolic sine
sprintf	formatted conversion to a string
sqrt	returns square root
srand	sets the seed for **rand**
sscanf	formatted conversion from a string
strchr	finds character in a string
strcmp	compares two strings
strcoll	transforms a string with non-ASCII characters
strcpy	copies a string to another string
strcspn	finds length of string with multiple ending characters
strerror	converts a file error to a string
strftime	formatted conversion of a time structure to a string
strlen	computes the length of a string
strcat	concatenates two strings
strncat	concatenates two strings up to a number of characters
strncmp	compares two strings up to a number of characters
strncpy	copies a string to another string up to a number of characters
strpbrk	finds string within a string
strrchr	finds last occurrence of character in a string
strspn	finds length of string of selected characters
strstr	searches for a string in a string
strtod	converts a string to a double with error setting

Table B.2. *Continued*

Name	Use
strtok	breaks a string into tokens one at a time
strtol	converts a string to a long with error setting
strtoul	converts a string to a long with error setting
strxfrm	transforms a string using the locale setting
system	calls the operating system
tan	returns tan
tanh	returns hyperbolic tangent
time	returns the current calendar time
tmpfile	creates a temporary file
tmpnam	generates a unique filename
tolower	returns lower case of character
toupper	returns upper case of character
ungetc	pushes a character back onto an input file
vfprintf	formatted output to a file using array of values
vprintf	formatted output to standard output using array of values
vsprintf	formatted conversion to a string using array of values

HEADER FILES

Each library function has an associated header file that accompanies it. You should include the header file if you use the function. Each file includes **typedefs**, **#defines**, and function prototypes. The contents of the header files are listed in Table B.3.

Table B.3. Table of library **defines** and macros.

Defines

Name*	Header file	Use
__DATE__	predefined	date of compilation
__FILE__	predefined	source filename
__LINE__	predefined	line number

*All names beginning with an underscore are reserved.

Table B.3. *Continued*

Name	Header file	Use
__STDC__	predefined	standard version
__TIME__	predefined	time of compilation
_IOFBF	stdio.h	setvbuf
_IOLBF	stdio.h	setvbuf
_IONBF	stdio.h	setvbuf
assert()	assert.h	
BUFSIZ	stdio.h	
CHAR_BIT	limit.h	
CHAR_MAX	limit.h	
CHAR_MIN	limit.h	
CLK_TCK	time.h	number of seconds for a clock tick
DBL_DIG	float.h	
DBL_EPSILON	float.h	
DBL_MANT_DIG	float.h	
DBL_MAX	float.h	
DBL_MAX_EXP	float.h	
DBL_MAX_10_EXP	float.h	
DBL_MIN	float.h	
DBL_MIN_EXP	float.h	
DBL_MIN_10_EXP	float.h	
errno	errno.h	global variable for errors
EDOM	errno.h	floating point error
EOF	stdio.h	end-of-file value
ERANGE	errno.h	floating point error
EXIT_FAILURE	stdlib.h	
EXIT_SUCCESS	stdlib.h	
FILE	stdio.h	file type
FILENAME_MAX	stdio.h	length of filename
FLT_DIG	float.h	
FLT_EPSILON	float.h	
FLT_MANT_DIG	float.h	

Table B.3. *Continued*

Name	Header file	Use
FLT_MAX	float.h	
FLT_MAX_EXP	float.h	
FLT_MAX_10_EXP	float.h	
FLT_MIN	float.h	
FLT_MIN_EXP	float.h	
FLT_MIN_10_EXP	float.h	
FLT_RADIX	float.h	
FLT_ROUNDS	float.h	
FOPEN_MAX	stdio.h	number of possible open files
HUGE_VAL	math.h	floating point error
INT_MAX	limit.h	arithmetic limit
INT_MIN	limit.h	arithmetic limit
L_tmpnam	stdio.h	tmpnam
LC_ALL	locale.h	
LC_COLLATE	locale.h	
LC_CTYPE	locale.h	
LC_NUMERIC	locale.h	
LC_MONETARY	locale.h	
LC_TIME	locale.h	
LDBL_DIG	float.h	
LDBL_EPSILON	float.h	
LDBL_MANT_DIG	float.h	
LDBL_MAX	float.h	
LDBL_MAX_EXP	float.h	
LDBL_MAX_10_EXP	float.h	
LDBL_MIN	float.h	
LDBL_MIN_EXP	float.h	
LDBL_MIN_10_EXP	float.h	
LONG_MAX	limit.h	
LONG_MIN	limit.h	
MB_CUR_MAX	stdlib.h	
MB_LEN_MAX	limits.h	

Table B.3. *Continued*

Name	Header file	Use
NDEBUG		not defined, used in assert.h
NULL	stddef.h	null pointer value (also in stdio.h and string.h)
offsetof	stddef.h	offset in structure
RAND_MAX	stdlib.h	
SCHAR_MAX	limit.h	
SCHAR_MIN	limit.h	
SEEK_CUR	stdio.h	fseek
SEEK_END	stdio.h	fseek
SEEK_SET	stdio.h	fseek
SHRT_MAX	limit.h	
SHRT_MIN	limit.h	
stderr	stdio.h	standard error
stdin	stdio.h	standard input
stdout	stdio.h	standard output
SIG_DFL	signal.h	
SIG_ERR	signal.h	
SIG_IGN	signal.h	
SIGABRT	signal.h	
SIGFPE	signal.h	
SIGILL	signal.h	
SIGINT	signal.h	
SIGSEGV	signal.h	
SIGTERM	signal.h	
TMP_MAX	stdio.h	tmpnam
UCHAR_MAX	limit.h	
UINT_MAX	limit.h	
ULONG_MAX	limit.h	
USHRT_MAX	limit.h	
va_start()	stdarg.h	
va_arg()	stdarg.h	
va_end()	stdarg.h	

Table B.3.   *Continued*

Typedefs

Name	Header file	Use
clock_t	time.h	time
div_t	stdlib.h	div()
fpos_t	stdio.h	file position
jmp_buf	setjmp.h	setjmp/longjmp
ldiv_t	stdlib.h	ldiv()
prtdiff_t	stddef.h	difference in two pointers
sig_atomic_t	signal.h	variables for signals
size_t	stddef.h	result of sizeof (also in stdio.h)
time_t	time.h	time
va_list	stdarg.h	variable parameter list

Structure Tags

tm	time.h	structure for time

Additional identifiers may be reserved in the future. These include

1. Function names beginning with "is" and "to" followed by a lower case letter may be added for character testing functions.
2. Current function names with a suffix of **f** or **l** (for float and long double) may be added.
3. Macros beginning with SIG and an upper case letter may be added for signal handling.
4. Function names beginning with "str" and "mem" may be added to string handling and memory functions.
5. All external identifiers and macros beginning with an underscore (_) are reserved.
6. Macros beginning with E and an upper case letter may be added for definitions of errors by a compiler.

7. Macros beginning with LC_ and an upper case letter may be added for definitions of locale.

LIBRARY USAGE

There is no error checking on values passed to standard functions. Functions may be macros or actual functions. Using **#undef** to delete a function name or surrounding it with parentheses ensures that the actual function is called, if it exists. For example, with the standard header alone

```
#include <stdlib.h>
...
i = func();
```

func may be a macro. However, if you code either

```
#include <stdlib.h>
#undef func
...
i = func();
```

or

```
i = (func)();
```

then **func** will be a function call, if it was a macro. Note that the parentheses inhibit the preprocessor from expanding **func**.

You may explicitly declare a function prototype or allow the compiler to determine it implicitly. Using the header files for the prototypes will save work.

```
extern int func( parm_list );   explicit declaration
i = func();                     implicit declaration
```

stddef.h

This standard header file has common **typedefs** and **#defines** that are useful in program writing. They are:

ptrdiff_t	typedef	difference between two pointers
size_t	typedef	result of **sizeof**
NULL	define	null pointer
offsetof(struct_type, member)	define	offset in bytes of member in a structure of **struct_type**

errno.h

This header file contains three useful definitions for error handling:

errno	external	error value for some library functions
EDOM	define	domain error value
ERANGE	define	range error value

float.h

This is one of two header files that contain the limits of numbers for a particular compiler. If you define a floating point number as

$$sign * base^{exp} * mantissa$$

$$exponent\ min <= exponent <= exponent\ max$$

then the values in this header file give the limits for this representation:

FLT_RADIX	base of exponent, defined as 2
FLT_ROUNDS	type of addition
	>0 rounds
	=0 chops
	−1 indeterminate

FLT_MANT_DIG	number of bits in mantissa
DBL_MANT_DIG	
LDBL_MANT_DIG	
FLT_EPSILON	smallest number such that 1.0 + epsilon does not equal 1.0
DBL_EPSILON	
LDBL_EPSILON	
FLT_DIG	number of decimal digits in mantissa
DBL_DIG	
LDBL_DIG	
FLT_MIN_EXP	smallest negative power of 2 that can be expressed
DBL_MIN_EXP	
LDBL_MIN_EXP	
FLT_MIN	smallest positive floating point number
DBL_MIN	
FLT_MIN_10_EXP	smallest negative power of 10 that can be expressed
DBL_MIN_10_EXP	
LDBL_MIN_10_EXP	
FLT_MAX_EXP	largest power of 2 that can be expressed
DBL_MAX_EXP	
LDBL_MAX_EXP	
FLT_MAX	largest number
DBL_MAX	
LDBL_MAX	
FLT_MAX_10_EXP	largest power of 10 that can be expressed
DBL_MAX_10_EXP	
LDBL_MAX_10_EXP	

limits.h

This file gives the limits for integer data types.

CHAR_BIT	number of bits in a char
SCHAR_MIN	minimum value for signed char
SCHAR_MAX	maximum value for signed char
UCHAR_MAX	maximum value for unsigned char
CHAR_MIN	minimum value for a plain char
CHAR_MAX	maximum value for a plain char

    if sign extension
        CHAR_MIN==SCHAR_MIN and
        CHAR_MAX==SCHAR_MAX
    if no sign extension **CHAR_MIN=0** and
        CHAR_MAX==UCHAR_MAX

SHRT_MIN	minimum value for a short
SHRT_MAX	maximum value for a short
USHRT_MAX	maximum value for an unsigned short
INT_MIN	minimum value for an int
INT_MAX	maximum value for an int
UINT_MAX	maximum value for an unsigned int
LONG_MIN	minimum value for a long
LONG_MAX	maximum value for a long
ULONG_MAX	maximum value for an unsigned long

MATHEMATICAL FUNCTIONS

These functions share a common way of reporting errors. If there is an error, a value of either **EDOM** or **ERANGE** is put into **errno**.

EDOM	if input argument is outside of the domain for which the function is valid. Return value is undefined.
ERANGE	if result cannot be represented as a double. **HUGE_VAL** will be returned if the magnitude is too great.
0	is returned if the magnitude underflows.

For example,

```
sqrt(-1.0)           would put EDOM in errno,
                     return value undefined.

pow(10., 10000.)     would put ERANGE in errno
                     and return HUGE_VAL as result.
```

math.h

This file contains the prototypes for all mathematical functions and the following definitions.

EDOM   value for **errno** for domain errors
ERANGE   value for **errno** for range errors
HUGE_VAL   value for a return if result overflows

Trigonometric Functions

The trigonometric functions include the regular functions, the arc functions, and the hyperbolic functions. Many of them return a domain error if the parameters are out of a given range.

Regular Functions

```
#include <math.h>
double cos(double angle)
```

This function returns the cosine of **angle**, which is in radians. If **angle** is large, the result may be off, so you should use **fmod(angle, (2*PI))** as the argument.

```
#include <math.h>
double sin(double angle)
```

This function returns the sine of **angle**, which is in radians. If **angle** is large, the result may be off, so use **fmod(angle, (2*PI))** as the argument.

```
#include <math.h>
double tan(double angle)
```

This function returns the tangent of **angle**, which is in radians. If **angle** is large, the result may be off, so use **fmod(angle, (2*PI))** as the argument.

Arc Functions

```
#include <math.h>
double acos(double value)
```

This computes the arccosine of **value**. It returns an angle from 0.0 to PI. If **value** is not between −1.0 to 1.0, **errno** is set to **EDOM**.

```
#include <math.h>
double asin(double value)
```

This function computes the arcsine of **value**. It returns an angle from −PI/2 to PI/2. If **value** is not between −1.0 to 1.0, **errno** is set to **EDOM**.

```
#include <math.h>
double atan(value)
double value;
```

This function computes the arctangent of **value**. It returns an angle from −PI/2 to PI/2.

```
#include <math.h>
double atan2(opposite, adjacent)
double opposite;
double adjacent;
```

This function computes the arctangent of **opposite/adjacent**. It returns an angle from −PI to PI, based on the signs of **opposite** and **adjacent**. If both **opposite** and **adjacent** are 0.0, **errno** is set to **EDOM**.

Hyperbolic Functions

```
#include <math.h>
double cosh(value)
double value;
```

This returns the hyperbolic cosine of **value**. If **value** is too large, **errno** is set to **ERANGE**.

```
#include <math.h>
double sinh (value)
double value;
```

This returns the hyperbolic sine of **value**. If **value** is too large, **errno** is set to **ERANGE**.

```
#include <math.h>
double tanh(value)
double value;
```

This returns the hyperbolic tangent of **value**. If **value** is too large, **errno** is set to **ERANGE**.

Exponential Functions

These functions return various powers and logarithms of numbers.

```
#include <math.h>
double exp(double power);
```

This function returns *e* raised to **power**. If **power** is too large, **errno** is set to **ERANGE**.

```
#include <math.h>
double log(double value);
```

This function returns the natural logarithm of **value**. If **value** is negative, **errno** is set to **EDOM**. If **value** is 0.0, **errno** is set to **ERANGE**.

```
#include <math.h>
double log10(double value);
```

This function returns the base-ten logarithm of **value**. If **value** is negative, **errno** is set to **EDOM**. If **value** is 0.0, **errno** is set to **ERANGE**.

```
#include <math.h>
double pow(double base, double exponent);
```

This function returns **base** raised to the **exponent** power. If the **base** is 0.0 and **exponent** is less than or equal to 0.0, or if **base** is less than 0.0 and **exponent** is not an integer, **errno** is set to **EDOM**. For some pairs of parameters, **errno** may be set to **ERANGE**.

```
#include <math.h>
double ldexp(double number, int exponent);
```

This function returns the value of **number** * 2 $^{**\ exponent}$. If the result is too large, **errno** is set to **ERANGE**.

```
#include <math.h>
double sqrt(double value);
```

This function returns the square root of **value**. If **value** is less than 0.0, **errno** is set to **EDOM**.

Floating Point Numbers

These functions evaluate a floating point value in different ways.

```
#include <math.h>
double frexp(double number, int *pexponent);
```

This function breaks **number** into a normalized fraction and a power of 2. The return value is between 0.5 and 1.0. The pointer ***pexponent** is set such that **number = return_value * 2** $^{**(*pexponent)}$. If **number** is 0.0, both the return value and ***pexponent** are set to 0.

```
#include <math.h>
double modf(double number, double *pinteger);
```

This function breaks **number** into an integer part and a fractional part. The return value is the fractional part. The integer part is put where **pinteger** points.

Miscellaneous

These functions compute the ceiling (**ceil**) and **floor** values and find absolute and modulus values.

```
#include <math.h>
double ceil(double value);
```

This function returns the smallest integer not less than **value**. This is the ceiling.

```
#include <math.h>
double floor(double value);
```

This function returns the largest integer not greater than **value**. If **ceil(value)** equals **floor(value)**, then **value** is an integer.

```
#include <math.h>
double fabs(double number);
```

This function returns the absolute value of **number**.

```
#include <math.h>
double fmod(double number, double mod);
```

This function returns the floating point remainder of **number/mod**. If **mod** is zero, then zero is returned. The remainder has the same sign as **number**.

INPUT/OUTPUT FUNCTIONS

Input and output functions operate on data streams. These are series of characters read from or output to files or devices. Basically, it makes no difference in operation whether these functions refer to a disk file or an input/output device, unless a particular device cannot support a particular operation (e.g., the keyboard cannot be rewound).

There are two types of streams—text and binary. Text streams contain new-line characters, which terminate lines. A text stream assumes printable characters and white space characters are being written to it. If you write control characters to a text stream and attempt to read the stream, you may not input equivalent characters. Spaces just before new- lines may not be written out. New-line characters may be converted on output to a sequence of characters (e.g., carriage return, line feed). When this sequence is read in, it is converted back to a single new-line character. Usually, one character, the end-of-file character, terminates the stream and forces functions to return the end-of-file indicator (**EOF**).

Binary streams are simple sets of character. There are no conversions and what is output to a stream will match what is input later from that stream. An input binary stream may have NUL characters appended to it.

You associate a stream with a file or device by opening the stream. The open functions return a pointer to a typedef **FILE**. This pointer is used by subsequent calls to other functions on the stream. When a stream is opened, it is positioned to the first character. A stream may be created and opened at the same time. If a prior file exists with the same name, its contents are erased. The type of stream—text or binary—is specified depending on whether the stream is opened by **fopen** or **freopen**.

A stream may be buffered in three ways: block, line, or none. With block buffering, a block of characters is transmitted to or from the file whenever the corresponding buffer is full. Line buffering forces the characters to be transmitted when a new-line character is encountered or when the buffer is full. If you choose no buffering, the characters are sent as soon as possible. You may use **setbuf** or **setvbuf** to set the buffering for a particular stream. Buffering is performed by the library functions. The operating system may have its own internal buffers which are not affected by **setvbuf** and **setbuf**.

Closing a stream disassociates it from a particular file or device. If anything remains in an output stream buffer, it is written out before closing. The **exit** function (or equivalently, ending the **main** function) forces a close on all open files. The **abort** function or an abnormal program termination may not necessarily close files properly.

Three streams are opened when the **main** function starts: the standard input (**stdin**), standard output (**stdout**), and standard error (**stderr**) streams. These streams are normally associated with the keyboard (**stdin**) and the terminal screen (**stdout** and **stderr**). You may redirect **stdin** and **stdout** on the command line to other files or devices on those operating systems that support redirection.

Each stream has a file position value that indicates where the next characters will be read or written. The **ftell** and **fgetpos** functions return the current file position. The **fseek** and **fsetpos** set the current file position.

stdio.h

This file includes several definitions used by the input and output functions, and function prototypes.

FILE	typedef	structure that holds stream information
fpos_t	typedef	file position type for **fgetpos** and **fsetpos**
_IOFBF	macro	
_IOLBF	macro	used by **setvbuf**
_IONBF	macro	
BUFSIZE	macro	size of buffer used by **setbuf**
EOF	macro	end of file indicator
L_tmpnam	macro	size of array required to hold name returned by **tmpnam**
FOPEN_MAX	macro	number of files that may be opened simultaneously
FILENAME_MAX	macro	maximum length for a filename
SEEK_CUR		
SEEK_END	macros	used by **fseek**
SEEK_SET		
TMP_MAX	macro	number of unique filenames that **tmpnam** can generate
stdin		
stdout		point to structures of type **FILE** for standard input, standard output, and standard error
stderr		

The use of a leading 0 in format specifiers to specify padding with zeros may not be supported in the future. Other lower case letters may be added to the format specifiers for **fprintf** and **fscanf**.

File Manipulations

```
#include <stdio.h>
FILE *fopen(char *file_name, char *open_mode);
```

This opens a file or device with the name to which **file_name** points. The value to which **open_mode** points states how to open the file and whether to create it or not.

A file may be opened for reading, writing, or appending. An attempt to open a nonexistent file for reading will fail. Opening a file for appending forces all writes to the file to be at the current end-of-file. Both reading and writing may be performed on a file opened for updating. However, calls to input and output functions must be separated by a call to **fflush** or a file positioning function (**fseek**, **fsetpos**, or **rewind**). The stream is fully buffered unless it refers to an interactive device. The characters to which **file_name** and **open_mode** point will not be modified.

Values for **open_mode** are

Text Streams	Binary Streams	Action
r	**rb**	open stream for reading
w	**wb**	create stream for writing
a	**ab**	open stream or create stream for appending (writes appended to end)
r+	**r+b** or **rb+**	open stream for updating
w+	**w+b** or **wb+**	create stream for updating

a+	**a+b** or **ab+**	open stream or create stream for updating (writes appended to end)

Using **fopen** returns a pointer to a type **FILE** for subsequent function calls on the stream. It returns **NULL** if an error occurs. If the mode is updating, a call to **fflush**, **fseek**, **fsetpos**, or **rewind** must occur between calls to input functions and calls to output functions.

```
#include <stdio.h>
FILE *freopen(char *file_name, char *open_mode,
   FILE *file_pointer);
```

This function opens a file or device using the name to which **file_name** points. The value pointed to by **open_mode** states how to open the file and whether to create it or not. The values for **open_mode** are the same as for **fopen**. The function first closes the file specified by **file_pointer**.

The function **freopen** returns a pointer to a type **FILE** for subsequent function calls on the stream. It returns **NULL** if an error occurs. The primary use of **freopen** is to reassign the file associated with **stdin**, **stdout**, or **stderr**. The characters to which both **file_name** and **open_mode** point will not be modified.

```
#include <stdio.h>
fflush(FILE *file_pointer);
```

This function flushes the output buffer to the operating system. If **file_pointer** is an input stream, **fflush** undoes the effect of any preceding **ungetc** calls. It returns zero if no error occurs, and nonzero if any write error occurs.

```
#include <stdio.h>
int fclose(FILE *file_pointer);
```

This function closes the stream to which **file_pointer** points. The stream is disassociated from the file specified in the **fopen** or **freopen** function. The output buffer, if any, is flushed before the close. If successful, **fclose** returns a value of zero. If an error occurs or the stream was already closed, it returns a nonzero value.

```
#include <stdio.h>
int remove(char *file_name);
```

This function removes from the operating system the file with the name to which **file_name** points. The file should not be open when **remove** is called. If successful, **remove** returns a value of zero. If not, it returns a nonzero value. The characters to which **file_name** points will not be modified.

```
#include <stdio.h>
rename(char *old_name, char *new_name);
```

This function renames the file with the name indicated by **old_name** to the name indicated by **new_name**. If there is already a file with the name **new_name**, then the result is uncertain. If successful, **rename** returns zero. If not, it returns a nonzero value. The characters to which **old_name** and **new_name** point will not be modified.

```
#include <stdio.h>
FILE *tmpfile();
```

This function creates a temporary binary stream, opened for update. The stream disappears when it is closed or when the program terminates. This function returns a pointer to the temporary stream. It returns **NULL** if it cannot create a temporary stream.

```
#include <stdio.h>
char *tmpnam(char *name);
```

This function generates a string that is not the same as an existing file name, and returns a pointer to the string. If **name** is not **NULL**, then it places the string into the location and returns the value of **name**.

The variable **name** should be an array of at least **L_tmpnam** characters. This function may be called at least **TMP_MAX** (minimum of 25) times, each time generating a new name. It is useful for creating file names for interprogram files.

File Errors

Two flags for each file may be set by the input/output functions. These are the end-of-file flag and the error indication flag. The end-of-file flag is set if an end-of-file is read on input. The error flag is set if an error occurs during reading or writing. Both flags are reset when a file is opened and when **clearerr** or **rewind** is called.

```
#include <stdio.h>
int ferror(FILE *file_pointer);
```

This function tests the error flag for the file to which **file_pointer** points. It returns zero if no error has occurred or nonzero if an error has occurred.

```
#include <stdio.h>
void clearerr(FILE *file_pointer);
```

This function clears the error and end-of-file flags for the file to which **file_pointer** points.

```
#include <stdio.h>
int feof(FILE *file_pointer);
```

This function tests the end-of-file flag for the file to which **file_pointer** points. It returns zero if end-of-file has not been reached or nonzero if it has been reached.

File Buffering

```
#include <stdio.h>
setvbuf(FILE *file_pointer, char *buffer, int type,
  size_t size);
```

The function **setvbuf** sets the type of buffering on a file. If used, it must be called after the file pointed to by **file_pointer** is opened and before reading from or writing to it. The type of buffering is specified by **type**. The values are

_IOFBF	fully buffered
_IOLBF	line buffered (new-line written, buffer is full, or input is requested)
_IONBF	completely unbuffered

If **buffer** is not **NULL**, it will be used as a buffer. The **fopen** function will not allocate a buffer. The value of **size** should be the length of **buffer**. The function returns nonzero if **mode** or **size** is invalid or if the file cannot be buffered in the requested type. It returns zero if successful.

```
#include <stdio.h>
void setbuf(FILE *file_pointer, char *buffer);
```

This function is equivalent to calling **setvbuf(file_pointer, buffer, _IOFBF, BUFSIZE)**. If **buffer** has a value of **NULL**, this function is equivalent to calling **setvbuf(file_pointer, buffer, _IONBF, 0)**.

File Positioning

```
#include <stdio.h>
long int ftell(FILE *file_pointer);
```

This function returns the current file position for the file to which **file_pointer** points. If there is a failure, it returns -1L and sets the value of **errno**. For a binary file, the position is the number of characters from the beginning of the file. For a text file, it may not necessarily be the number of characters. However, in either case, the value returned may be used in a call to **fseek** to position the file to the same place.

```
#include <stdio.h>
int fseek(FILE *file_pointer, long offset, int mode);
```

This function changes the current file position for the file to which **file_pointer** points. For a binary file, the **mode** may be one of three values, which will determine how **offset** is used. These are:

SEEK_SET   offset from beginning of file
SEEK_END   offset from end of file
SEEK_CUR   offset from current position

For a text file, the mode must be **SEEK_SET**, and **offset** must be either a value returned by a call to **ftell** or 0.

```
#include <stdio.h>
int fgetpos(FILE *file_pointer, fpost_t *pposition);
```

This function returns the current file position for the file pointed to by **file_pointer** in the location pointed to by **pposition**. If there is a failure, **fgetpos** returns a nonzero value and sets the value of **errno**. This value may be passed to **fsetpos** to set the position of the file. This function and **fsetpos** are for files that may have more bytes than can be represented in the **long** offset value used by **fseek** and **ftell**.

```
#include <stdio.h>
int fsetpos(FILE *file_pointer, fpos_t *position);
```

This function sets the current file position for the file pointed to by **file_pointer** to the value in the location pointed to by **pposition**. If there is a failure, **fsetpos** returns a nonzero value and sets the value of **errno**. This must be a value returned by **fgetpos**. The value pointed to by **position** will not be modified.

```
#include <stdio.h>
void rewind(FILE *file_pointer);
```

This function sets to 0 the current file position for the file pointed to by **file_pointer**. No errors can occur. It is equivalent to **fseek(file_pointer, 0L, SEEK_SET)**;

```
#include <stdio.h>
int ungetc(int chr, FILE *file_pointer);
```

This function "ungets" the value of **chr** on the input file to which **file_pointer** points. This value will be returned by the next read from the file. If a file positioning function or **fflush** is called before the character is read, the character is thrown away. If the value of **chr** is **EOF**, then nothing occurs. The function returns the value of **chr** or **EOF** if it fails.

For a binary file, the file position is decremented by a call to **ungetc**. For a text file, the file position is indeterminate. When all the "ungotten" characters have been read, the file position is the same as prior to any **ungetc** calls. Some compilers allow stacking of "ungotten" characters.

Formatted I/O

```
#include <stdio.h>
int fprintf(FILE *file_pointer, char *format, values);
```

This function outputs characters to the file to which **file_pointer** points. The **format** is a string of characters that specifies what is to be written. The string consists of ordinary characters, written without change, and format specifiers. The specifiers begin with % and notify **fprintf** that a corresponding value is being passed, and how to convert it and output it. If you pass fewer values than you have conversion specifiers, the output characters remain undefined. The string to which **format** points will not be modified.

Format Specifier

%

flags: characters (optional)

width: a number (optional)

precision: decimal point followed by a number (optional)

data width: a character (optional)

conversion type: a character

Flag Characters

-     Left justify.
- +   Begin a signed conversion with a "+" or "–".
- " " Begin a signed conversion with a space (for positive values) or "–".
- #   Convert to an alternate form.

For conversion types:

c, d, i, s, and **u**
No effect.

o
Nonzero will have **0** beginning.

x or **X**
Nonzero will have **0x** or **0X** beginning.

e, E, f, g, G
Include decimal point even if not needed for **g** and **G**; do not remove trailing zeros.

0 Pad left side with leading zeros.

Width. This value establishes the minimum field width. If more characters are required, they will be output. If fewer characters are required, the field will be right-justified (padded on the left with spaces). If the "–" flag is included, it will be left-justified (padded on the right with spaces). If the width starts with a zero digit, the padding will be zero characters.* If the width is specified by *, then the width will be taken from the corresponding *values*.

Precision. Precision is a decimal point followed by a value. The value is interpreted differently depending on the conversion type.

d,i,o,u,x,X
Specifies the minimum number of digits to be output. If the value can be represented in fewer digits, then leading zeros will be appended.

e,E,F
Specifies the number of digits after the decimal point.

g,G
Specifies the maximum number of significant digits.

s

---

*The use of precision is replacing this method of specifying zero padding characters.

Specifies the maximum number of characters.

If the precision is specified by a *, then it will be taken from the value supplied in *values*.

Data width. The data width is an optional modifier on the conversion type. The values are

- **h** for **d,i,o,u,x,X**
  The value is converted to a short or an unsigned short int before outputting.
- **l** for **d,i,o,u,x,X**
  The corresponding value is a long int or a long unsigned int.
- **L** for **e,E,f,g,G**
  The corresponding value is a long double.

Conversion types.

- **d** or **i** Value output as signed int (decimal)
- **o**   Value output as octal
- **u**   Value output as unsigned int
- **x**   Value output as hexadecimal with lower case digits
- **X**   Value output as hexadecimal with uppercase digits.

  For all of the preceding conversion types, the default precision is one. If precision is zero and value is zero, no characters are output. The value should be of type **int** or unsigned **int**.

- **e,E** Value output as (–)d.dddddde(+/–)dd. There is one nonzero digit before the decimal point. The precision specifies the number of digits after the decimal point. If the precision is zero, no decimal point appears. The default precision is six. The value is rounded to the number of digits specified. For "E", the number will contain "E" rather than "e". The value type should be **float** or **double**.

- **f**   Value output as (–)ddd.dddddd. The precision specifies the number of digits after the decimal point. The default precision is six. If the precision is zero, no decimal point appears. The value is rounded to the num-

ber of digits specified. The value type should be **float** or **double**.
- **g,G** Value output as **f** or **e**, depending on which takes fewer characters. The value type should be **float** or **double**.
- **c** Value output as a character. Value type should be **char** or **int**.
- **s** Value must be a pointer to a string. Characters are output up to, but not including, the terminating NUL. The precision, if specified, is the maximum number of characters output.
- **p** Value is a pointer to void. The value is output as a sequence of compiler-defined characters.
- **%** Output is "%". No value is converted.
- **n** Corresponding value is a pointer to an **int**. The number of characters output to that point by **fprintf** is written to the location.

The function returns the number of characters output, or a negative value if an error occurred. With **fprintf**, you may output at least 509 characters per call. Table B.4 presents sample output obtained using **fprintf**.

```
#include <stdio.h>
int printf(char *format, values);
```

The function **printf** acts as does **fprintf**, but sends all output to the standard output file. Its format is like the call **fprintf(stdout**, **format**, *values*), and it returns the number of characters output or a negative number if there is an error.

```
#include <stdio.h>
int sprintf(char *string, FILE *file_pointer, char
  *format, values);
```

The function **sprintf** acts just like **fprintf**, but all output goes to the string specified. A NUL character is written at the end of the string. It returns the number of characters written to the string or a negative number if there is an error.

FUNCTION LISTING   257

Table B.4.   Sample output by **fprintf**.

Value	Format	Output* Column
		0 1
		1234567890123
"abc"	%s	abc_
"abc"	%10s	abc_
"abc"	%.2s	ab_
"abc"	%-10s	ab _
354	%d	354_
354	%5d	354_
354	%5.5d	00354_
354	%+d	+354_
3.5	%f	3.500000_
3.5	%10.2f	3.50_
3.0	%.0f	3_
3.1	%.1f	3.1_
3.2	%.1f	3.20_

*Underscore shows where next character may be output.

```
#include <stdio.h>
int fscanf(FILE *file_pointer, char *format, addresses);
```

This expression inputs characters from the file to which **file_pointer** points. It scans the input characters for values to convert. The **format** is a string of characters specifying what is to be read. This string consists of ordinary characters and format specifiers. Ordinary characters are read as is. Format specifiers begin with %, and tell **fscanf** that a corresponding address is being passed. The function then converts the input and places the resulting value at the address. If you pass fewer addresses than you have conversion specifiers, the function will place the resulting values as garbage locations, but will not modify the string to which **format** points.

The function will stop scanning the input when there is no more input or when the input is not appropriate for the value type being converted (a matching failure). It returns the number of values converted and assigned, or **EOF** if an error occurs before any values are assigned.

If the ordinary character is a space or white space (tabs, etc.), then function reads the input characters until it encounters a non-white space. The function does not read this character, but pushes it back onto the input. If there are no white-space characters, then the scanning fails.

Any ordinary character that is not a format specifier must match the input character. If it does not, then the input character remains unread, and the scanning fails.

If the format is a specifier, then the function reads the input characters until the value to be converted is input or the scanning fails. Except for "c," "n," and "[", leading spaces are read and ignored. The function reads the characters until a character that could not be part of the value is input. That character remains unread and the characters up to that point are converted. If the number of characters per item that the function reads equals zero, then there is a matching failure and the scanning stops.

Format specifiers consist of:

%

flag: assignment suppression (optional)

width: a number (optional)

precision: decimal point followed by a number (optional)

data width: a character (optional)

conversion type: a character

Flags. The flag character is

- * convert the input, but do not place the result anywhere

Width. This is the maximum field width, or number of characters, that the function will read for a given input value. If the width is specified, then scanning stops after the function reads that number of characters or encounters a character that cannot be part of the converted type. If the field width is not specified, then the scan continues until it encounters a nonconvertible character.

Data Width. This optional modifier on the conversion type has the values:

- **h**   For **d,i,n,o,** and **x,**
    the address points to a **short int**.
    For **u,**
    the address points to an **unsigned short int**.
- **l**   For **d,i,n,o,** and **X,**
    the address points to a **long int**.
    For **u,**
    the address points to an **unsigned long int**.
    For **e,f,** and **g,**
    the address points to a **double**, rather than a **float**.
- **L**   For **e,f,** and **g,**
    the address points to a **long double**.

Conversion Types

- **d**   Input value is an integer.
- **i**   Input value is an integer with decimal, octal or hexadecimal representation.
- **o**   Input value is an octal number.
- **u**   Input value is an unsigned integer.
- **x**   Input value is a hexadecimal number.

For the all of the above, the address should point to an **int** or unsigned **int**.

- **e,f,** and **g**   Input value is a valid floating point number of the form (–)ddd.ddd(E+/–dd). The address should point to a **float**.
- **c**   Input consists of 1 or characters. The field width states the number of characters and has a default of 1. The address should point to a character array large enough to hold the width. No NUL character is placed on the end of this array.
- **s**   Input value is a string of non-white space charac-

- **p**

  ters. The address should point to a character array large enough to hold the number of characters. A NUL character is placed on the end.

  Input value is a sequence of characters that represents a pointer value produced by **fprintf** using the **p** type, as defined by the compiler. The address should point to a pointer to void.

- **%** A % is expected. No conversion takes place.
- **n** The corresponding address is a pointer to an **int**. The number of characters input so far by **fscanf** is written to that location.
- **[** This starts a series of characters expected in the input string. The series terminates with a right bracket]. Characters that match a value in this series are read. The address should point to an array of characters that will contain the characters read and a NUL at the end. If the first character after the bracket is], then] is included in the series and the next] terminates the series. If the first character after the bracket is ^, then all values in the series are characters except those listed. If the first character after the ^ is], then] is included among the characters to be accepted and the next] terminates the series. Thus

  "%[abcdefghijklmnopqrstuvwxyz]"

  reads characters until a nonlower case character is read, and

  "%[^0123456789]"

  reads characters until a digit is read.

The function returns the number of input items assigned values, or **EOF** if an error occurred.

Table B.5 illustrates the conversions **fscanf** performs given the variables

```
int i;
float f;
char string[100];
```

Table B.5. Sample conversions performed by **fscanf**.

Input String	Format and Values	Values Converted
"123ABC"	"%d%s",&i,string	d = 123
		s = "ABC"
	"%2d%s",&i,string	d = 12
		s = "3ABC"
"ABC DEF",	"%s",string	s = "ABC"
	"%5c",string	s = "ABC D" (no NUL)
	"%[AB]",string	s = "AB"
"ABC DEF\n",	"%[^\n]",string	s = "ABC DEF"

```
#include <stdio.h>
int scanf(FILE *file_pointer, char *format, addresses);
```

The function **scanf** acts like **fscanf**, but all input comes from the standard input file. This function acts like the call **fscanf(stdin, format, *values*)**, returning the number of input items assigned values, or EOF if an error occurred.

```
#include <stdio.h>
int sscanf(char *string, char *format,addresses
```

The function **sscanf** also acts like fscanf, except that input comes from the specified string. If the NUL character at the end of the string is read, it acts like an end-of-file. The function returns the number of input items assigned values, or EOF if an error occurred.

Character I/O

```
#include <stdio.h>
int fgetc(FILE *file_pointer);
```

This function reads the next character from the file to which **file_pointer** points, and returns the character read, or **EOF** at the end of the file. If an error occurs, this function returns EOF and sets the error indicator for the file.

```
#include <stdio.h>
int getc(FILE *file_pointer);
```

This function is equivalent to **fgetc**, but it may act as a macro as well as an actual function call.

```
#include <stdio.h>
int getchar(void)
```

This function is equivalent to **getc(stdin)** and is usually a macro.

```
#include <stdio.h>
int fputc(int character,FILE *file_pointer);
```

This function writes **character** to the file to which **file_pointer** points, and returns the character written. It returns **EOF** and sets an error indicator for the file if an error occurs.

```
#include <stdio.h>
int putc(int character, FILE *file_pointer);
```

This function is equivalent to **fputc**, but it may act as a macro rather than an actual function call.

```
#include <stdio.h>
int putchar(int character);
```

This function is equivalent to **putc(stdout)**, and is usually a macro.

```
#include <stdio.h>
int ungetc(int character, FILE *file_pointer);
```

This function puts **character** back onto the input file to which **file_pointer** points. The next time the file is read, this character will be the first returned. This function does not actually write the character to the file, but returns the character pushed and, if successful, resets the end-of-file flag. It returns **EOF** if not successful.

The functions **fflush**, **fseek**, and **rewind** erase the character that was pushed. The "ungetting" of one character is supported by all compilers. However, multiple calls to **ungetc** without re-reading the file may not work.

For binary files, the file position value will be decremented by one for each **ungetc**. For a text file, the file position value is indeterminate. For both types, once all pushed characters are read, the file position value is the same as it was before any characters were pushed.

String I/O

```
#include <stdio.h>
char *fgets(char *string, int count, FILE *file_pointer);
```

This function reads one line of characters up to a new-line character from the file to which **file_pointer** points. The characters are placed into the array to which **string** points, with the new-line character and a terminating NUL at the end. If the function reads **count** −1 characters without encountering a new-line, it stops inputting and places a NUL at the end.

The function returns the value of string if successful. If the end-of-file comes before any characters are read, then no characters are placed in string and the function returns the **NULL** pointer. It also returns a **NULL** pointer if an error occurs.

```
#include <stdio.h>
char *gets(char *string);
```

This function reads a line of characters from the standard input file, **stdin**, until it encounters a new-line character or end-of-file. The characters read are placed into the array to which **string** points, and a terminating NUL character is placed at the end. The new-line character is not placed in the array.

This function returns the value of string if successful. If the end-of-file comes before any characters are read, then no characters are placed in **string** and the function returns the **NULL** pointer. It also returns a **NULL** pointer if an error occurs.

```
#include <stdio.h>
int fputs(char *string, FILE *file_pointer);
```

This function writes the characters in the array indicated by **string** to the file indicated by **file_pointer**. It does not include the terminating NUL, but does write a new-line character to the file. It returns zero if successful, or nonzero if an error occurs.

```
#include <stdio.h>
int puts(char *string);
```

This function writes the characters in the array indicated by **string**, up to the NUL character, to the standard output file **stdout**. It then writes a new-line character to the file. This function returns zero if successful or nonzero if an error occurs.

Direct I/O

These functions read one or more characters from a file without interpreting the meaning of the characters.

```
#include <stdio.h>
size_t fread(void *buffer, size_t element_size, size_t number_elements,
    FILE *file_pointer);
```

This function reads a number of characters from the file to which **file_pointer** points. It places the characters in the array starting at **buffer**. The number of characters read is **element_size** * **number_elements**, and the function returns this value. If an error or end-of-file occurs, this number may be less than **number_elements**. If either **element_size** or **number_elements** is zero, then no reading occurs and the contents of buffer remain unchanged.

```
#include <stdio.h>
size_t fwrite(void *buffer,size_t element_size, size_t number_elements,
    FILE *file_pointer);
```

This function writes a number of characters to the file to which **file_pointer** points. The characters are obtained from the array starting at **buffer**. The number of characters written is **element_size** * **number_elements**. It returns the number of elements written. If an error occurs, this number may be less than **number_elements**.

GENERAL UTILITY FUNCTIONS

These functions perform various conversions.

stdlib.h

This header file is required by the functions described in this section.

div_t	type returned by **div**
ldiv_t	type returned by **ldiv**
RAND_MAX	maximum value returned by **rand**
EXIT_FAILURE	values for **exit**
EXIT_SUCCESS	values for **exit**

String to Number Conversion

These routines convert character strings into numeric values in a double or signed int constant format.

```
#include <stdlib.h>
double atof(char *string);
```

This functions returns the value of **string** converted to a double without modifying **string**. If the result is out of range, there is no specified error return.

```
#include <stdlib.h>
int atoi(char *string);
```

This function returns the value of **string** converted to an integer without modifying **string**. If the value is out of range, there is no specified error return.

```
#include <stdlib.h>
long atol(char *string);
```

This function returns the value of **string** converted to a long integer without modifying **string**. If the value is out of range, there is no specified error return.

```
#include <stdlib.h>
double strtod(char *string, char **rest_of_string);
```

This function converts the characters in **string** to a double and returns the result. If no conversion can be performed, it returns 0.0. If the converted value overflows, this function returns **HUGE_VAL** and sets **errno** to **ERANGE**. If the converted value underflows, it returns 0.0 and sets **errno** to **ERANGE**.

If **rest_of_string** is not **NULL**, it will be set to point to the place in **string** where conversion stopped. Conversion stops when the function reaches the terminating NUL or a character that cannot be part of a double constant. This function does not modify **string**.

```
#include <stdlib.h>
long strtol(char *string, char **rest_of_string, int
   conversion_base);
```

This function returns **string** converted to a long constant with base **conversion_base**. If no conversion can be performed, it returns 0. If the converted value may overflow, **LONG_MAX** or **LONG_MIN** is returned and **errno** is set to **ERANGE**. This function does not modify **string**.

If **rest_of_string** is not **NULL**, it will be set to point to the place in the string where conversion stopped. Conversion stops when the function reaches the terminating NUL or a character that cannot be part of a long constant of the **conversion_base**. The digits for a given **conversion_base** run from 0 to 9, then A to Z. Lower case letters are converted to upper case. If the base is 16, then the constant may be preceded by 0x or 0X.

For example, for base 2, the only allowable digits are 0 and 1. For base 20, they are 0 to 9, A to J, and a to j.

```
#include <stdlib.h>
unsigned long strutol(char *string, char **rest_of_string,
   int conversion_base);
```

This function returns **string** converted to an unsigned long constant with base **conversion_base**. If no conversion can be performed, it returns 0. If the converted value may overflow, it returns **ULONG_MAX** and sets **errno** to **ERANGE**. It does not modify **string**.

If **rest_of_string** is not **NULL**, then it will be set to point to the place in the string where conversion stopped. Conversion stops when the function reaches the terminating NUL or a character that cannot be part of an unsigned long constant of the **conversion_base**. The digits for a given **conversion_base** run from 0 to 9, then A to Z. Lower case letters are converted to upper case. If the base is 16, then the constant may be preceded by 0x or 0X. For example, for base 2, the only allowable digits are 0 and 1. For base 20, they are 0 to 9, A to J, and a to j.

Random Number Functions

These functions provide random integer numbers, either in a set sequence or randomly.

```
#include <stdlib.h>
int rand();
```

This function returns a random number from 0 to **RAND_MAX**. The random number is computed using a random number generator. Unless you call **srand()**, the function returns the same sequence of random numbers each time it is called.

```
#include <stdlib.h>
void srand(unsigned int seed);
```

This function sets the seed for a sequence of random numbers returned by **rand()**. The default value for the **seed** is 1. If **srand** is called each time with the same value for **seed**, **rand()** will return the same sequence of random numbers.

Memory Management

These functions allocate memory for a program's use. The memory these functions return is suitable for storing any data, provided that the **sizeof** of the object is specified.

```
#include <stdlib.h>
void *malloc(size)
size_t size;
```

This function allocates a space of **size** bytes. It returns a pointer to the first memory location of that space. If space cannot be allocated, this function returns **NULL**. If either **number_element** or **sizeof_element** is zero, it may return either **NULL** or a unique pointer value.

```
#include <stdlib.h>
void *calloc(size_t number_element, size_t sizeof_element);
```

This function allocates space for an array of **number_elements**. Each element is **sizeof_element** bytes in length. The allocated space is set to zero. The function returns a pointer to the first memory location of the space. If space cannot be allocated, it returns **NULL**. If either **number_element** or **sizeof_element** is zero, it may return either **NULL** or a unique pointer value.

```
#include <stdlib.h>
void free(void *pointer);
```

This function deallocates the space indicated by **pointer**. That space is returned to the free memory pool for further allocation. If **pointer** has the value **NULL**, nothing occurs. If **pointer** has returned by **malloc**, **calloc**, or **realloc** a value other than one, or if the space has been freed, then what occurs is indefinite. If you try to reference the space indicated by **pointer** after **free** is called, what happens is also indefinite.

```
#include <stdlib.h>
void *realloc(void *pointer, size_t new_size);
```

This function allows you to change the size of an allocated space without altering the contents. The space to which **pointer** points increases or decreases to the **new_size**. The value of **pointer** must be a value returned by a previous call to **calloc**, **malloc**, or **realloc**. If **pointer** is **NULL**, the call is equivalent to calling **malloc** with **new_size**. If **new_size** is zero, the call is equivalent to **free(pointer)**.

Sorting and Searching

These two functions sort arrays and search arrays for a value. They both require a pointer to a user-supplied function that performs a comparison. This user-supplied function receives pointers to two values and must return a value less than zero, zero, or greater than zero depending on whether the first value is less than, equal to, or greater than the second. A prototype for this function is **int pcompfunc(void *, void *)**. For example, a typical comparison function for unsigned integers could look like

```
    comp_int( void *pelement1, void *pelement2)
/* Compares two unsigned integer values that are pointed
to */
        {
        int ret;
        ret = (* (unsigned int *) pelement1 -
            * (unsigned int *) pelement2);
        return ret;
        }
```

The comparison function determines the order in which an array is sorted.

```
#include <stdlib.h>
void *bsearch(void *key, void *base, size_t number_el,;
        size_t size_el, int (*pcompfunc)(void *, void
*));
```

This function searches an array for a matching value. The array begins at **base** and has **number_el** elements. The size of each element is **size_e**. The pointer **key** points to the value for which the function is searching. The function indicated by **pcompfunc** must point to a function that compares two pointers to elements. The array must be in ascending sorted order, based on **pcompfunc**. The pointer **key** and the array at **base** will not be modified. The function returns a pointer to the matching value or the **NULL** pointer if it finds no match.

```
#include <stdlib.h>
void qsort(void *base, size_t number_el, size_t size_el,
        int (*pcompfunc)(void *, void *));
```

This function sorts an array. The array begins at **base** and has **number_el** elements. The size of each element is **size_e**. The function indicated by **pcompfunc** must point to a function that compares two elements. You must call **qsort** for an array before using **bsearch** on the same array. This function will not modify the array at **base**.

Integer Arithmetic Functions

These functions compute absolute values and division remainders for integers.

```
#include <stdlib.h>
int abs(int number);
```

This function returns the absolute value of **number**. If **INT_MAX** is less than the absolute value of **INT_MIN**, then **abs(INT_MIN)** returns an undefined value.

```
#include <stdlib.h>
div_t div(int numerator, int denominator);
```

This function computes the quotient and the remainder of **numerator** divided by **denominator**. It returns a structure with these two values. The structure includes the members

```
int quot;         /* quotient */
int rem;          /* remainder */
```

```
#include <stdlib.h>
long labs(long number);
```

This function returns the absolute value of **number**. If **LONG_MAX** is less than the absolute value of **LONG_MIN**, then **abs(LONG_MIN)** returns an undefined value.

```
#include <stdlib.h>
ldiv_t div(long numerator, long denominator);
```

This function computes the quotient and the remainder of **numerator** divided by **denominator**. It returns a structure with these two values. The structure includes the members

```
long quot;         /* quotient */
long rem;          /* remainder */
```

STRING HANDLING

These functions operate on strings. If the destination is not large enough to hold the values transferred, errors may result.

string.h

This header file contains the prototypes for the functions that follow.

Copying

```
#include <string.h>
char *strcpy(char *destination, char *source);
```

This function copies the string from **source** to **destination**. If the **source** and **destination** overlap in memory, the copy may not be correct. The function returns the value of **destination**. The **source** is not modified, unless it overlaps the **destination**.

```
#include <string.h>
char *strncpy(char *destination, char *source, size_t
  max_number);
```

This function copies up to **max_number** characters from the string in **source** to **destination**. If these two overlap in memory, the copy may not be correct. If the string in **source** is less than **max_number** of characters long, NUL characters are added to the end of the string in **destination**. If the NUL character in the string in **source** comes after **max_number** of characters, then no NUL character will be copied into **destination**. This function returns the value of **destination**. The **source** is not modified, unless it overlaps the **destination**.

Concatenation

```
#include <string.h>
char *strcat(char *destination, char *source);
```

This function catenates a copy of the string from **source** to the string at **destination**. The NUL character of **destination** is overwritten by the first character copied from **source**. The NUL character from **source** is copied. This function returns the value of **destination**, and does not modify **source** unless **source** overlaps **destination**.

```
#include <string.h>
char *strncat(char *destination, char *source, size_t
  max_number);
```

This function catenates up to **max_number** of characters in a string from **source** to the string at **destination**. The NUL character of **destination** is overwritten by the first character copied from **source**. If the NUL character from **source** is not included in **max_number** of characters in **source**, a NUL character is added to **destination** anyway. This function returns the value of **destination**, and does not modify **source** unless **source** overlaps **destination**.

String Comparison

When the corresponding characters in two strings are compared, the result is based on the first pair of characters from the two strings that are not equal. If the high-order bit is set in one of the characters compared, the result may be erroneous.

```
#include <string.h>
int strcmp(char *string1, char *string2);
```

This function compares **string1** to **string2** and returns a value less than zero, zero, or greater than zero, depending on whether **string1** is less than, equal to, or greater than **string2**. Neither **string1** nor **string2** is modified.

```
#include <string.h>
int strncmp(char *string1, char *string2, size_t max_number);
```

This function compares up to **max_number** of characters in **string1** to **string2** and returns a value less than zero, zero, or greater than zero, depending on whether **string1** is less than, equal to, or greater than **string2**. Neither **string1** nor **string2** is modified.

String Search

```
#include <string.h>
char *strchr(char *string, int character);
```

This function searches **string** for the first occurrence of the specified **character**. It returns a pointer to the location containing **character**, or **NULL** if it does not find the character. It does not modify **string**.

```
#include <string.h>
char *strrchr(char *string, int character);
```

This function searches **string** for the last occurrence of the **character**. It returns a pointer to the location containing **character**, or **NULL** if it does not find the character. It does not modify **string**.

```
#include <string.h>
char *strpbrk(char *string, char *match_chars);
```

This function searches **string** for the first occurrence of a set of characters. The variable **match_chars** consists of an array of characters, terminating with the NUL character. The function returns a pointer to the first character in **string** that matches any character other than NUL in **match_chars**, or **NULL** if no characters in **match_chars** are in **string**. Neither **string** nor **match_chars** is modified.

```
#include <string.h>
size_t strspn(char *string, char *match_chars);
```

This function computes the number of contiguous characters in **string**, from the first character onward, that are *all* present in the character set in **match_chars**. It then returns that number. Neither **string** nor **match_chars** is modified.

```
#include <string.h>
size_t strcspn(char *string, char *match_chars);
```

This function computes the number of contiguous characters in **string**, from the first character onward, that are *not* present in the character set in **match_chars**. It then returns this number. Neither **string** nor **match_chars** is modified.

```
#include <string.h>
strstr(char *string, char *match_string);
```

This function searches **string** for the first occurrence of **match_string**, ignoring the NUL character. It returns a pointer to the starting location of the matching string, or **NULL** if it finds no match. Neither **string** nor **match_char** is modified.

```
#include <string.h>
char *strtok(char *string, char *delimited_chars);
```

This function breaks a string into tokens. Here, **delimited_chars** consists of an array of characters, terminating with the NUL character. The function searches **string** for the first character not present in **delimited_chars**. If it finds no nonmatching character, the result is no token. The function searches character by character for a nonmatching character in **delimited_chars**. If it finds one, it replaces it with a NUL character. If it finds none, the token ends at the NUL character at the end of string. The function does not modify **delimited_chars**. It returns a pointer to the first character of a token, or **NULL** if it finds no token.

The variable **strtok** places an internal pointer to the next character after the NUL character. To obtain the next token, a **NULL** value must be passed for **string,** so that **strtok** may use this internal pointer as the starting place for the search. For each call, the set of delimiting characters may be different. For example,

```
#include <string.h>
static char string[]="*abc*d, e";
static char delimiter1[]="*";
static char delimiter2[]="*, "
char *token;
```

```
token=strtok(string, delimiter1);      token points to
"abc"
token=strtok(NULL, delimiter2);        token points to "d"
token=strtok(NULL, delimiter2);        token points to "e"
token=strtok(NULL, delimiter2);        token is NULL
```

Miscellaneous

```
#include <string.h>
char *strerror(int error_number);
```

This function converts **error_number** to a pointer to a string. The contents of the string are system dependent.

```
#include <stdio.h>
void perror(char *string);
```

This function writes a line to the standard error file. The line consists of the string, a colon, and a space, and a compiler defined error message based on the contents of **errno**. The error message is equivalent to that returned by **strerror(errno)**. If **string** is **NULL** or has zero length, then only the error message is written. This function does not modify **string**.

```
#include <string.h>
size_t strlen(char *string);
```

This function returns the length of string, the number of characters before the NUL character. It does not modify **string**.

Memory Functions

These functions operate on arrays of bytes or characters. The NUL character, which terminates string functions, has no effect in these functions. Their result is based on the first two bytes that are not equal. If the high-order bit is set in a byte being compared, the result may be erroneous.

```
#include <string.h>
void *memcpy(void *destination, void *source, size_t number);
```

This function copies up to **number** bytes from **source** to **destination**. If these overlap in memory, the copy may not be correct. The function returns the value of **destination**, and does not modify **source** unless **source** overlaps **destination**.

```
#include <string.h>
void *memmove(void *destination, void *source, size_t number);
```

This function copies up to **number** bytes from **source** to **destination**. Even if these overlap in memory, the copy will be correct. The function returns the value of **destination**, and does not modify **source** unless **source** overlaps **destination**.

```
#include <string.h>
int memcmp(void *memory1, void *memory2, size_t number);
```

This function compares up to number bytes in **memory1** to **memory2**. It returns a value less than zero, zero, or greater than zero, depending on whether **memory1** is less than, equal to, or greater than **memory2**. If two structures are being compared, any holes caused by alignment may cause an erroneous result unless the structures were implicitly set to zero (e.g., external or static), or explicitly set once to zero (e.g., by **memset**). Neither **memory1** nor **memory2** is modified.

```
#include <string.h>
void *memchr(void *memory, int byte, size_t number);
```

This function searches for the first occurrence of the value of **byte** starting at **memory**. Only number of locations are searched. The function returns a pointer to the location containing **byte**, or **NULL** if it does not find byte. It does not modify **memory**.

```
#include <string.h>
void *memset(void *memory, int byte, size_t number);
```

This function sets **number** of locations starting at **memory** to the value of **byte**, converting **byte** to an **unsigned char** and returning the value of **memory**.

Table B.6. Summary of the features of *time.h*.

Feature	Type	Purpose
CLK_TCK	macro	conversion factor that transforms **clock_t** value into seconds
clock_t	typedef	represents the processor ticks returned by clock
time_t	typedef	represents a time value
struct tm	structure tag	contains the time members listed

DATE AND TIME

These functions deal with calendar time, which is the current date. Local time is the calendar time for a specific time zone. Daylight Savings Time(DST) is the local time changed, if necessary, for DST.

time.h

This header file contains the prototypes and other features summarized in Table B.6.

Time Members

```
struct tm
        {
        int tm_sec;      seconds (0 to 59)
        int tm_min;      minutes (0 to 59)
        int tm_hour;     hours (0 to 23)
        int tm_mday;     day of the month (1, 31)
        int tm_mon;      month since January (0, 11)
        int tm_year;     years since 1900
        int tm_wday;     weekday (0, 6); 0 is Sunday
        int tm_yday;     days since January 1 (0, 365)
        int tm_isdst;    flag for Daylight Savings Time;
                         positive if DST in
                         effect, zero if not, or negative
                         if unknown.
        };
```

Timing

```
#include <time.h>
clock_t clock(void);
```

This function returns the processor time used since the beginning of program execution. The value returned is only an approximate time, in units of clock ticks. The number of seconds is **clock()/CLK_TCK**. The function returns the value –1 if processor time is not available on a particular system.

```
#include <time.h>
time_t time(time_t *time_pointer);
```

This function returns the current calendar time. If **timer_pointer** is not **NULL**, this time value is also stored at the location indicated by the pointer. The function returns –1 if calendar time is not available on a particular system.

```
#include <time.h>
double difftime(time_t time1, time_t time2);
```

This function returns the difference between two calendar times **(time1 - time2)** in seconds.

Time Conversion

```
#include <time.h>
struct tm *localtime(time_t *time_pointer);
```

This function converts the calendar time indicated by **time_pointer** into a time structure, using local time. It returns a pointer to this structure and does not modify **time_pointer**.

```
#include <time.h>
struct tm *gmtime(time_t *time_pointer);
```

This function converts the calendar time indicated by **time_pointer** into a time structure using Greenwich Mean Time (GMT). It returns a pointer to this structure or NULL if the conversion to GMT is not available, and does not modify **time_pointer**.

```
#include <time.h>
time_t mktime(struct tm *time_pointer);
```

This function converts the values in the structure indicated by **time_pointer** into calendar time. The initial values for **tm_yday** and **tm_wday** are ignored. If the conversion is successful, these variables are set to the proper values. The function returns the calendar time if the values in the time structure can be converted, or the value −1 if they cannot.

```
#include <time.h>
char *asctime(struct tm *time_pointer);
```

This function converts the values in the time structure indicated by **time_pointer** into a string in the form

```
WWW MMM DD HH:MM:SS YYYY
```

where

WWW is the day of the week, one of:
                  Sun Mon Tue Wed Thu Fri Sat

MMM is the month, one of:
   Jan Feb Mar Apr May Jun Jul Aug Sep Oct Nov Dec

DD is the day of the month

HH is the hour

MM is the minute

SS is the second

YYYY is the year

A new-line and a NUL character terminate the string, and the function returns a pointer to it.

```
#include <time.h>
char *ctime(time_t *time_pointer);
```

This function converts the calendar time indicated by **time_pointer** into a string, and returns a pointer to that string. It does not modify **time_pointer**. This function is the equivalent of **asctime(localtime(time_pointer));**.

CHARACTER HANDLING

These functions test to determine whether character values are of a particular type and convert alphabetic characters from one case to another. Even though these functions take **int** arguments, the values of the characters tested must be representable by an **unsigned char** or have the value of **EOF**.

Printing characters are those that have graphic representations, including the space character. Control characters are all other characters.

ctype.h

This header file contains the prototypes and the macros, if any, for these functions.

Character Conversion

```
#include <ctype.h>
int toupper(int character);
```

This function returns the upper-case value for **character**. If **character** is not a letter or is already upper case, the function returns the value of **character**.

```
#include <ctype.h>
int tolower(int character);
```

This function returns the lower-case value for **character**. If **character** is not a letter or is already lower case, the function returns the value of **character**.

Character Testing

The following functions all receive an integer. They return nonzero (true) if the value of the integer tested represents a character of the type specified in the function statement, or zero if it does not. These functions all have the form

```
is____(int character);
```

Table B.7. Standard ASCII character set groups.

Character Group	ASCII Values
control characters	0 to 8, 14 to 31, and 127
punctuation characters	33 to 47, 57 to 64, 91 to 96 and 123 to 126
white space characters	' ','\f','\n','\r','\t','\v'
digits	'0' to '9'
lowercase letters	'a' to 'z'
uppercase letters	'A' to 'Z'
implementation defined	values greater than 127

The character set is divided into several groups, depending on the computer and the locale. The groups for standard ASCII appear in Table B.7. For other values, the implementation defines the character type.

```
#include <ctype.h>
isdigit(int character);
```

Tests **character** to determine whether it is a digit.

```
#include <ctype.h>
isxhdigit(int character);
```

Tests **character** to see if it is a hexadecimal digit (0 to 9, a to f, and A to F).

```
#include <ctype.h>
isupper(int character);
```

Tests **character** to see if it is an upper case letter.

```
#include <ctype.h>
islower(int character);
```

Tests **character** to see if it is a lower case letter.

```
#include <ctype.h>
isalpha(int character);
```

Tests **character** to see if it is an upper or lower case letter.

```
#include <ctype.h>
isalnum(int character);
```

Tests **character** to see if it is an upper or lower case letter, or a digit.

```
#include <ctype.h>
iscntrl(int character);
```

Tests **character** to see if it is a control character.

```
#include <ctype.h>
isprint(int character);
```

Tests **character** to see if it is a printable character (a non-control character).

```
#include <ctype.h>
isgraph(int character);
```

Tests **character** to see if it is a printable character (a non-control character) other than the space character ' '.

```
#include <ctype.h>
ispunct(int character);
```

Tests **character** to see if it is a punctuation character or a white space character other than the space character ' '.

```
#include <ctype.h>
isspace(int character);
```

Tests **character** to see if it is any white space character.

ENVIRONMENT

These functions terminate programs and communicate with the operating system to perform operations.

stdlib.h

This header file contains the prototypes for the following functions.

```
#include <stdlib.h>
void abort();
```

This function forces the program to terminate abnormally, and may or may not close open files, depending on the system. Calling this function is the equivalent of **raise(SIGABRT)**. The function never returns to the caller.

```
#include <stdlib.h>
int at_exit(int (*pfunc)(void));
```

This function sets up a list of functions to execute when you call the **exit** function. Each time you call this function, it adds the function to which **pfunc** is pointing to the list.

```
#include <stdlib.h>
void exit(int status);
```

This function normally terminates a program, calling all functions passed to **atexit**. The last function added to **atexit** is the first it calls. In addition, it flushes all output streams, closes all open streams, and removes all temporary files. Finally, it returns the value of **status** to the operating system.

    A **status** of zero or **EXIT_SUCCESS** causes the return of a successful termination value. A **status** of **EXIT_FAILURE** causes the return of an unsuccessful termination value.

```
#include <stdlib.h>
char *getenv(char *name);
```

This function returns a pointer to a string associated with **name**. The value of **name** must appear in the environment of the operating system. If it does not, then the function returns **NULL**.

```
#include <stdlib.h>
int system(char *string);
```

This function passes **string** to the operating system. The operating system executes **string** as if it were a command typed directly to the system. The return value is system-dependent. If **string** has the value **NULL**, then the function returns zero if there is no command processor; otherwise it returns nonzero.

DIAGNOSTIC

This macro allows you to put diagnostics into a program for debugging purposes.

assert.h

This header file contains the **assert** macro.

```
#include <assert.h>
void assert(int expression);
```

If the expression is false, this function writes information on name of source file (__FILE__) and line number (__LINE__) to **stderr** and calls **abort**. If the expression is true, the function takes no action. If you define **NDEBUG** in the source file before **#include <assert.h>**, then this macro has no effect.

NONLOCAL JUMPS

The following two functions allow you to set a spot in a program and to return to that spot from anywhere in the program. Thus they resemble a **goto** that can go to a label in any function.

Use these functions only to handle error conditions that may occur in deeply nested, low-level routines. These functions can help you avoid having to check each level of such routines for errors. However, you must exercise great care when using these and all other programming constructs that favor speed or decreased code over readability.

setjmp.h

This header file contains the necessary prototypes for these two functions and the following definition.

jmp_buf   type of variable passed to **setjmp** and **longjmp**

```
#include <setjmp.h>
int setjmp(jmp_buf environment);
```

This function sets a place holder to which a subsequent call to **longjmp** will go. It saves the current status in **environment** for later use by **longjmp**. Part of what is saved in **environment** is the value of the call's program counter, which **longjmp** uses to return to the set place. You must call **longjmp** either from the same routine where the corresponding **setjmp** appears, or from another routine that this routine has called. All objects in the routine containing **setjmp** should be declared **volatile** to ensure that they retain the proper values. When you call **setjmp** directly from a function, **setjmp** returns a 0 value. If **setjmp** returns via a **longjmp** call, it returns a non-zero value.

```
#include <setjmp.h>
longjmp(jmp_buf environment, int value);
```

This function executes a jump to the last **setjmp** called with the corresponding **environment**, and returns **value** to the **setjmp** call.

If no **setjmp** exists with that **environment**, or if the function containing the **setjmp** has executed a return, then undefined behavior occurs. Variables not typed **volatile** may not have the proper values the next time your routine returns to **setjmp**. If **longjmp** tries to return zero, the return from **setjmp** is forced to one.

The following example illustrates how to use **setjmp** and **longjmp**.

```
#include <setjmp.h>
jmp_buf save_env;
int ret;
...
ret=setjmp(save_env)
if (ret==0)
        {
        /* do normal processing */
        }
```

```
else {
        /* This is a return from longjmp */
        /* do appropriate processing */
        if (ret==3)
                /* Return from the example of longjmp */
        }
```

In this or another file, you may then do a **longjmp** back to the **setjmp** shown above using

```
extern jmp_buf save_env;
...
longjmp(save_env, 3);
```

SIGNAL HANDLING

Signals are interrupts that occur during the execution of a program. These interrupts may occur from within the program, for instance, when a routine attempts to divide by zero, or they may be external to the program, such as a user pressing a break key on the terminal. A call to **raise** may also generate an interrupt.

You may call functions that handle signals anytime during a program's execution. Usually the operating system, rather than the program itself, calls these functions. You must write functions that handle signals carefully to ensure that the program will continue to run after they return. Writing interrupt handlers is beyond the scope of this text, but the routines needed to do so appear here for the sake of completeness.

signal.h

This header file supplies **defines** for various signals. These **defines** are used by both **signal** and **raise**.

sig_atomic_t	type of variable used by a function that handles a signal
SIG_DFL	default action for a signal
SIG_IGN	ignores a signal
SIG_ERR	returns value of signal if an error occurs

SIGABRT abnormal termination signal
SIGFPE   floating point error signal
SIGILL   invalid program in core
SIGINT   interrupt signal from user
SIGSEGV segment violation (invalid storage access) signal
SIGTERM termination request signal

```
#include <signal.h>
void (*signal (int signal_type, void
  (*function_pointer)(int))) (int);
```

This function supplies a handler for a signal. The **signal_type** is one of the **defines** listed in **signal.h**. The address of the function called when **signal_type** occurs is **function_pointer**. If **SIG_DFL** is the value passed to **function_pointer**, the function calls the default handler for the operating system. If **SIG_IGN** is the value passed, then the function ignores **signal_type**.

The function returns the address of the function previously handling the signal. If an error occurs, it returns **SIG_ERR**.

When the signal occurs, the function first resets the signal handler to the default handler. Then it calls the function addressed by **function_pointer**. That function may in turn call **abort**, **exit**, or **longjmp** to end. If it uses a **return** to end and the value of the signal was not **SIGFPE**, then the program executes normally. With **SIGFPE**, the result of the arithmetic computation is unknown, so the program may not execute properly. You should not use a signal handler to call the standard library functions, as there is no guarantee they will reenter. Also, the signal handler may assign values to variables of type **sig_atomic_t**.

```
#include <signal.h>
int raise(int signal_type);
```

This raises a signal of **signal_type**. If successful, it returns zero, otherwise it returns a nonzero value.

VARIABLE ARGUMENTS

The macros and function described in this section go through lists of arguments whose type and number can be variable. The library functions, **fprintf** and **fscanf**, and their related functions all rely on these essential macros for program writing in C.

Using functions with a variable number of arguments can be a source of errors. You can write most functions that might require a variable number using a fixed number, an array of objects and a count as the parameters. These functions are only presented for completeness.

The value **va_list** is a typedef for an object holding information for these functions. The type of the object you declare must match that of this information. You then call **va_start** to initialize the variable list. Each argument is accessed using **va_arg**. Before returning from the variable argument function, you should call **va_end**.

stdarg.h

This header file contains the prototypes, macro definitions, and

va_list   typedef for object for holding variable parameters

```
void va_start(va_list argument_list, last_parameter)
```

This macro initializes **argument_list** for use by **va_arg** and **va_end**. The *last parameter* is the name of the rightmost parameter in the list (the one just before the ellipses).

```
#include <stdarg.h>
type va_arg(va_list argument_list, type)
```

This argument returns the next value in the parameter list converted to the value *type*. If value cannot be converted to *type*, the result is undefined. The first time you call this function, it returns the first value after the *last parameter* in the call. Each subsequent call returns the next value.

```
#include <stdarg.h>
void va_end(va_list argument_list);
```

This argument sets up the function for a normal return. You should call it after **va_arg** has accessed all the arguments and before the return from the function.

```
#include <stdio.h>
#include <stdarg.h>
vfprintf(FILE *file_pointer, char *format,va_list
  argument_list);
```

This function is equivalent to calling **fprintf** where the variable argument list (*values*) has been initialized by a call to **va_start**. It returns the number of characters output, or a negative number if an error occurred, without modifying **format**.

```
#include <stdio.h>
#include <stdarg.h>
vprintf(char *format, va_list argument_list);
```

This function is equivalent to calling **printf** where the variable argument list (*values*) has been initialized by a call to **va_start**. It returns the number of characters output or a negative number if an error occurred.

```
#include <stdio.h>
#include <stdarg.h>
vsprintf(char *string, char *format, va_list argument_list);
```

This function is equivalent to calling **sprintf** where the variable argument list (*values*) has been initialized by a call to **va_start**. It returns the number of characters placed in **string** or a negative number if an error occurred.

INTERNATIONALIZATION ISSUES

To make C international, additional features have been added to it. These include provisions for characters that cannot fit in a byte and multiple forms for displaying time. The following descriptions of some of these features are adapted from the ANSI standard.

Characters

A single **char** may represent multiple characters. For example, **'AB'** may produce a single character that represents a foreign language character. The data type **wchar_t** represents the size

Table B.8. Summary of commonly used trigraphs and the C characters they represent.

Sequence	Character
??=	#
??(	[
??/	\
??)	]
??'	^
??<	{
??!	|
??>	}
??-	~

of a multi-byte, or wide, character. You may also prefix strings with an 'L' to make them strings of multi-byte characters, each of type **wchar_t**.

Trigraphs are sets of three characters representing a single character. These have been created to allow terminals that do not have keys for certain C punctuation to produce C programs. Table B.8 summarizes some of the most common of these trigraphs and the C characters they represent.

Supporting Functions

Some functions in the library, aid in creating a program that will work with a number of different character sets. These functions deal with the ordering of characters as viewed by the string functions. The locale is the foreign language or custom environment under which the C program is operating.

Also included is a set of functions for operating on multibyte characters and transforming regular strings to multibyte strings.

Header File

The header file **locale.h** contains several macros that **setlocale** uses with these international functions.

| LC_ALL | LC_CTYPE | LC_NUMERIC |
| LC_COLLATE | LC_MONETARY | LC_TIME |

This header file also contains the structure tag **struct lconv**, described in **localeconv**.

Locale

```
#include <locale.h>
char *setlocale(int category, char *setting);
```

This function sets those program functions dependent on the area of the world in which the program runs. The value of **category** states which of these functions to alter:

LC_ALL	entire set of functions
LC_COLLATE	collation sequence for **strcoll** and **strxfrm**
LC_CTYPE	character handling functions
LC_MONETARY	monetary information
LC_NUMERIC	decimal point character
LC_TIME	for **strftime** function

The value of **setting** tells how to alter them. The value for a standard C environment is **C**. The null string ("") and all other values are for implementation defined environments. The function returns a pointer to a string referencing the current locale, or NULL if there is no matching locale. If the value of **setting** is the NULL pointer, then the function returns a pointer to the current locale, and **setting** remains unmodified.

Collation Sequence

```
#include <locale.h>
strcoll(char *string1, char *string2);
```

This function compares **string1** to **string2** and returns a value less than zero, zero, or greater than zero, depending on whether **string1** is less than, equal to, or greater than **string2**. It performs the comparison of the strings after transformation according to the program's locale, but does not modify **string1** and **string2**.

```
#include <locale.h>
size_t strxfrm(char *destination, char *source,size_t
  max_number);
```

This function transforms strings that may not be in the computer's normal sorting sequence (e.g., that used for **strcmp**), basing the transformation on the locale. Following transformation of the two strings, **strcmp** can compare them. Transformed strings may be twice as long as source strings. The content of **source** remains unmodified.

The function transforms the string in **source** into a string in **destination**. No more than **max_number** of characters, including the NUL, is put in **destination**. If the transformed source cannot fit in **max_number** of characters, the contents of **destination** are undetermined. The function returns the number of characters in **destination**, or zero if the transformed string did not fit.

Time Transformation

```
#include <locale.h>
size_t strftime(char *string, size_t size, char *format,
        struct tm *time);
```

This converts **time** into a string under format control. The format works much like **sprintf**, placing values from the **time** structure in the string. No more than **size** characters including the terminating NUL, are placed in string. Both **format** and the structure pointed to by **time** remain unmodified. The format specifiers are:

a	abbreviated weekday name
A	full weekday name
b	abbreviated month name
B	full month name
c	locale's date and time

d	day of the month (01–31)
H	hour (00–23)
I	hour (01–12) using the twelve-hour clock
j	day of year (001–366)
m	month (01–012)
M	minute (00–59)
p	locale's A.M. or P.M.
S	second (00–59)
U	week number of year (00–52) with Sunday as first day
w	weekday (0–6) with Sunday as 0
W	week number of year (00–52) with Monday as first day
x	locale's date
X	locale's time
y	year (00–99)
Y	year with century (0000–9999)
Z	time zone name (if any)
%	The % character

The function returns the number of characters converted, or zero if the converted string cannot fit in size characters.

Monetary Information

```
#include <locale.h>
struct lconv *localeconv(void);
```

This function returns a pointer to a structure of type **lconv**. That structure contains the following information, useful in formatting monetary and other quantities.

```
struct lconv
    {
    char *decimal_point;      /* Decimal point character for
                                 non-monetary*/
    char *thousands_sep;      /* Thousand separator for
                                 nonmonetary */
```

```
    char *grouping;            /* Size of groups that are
                                  separated */
    char *int_curr_symbol;     /* International currency
                                  symbol */
    char *currency_symbol;     /* Local currency symbol */
    char *mon_decimal_point;   /* Decimal point character for
                                  monetary */
    char *mon_thousands_sep;   /* Thousand separator for
                                  monetary */
    char *mon_grouping;        /* Size of groups that are
                                  separated */
    char *positive_sign;       /* Positive sign */
    char *negative_sign;       /* Negative sign */
    char *int_frac_digits;     /* Number of fractional digits
                                  for international */
    char *frac_digits;         /* Number of fractional digits
                                  for local */
    char p_cs_precedes;        /* True if positive sign
                                  precedes value */
    char p_sep_by_space;       /* True if positive sign is
                                  separated by a space from
                                  value */
    char n_cs_precedes;        /* True if negative sign
                                  precedes value */
    char n_sep_by_space;       /* True if negative sign is
                                  separated by a space from
                                  value */
    char p_sign_posn;          /* Indicates position of
                                  positive sign */
    char n_sign_posn;          /* Indicates position of
                                  negative sign */
}
```

String Operations

Some multibyte strings depend on a shift state. Each call to the functions in this section has its own shift state memory. The internal shift state is altered if a shift character appears in the string passed to the function. When the string passed to a function is **NULL**, then the function returns a nonzero if multibyte strings have shift states. Arrays of type **wchar_t** store multibyte codes in them, each with a regular character (**char**) string representation, using multiple characters to represent the same code. These functions convert between the **wchar_t** and **char** representations.

```
#include <locale.h>
int mblen(wchar_t *multi_pointer, size_t size);
```

This function computes the number of bytes in the multibyte string passed to it, returning −1 if the string contains invalid multibyte codes.

```
#include <locale.h>
int mbtowc(wchar_t *multi_pointer, char *string, size_t size);
```

This function computes the number of bytes in the multibyte character representation to which **string** points. If **multi_pointer** is not NULL, it stores the code for that character at that address. It also returns the number of bytes of **string** used for the multibyte character, 0 if the character was NUL, or −1 if there was no valid multibyte character.

```
#include <locale.h>
int wctomb(char *string, wchar_t multi_char);
```

This function computes the number of bytes needed to represent the code stored in **multi_char**. If **string** is not **NULL**, the function stores the character representation at that address.

```
#include <locale.h>
size_t mbstowcs(wchar_t multi_pointer, char *string, size_t
   size);
```

This function converts the characters in **string** to a sequence of codes in **multi_pointer**. At most, the function stores **size** codes and returns the number of codes stored, or −1 if there was an invalid character representation.

```
#include <locale.h>
size_t wcstombs(char *string, wchar_t *multi_pointer, size_t
   size);
```

This function converts the sequence of codes in **multi_pointer** into a sequence of characters stored at **string**. At most, the function stores **size** bytes in **string** and returns the number of bytes stored, or −1 if there was an invalid multibyte code.

Appendix C
Linking and Compiling

If you have never written a C program, the best way to learn is to try executing the following simple example.

Example C.1

```
#include <stdio.h>

main()
        {
        printf("\n Hi everybody");
        }
```

Enter this program into your computer using the word processor or text editor that you use for other languages: "kedit" on a mainframe IBM, or "vi" or "ed" with UNIX. Save this program as "hello.c".

Compile the program by invoking the compiler. On almost all systems, the name of the compiler is "cc". To compile a program, simply type the program name after the "cc". For the program in Example C.1, type "cc hello.c".

The compiler translates this program file, called the source file, and creates a machine language or object file that represents

Table C.1. Linker commands for various systems.

MS/DOS	link hello
UNIX	cc hello.c (linker called implicitly)
VMS	link hello

the program in the native instructions of your computer. This object file's name is usually the first part of the source file's name followed by ".o" or ".obj". Thus the object file name for Example C.1 would be "hello.obj".

If the compiler cannot translate your program, it will report one or more errors. Compiler errors may be due to incorrect program entry. Your word processor may add formatting characters to the source file that the compiler does not understand.

If the compiler reports an error such as "Cannot find include file," you may have improperly entered the line **#include <stdio.h>**, or the file "stdio.h" supplied with your compiler may not be in the proper disk directory.

Link your object file with the library. The library contains routines that help start and end this program and help it perform input and output. Each operating system has its own linker. On UNIX, the C compiler automatically invokes the linker. On many other systems, you must run the linker manually. Specify the name of your object file and the name of the library. Table C.1 shows examples of link commands.

The linker combines the object file and the necessary routines in the library, and produces an executable file. This file's name is customarily the first part of the object file's name with the suffix ".exe" or ".com", so the name of the test program in Example C.1 would ordinarily be "hello.exe". On UNIX systems, however, it would be "a.out".* Figure C.1 illustrates the compile/link process.

The library function **printf** outputs on the terminal whatever you key in as inputs to it. If the linker reports an error such as "print undefined," you probably misspelled the name **printf** in the program. In such cases, go back to the editor, list your pro-

---

*You can use the UNIX compiler option "–o" to give the file a different name. For example, "cc –o hello hello.c" will produce an executable file called "hello".

LINKING AND COMPILING **299**

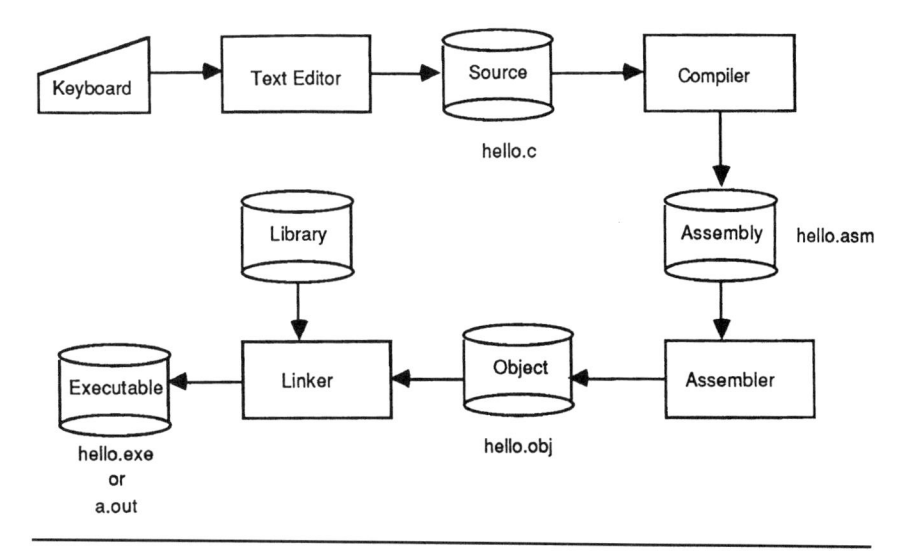

Figure C.1. The compile/link process.

gram, find and correct your error, and then recompile and try to link your program again.

To run your program, type its file name. For the program in Example C.1, type "hello", or "a.out". The computer will load and run your program, and you should see

```
Hi everybody
```

on your terminal.

MULTIPLE SOURCE FILES

You may compile two source files and link them into a single program either in separate steps or in one step. Suppose you have the two source files in Example C.2.

Example C.2

```c
/* Source file hello.c */

#include <stdio.h>
int my_function();
```

```
main()
        {
        my_function();
        printf("\n Hi everybody");
        }

/* Source file myfunc.c */

int my_function()

   {
   printf("\n Hi everybody");
   }
```

You may compile the files using either

```
cc hello.c myfunc.c
```

or

```
cc -c hello.c
cc -c myfunc.c
```

In the first case, the compiler compiles both files and implicitly calls the linker if it offers this feature. In the second case, the "–c"

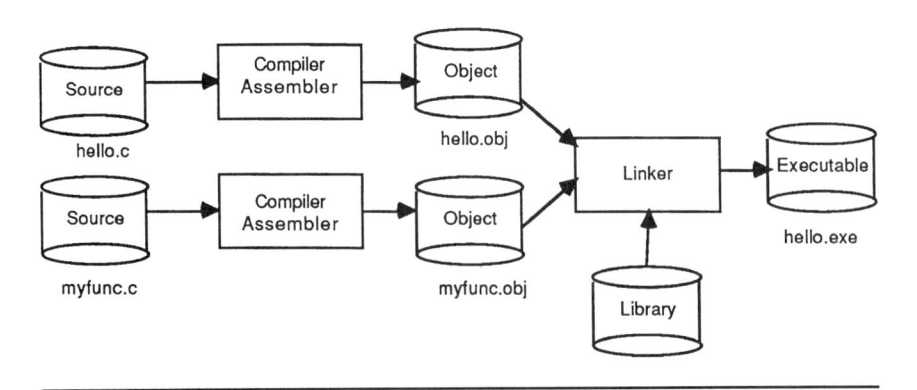

Figure C.2.   The compile/link process involving two source files.

option specifies that you simply want to compile the files. The compiler will not implicitly call the linker in this case, so you must call it, using the object filenames as in

```
link hello myfunc
```

or

```
cc hello.o myfunc.o
```

This process is shown in Figure C.2.

Appendix D
Bits, Bytes, and Numbers*

BIT VALUES

The value of a bit, binary digit, may be 0 or 1. Any given string of bits has a corresponding arithmetic value. Each bit position in a string has a value equal to twice that of the bit position to its right. Using the value of the bit position for each bit with a value of 1, you may compute the arithmetic value of a string of bits. For example, the arithmetic value of "01101010" is determined based on

```
Bit position            7   6   5   4   3   2   1   0
Value of bit position  128 64  32  16   8   4   2   1
Example bit string      0   1   1   0   1   0   1   0
```

and the decimal value of the bit string is

64 + 32 + 8 + 2 = 100.

Typically computers use strings of 8, 16, or 32 bits to store numbers. The leftmost bit, called the most significant bit or MSB, may be used to store the number's sign, which is generally 0 for

---

*This appendix is adapted from Kenneth Pugh: *C Language for Programmers*, Chicago: Scott Foresman, 1989, and used with permission of the publisher.

Table D.1. Representation of corresponding positive and negative values using one's complement and two's complement.

Positive Value	Negative Value	
	One's Complement	Two's Complement
00000001	11111110	11111111
01111111	10000000	10000001

positive numbers and 1 for negative numbers. The bit string for a negative number may be the complement of that for the positive number; that is, each negative bit is the negation (0 for 1 and 1 for 0) of the corresponding positive bit. This format for representing positive and negative numbers is called one's complement. An alternative format, called two's complement, adds a value of 1 to negative numbers. Table D.1 illustrates how computers represent and store corresponding positive and negative values using one's complement and two's complement.

The compiler may treated **char** values as either signed or unsigned. By default, **int** values are signed. The **unsigned** data type modifier makes the compiler treat a variable's MSB as a value bit, so that the compiler holds only positive numbers.

Sign Extension

If a string of bits is expanded to a longer string, the leftmost bits in the expanded string may either be set to 0 or depend on the sign bit in the smaller string. The latter case is called sign extension. If the sign bit of the small string is a 1, then the leftmost bits in the expanded string will be set to 1, as Table D.2 shows.

Note that the difference in the result occurs only if the original string has a negative sign. There is no sign extension for unsigned integer types, but only for signed integer types. If your compiler treats **char** variables as signed variables, they are signed extended.

Shifts

A bit string can shift left or right. If the string shifts left, the rightmost bit (least significant bit or LSB) is set to 0. If the string

BITS, BYTES, AND NUMBERS 305

Table D.2. String expansion with and without sign extension.

| 8-bit string | 16-bit string ||||
	Without Sign Extension		With Sign Extension	
01101110	00000000	01101110	00000000	01101110
10010000	00000000	10010000	11111111	10010000

shifts right, the sign bit (MSB) may either be set to 0 (termed a logical shift) or keep its starting value (termed an arithmetic shift). Table D.3 summarizes the results of left and right bit string shifts. These two types of shifts differ if the sign bit is 1.

Shifts of unsigned integer values are always logical shifts. Shifts of signed values may be either arithmetic or logical, depending on the compiler.

Memory Locations

A memory location has two associated numeric values: its address and the value that it contains. In a typical computer, each memory location contains one byte (eight bits) of information. The address uniquely identifies a memory location. Addresses typically start at zero and go up to one less than the number of bytes in the computer.

Each **char** value occupies one memory location, or one byte. Depending on the computer, **int** values occupy either two or four bytes. The order in which the bytes are stored is also computer dependent. Either the low-order byte (the one with the LSB) or the most significant byte (the one with the MSB) may occupy the first memory location. Finally, **double** values occupy eight or

Table D.3. Results of left and right shifts of 8-bit strings.

| 8-Bit String | Logical Shift || Arithmetic Shift Right |
	Left	Right	
01001001	10010010	00100100	00100100
10011000	00110000	01100000	11001100

more bytes, depending once again on the computer. The representation of floating point values (exponent and mantissa) is dependent on the processor.

When a routine allocates memory to a variable, it assigns that variable successive memory locations. The addresses of the memory locations for **static** and external variables are fixed while the program is executing. The memory locations for automatic variables are assigned when a function is entered. When the function returns, automatic variables in other functions may reuse those memory locations. The address operator applied to a variable name computes the address of the first memory location where the variable is stored.

Elements in an array are stored in successive bytes. Thus the second element in an array of **char** is stored in the memory location with the address one greater than the first element; the third element is stored at an address one greater than the second, etc. For an **int** array, each element is stored at an address either two or four greater than the previous element, depending on the amount of storage the computer requires for an **int**.

A pointer variable occupies two or four bytes, again depending on the computer. The value it contains does not appear any different than values stored in other variables, such as **ints**. If a routine refers to a pointer variable without including any operators, it accesses the value at the pointer's memory location. If the routine applies an indirection operator to a pointer variable, it first retrieves the contents of the pointer's memory location. The routine then treats that value as an address of another variable and accesses the contents at that address.

Appendix E

Summary of C

This summary is adapted from the ANSI C Standard.

DATA TYPES

Integer Types

char	single character
signed char	char that contains negative and positive numbers
unsigned char	**char** that contains only positive numbers
short	integer with range less than or equal to **int**
signed short int	same as **short**
unsigned short int	short that contains only positive numbers
int	integer
signed int	same as **int**
unsigned int	**int** that contains only positive numbers

long — integer with range equal to or greater than **int**.

signed long int — same as long

unsigned long int — **long** that contains only positive numbers.

Floating Point Types

float — floating point

double — floating point with equal or extended range over **float**

long double — floating point with equal or extended range over **double**

Void Type

void — used for functions that do not return values; pointers to **void** are universal pointers

Enumerated Type

enum — takes on restricted list of values

Example

```
enum tag-type    { enum-values };
```

Type Modifiers

const — variable that does not change value

volatile — variable that should not be optimized

Examples

```
int const i;      i is constant

int volatile i;   i is volatile
```

Examples

```
int const *name;   or  const int *name;
                   (pointer to an int that is constant)

int * const name;  variable that is constant
                   pointing to an int.
```

Aggregates and Derived Types

structure	struct *tag-type*
	{
	declarations-of-members
	};
union	union *tag-type*
	{
	declaration-of-members
	};
array	*data-type name*[ ]
pointers	*data-type *name*

data-type name( )   function returning data-type

You can recursively apply the preceding derived types.

- **typedef** assigns a new name to a data type, e.g., **typedef** *data-type TYPE*;
- Integral types are integer and enumerated types
- Arithmetic types are integral and floating point types
- Scalar types are arithmetic and pointer types
- Constants
    Integer Constant
        Decimal   non-zero starting char
        Octal   0 followed by 0 to 7
        Hexadecimal   0x or 0X followed by 0 to 9, A to F, or a to f

unsigned	u or U suffix
long	l or L (or value cannot fit in int)
Floating Constant	Number with decimal point and optional exponent
Type suffixes:	
double	no suffix
float	f or F suffix
long double	l or L suffix
Enum Constant	must have been listed in enum declaration
Char Constant	surrounded by single quotes.
Escape Characters	
Sequence	*Meaning*
\a	alert (bell)
\b	back-space
\t	tab (horizontal)
\n	new-line
\v	vertical tab
\f	form-feed
\r	carriage-return
\"	quote (in a string)
\'	single quote (as a character constant)
\?	question mark
\\	backslash (the character itself)
String Literals	Characters surrounded by double quotes.* \new-line allows you to continue to next line; two adjacent string literals are concatenated

- Comments   Surrounded by /* */

---

*If preceded by an **L**, a string literal is of **wchar_t** type.

may not appear within character constant, string literal, or another comment

- Variables storage classes

  automatic   inside a function; no key word or auto; can be initialized with any expression; does not retain values between calls to function

  register   inside a function; key word is **register**; can be initialized with any expression; cannot take address of register variable; does not retain values between calls to function

  static   inside a function; key word is **static**; can be initialized with constant expression; if no explicit initializer, initialized to zero; retains values between calls to function

  external   outside a function with no key word; outside or inside function with key word **extern**; can be initialized with constant expression; if no explicit initializer, initialized to zero; can be referenced by functions in other files

  static external   outside a function with key word **static**;* can be initialized with constant expression; if no explicit initializer, initialized to zero

---

*You can reference static externals from inside a function using the key word **extern**, but this is usually unnecessary.

OPERATORS

Bitwise operators must have integral type operands. Table E.1 summarizes operators, their associativity, and their precedence.

Table E.1. Operators and their associativity and precedence.

Operator	Use	Associativity
()	function call	left to right
[]	array element	
->	pointer to structure member	
.	member of structure	
!	logical negation	right to left
~	one's complement	
++	increment	
--	decrement	
-	unary minus	
+	unary plus	
(type)	cast	
*	indirection (pointer)	
&	address	
sizeof	size of object	
*	multiplication	left to right
/	division	
%	modulus	
+	addition	left to right
-	subtraction	
<<	left shift	left to right
>>	right shift	
<	less than	left to right
<=	less than or equal to	
>	greater than	
>=	greater than or equal to	

Table E.1.   *Continued*

Operator	Use	Associativity
==	equality	left to right
!=	inequality	
&	bitwise AND	left to right
^	bitwise XOR	left to right
|	bitwise OR	left to right
&&	logical AND	left to right
||	logical OR	left to right
? :	conditional	right to left
=	assignment	right to left
op=	shorthand assignment	
,	comma	left to right

Order of evaluation is not specified for operators except that it is left to right for comma, conditional, logical OR, and logical AND.

STATEMENTS
Simple

```
expression;
```

Compound

```
{
zero-or-more-statements
}
```

Control
if

```
if (condition)
        statement
```

if-else

```
if (condition)
        statement
else
        statement
```

while

```
while (condition)
        statement
```

do-while

```
do
        statement
        while (condition);
```

for

```
for (expression1;expression2;expression3)
        statement
```

switch

```
switch(integral_expression)
         {
    case integral-constant:
    ....
    default:
    ...
         }
```

break. Exits the **while**, **do-while**, and **for** loops and the **switch** statement.

continue. goes to the test condition in the **while** and **do-while** loops; goes to *expression3* in the **for** loop.

FUNCTIONS

```
data-type function-name(parameter-list)
declarations-of-parameters
        {
        declaration-of-local-variables
        statements
        }
```

main() function	**argc** and **argv** passed to it
exit(value)	ends the program and returns *value* to the operating system

PREPROCESSOR

#define *NAME*	defines a name
#define *NAME* (*tokens*)	defines a macro
#undef *NAME*	undefines a name or macro
#ifdef	tests for **#define**
#ifndef	tests for no **#define**
#if *expression*	tests expression
#else	other half of test
#endif	end of **#if**, **#ifdef**, and **#ifndef**
#elif	else-if
#line	sets up a line number
#error	creates an error in compilation
#pragma	local feature to a compiler
#	null directive
new-line	directive for continuation of preprocessor statements
defined(*NAME***)**	tests for **#define**—for use in **#if**
#	quoting operator
##	token pasting operator

KEY WORDS

List of Key Words

Key Words	Usage
auto	storage type
break	control flow (in **for, while, do-while, switch**)
case	control flow (in **switch**)
char	data type
const	data type modifier
continue	control flow (in **for, while, do-while**)
default	control flow (in **switch**)
do	control flow
double	data type
else	control flow (with **if**)
enum	data type
extern	storage type
float	data type
for	control flow
goto	control flow
if	control flow
int	data type
long	data type modifier
register	storage type
return	control flow (in function)
short	data type modifier
signed	data type modifier
sizeof	built-in operator
static	storage type
struct	aggregate data type
switch	control flow
typedef	data type declarator
union	aggregate data type
unsigned	data type modifier

void	data type	
volatile	data type modifier	
while	control flow	

List of Symbols and Their Meanings

Symbol	*Meaning*
+	addition
	(++) auto increment
	unary +
−	subtraction
	negation
	(−−) auto decrement
/	divide
	(/*) comment start
	(*/) comment end
*	multiply
	(/*) comment start
	(*/) comment end
%	modulus
!	not logical
	(!=) not equal
|	**or** bitwise
||	**or** logical
~	one's complement bitwise
^	exclusive or bitwise
&	**and** bitwise
	address of (as a unary operator)
&&	**and** logical
(	associativity
	function parameter list start
)	associativity
	function parameter list end

'	character constant start and end
"	string constant start and end
?	conditional operator (with :)
,	comma operator
	function parameter list separator
	data initialization separator
<	less than operator
<=	less than or equal to operator
>	greater than operator
>=	greater than or equal to operator
=	assignment operator
	(with +,–,etc.) shorthand assignment
==	equality operator
<=	less than operator
>=	greater than operator
:	conditional operator (with ?)
	label **switch**
	label **goto**
#	preprocessor command—quote
##	preprocessor command—token concatenation
[	starts an array index
]	ends an array index
{	starts a block (compound statement)
	starts an initialization list
}	ends a block (compound statement)
	ends an initialization list
\	escape character
;	statement terminator

Scope of Identifiers

- program
- function   goto label—identifier followed by ':'
- file   if outside a function or block, extends to end of source file
- block   in a block '{' or in list of function parameters; any identifiers redeclared in a block are instances of new identifiers.
- function prototype   only within the function prototype parameter list.

Linkage of Identifiers

- External linkage   In a set of files and libraries that make up the program, the same identifier denotes the same object identifiers for functions and objects declared outside of functions.
- Internal linkage   If the word **static** precedes the function or object identifier, then it is known only within the source file.
- extern   If the identifier was previously declared as internal linkage (**static**), then **extern** has no effect. Otherwise, it declares the identifier to have external linkage. If the identifier is not called in the source file, then no external reference need be made for it.
- volatile   These values must be intact when a sequence point is reached (i.e., they cannot be optimized out of a loop, and any interrupt must ensure that they are intact). Sequence points are function calls, unary + operator, comma operator, logical OR and logical AND, and conditional operator.

Appendix F
ASCII Chart

This chart shows the integer equivalents of ASCII characters.

Decimal	Octal	Hexadecimal	Binary	Character	Note
0	000	00	0000000	NUL	null character
1	001	01	0000001	SOH	
2	002	02	0000010	STX	
3	003	03	0000011	ETX	
4	004	04	0000100	EOT	
5	005	05	0000101	ENQ	
6	006	06	0000110	ACK	
7	007	07	0000111	BEL	produces beep or bell
8	010	08	0001000	BS	backspace (\b)
9	011	09	0001001	HT	horizontal tab (\t)
10	012	0A	0001010	LF	line feed (\n)
11	013	0B	0001011	VT	vertical tab
12	014	0C	0001100	FF	form feed (\f)

Decimal	Octal	Hexadecimal	Binary	Character	Note
13	015	0D	0001101	CR	carriage return (\r)
14	016	0E	0001110	SO	
15	017	0F	0001111	SI	
16	020	10	0010000	DLE	
17	021	11	0010001	DC1	
18	022	12	0010010	DC2	
19	023	13	0010011	DC3	
20	024	14	0010100	DC4	
21	025	15	0010101	NAK	
22	026	16	0010110	SYN	
23	027	17	0010111	ETB	
24	030	18	0011000	CAN	
25	031	19	0011001	EM	
26	032	1A	0011010	SUB	
27	033	1B	0011011	ESC	escape
28	034	1C	0011100	FS	
29	035	1D	0011101	GS	
30	036	1E	0011110	RS	
31	037	1F	0011111	VS	
32	040	20	0100000	SP	space
33	041	21	0100001	!	
34	042	22	0100010	"	
35	043	23	0100011	#	
36	044	24	0100100	$	
37	045	25	0100101	%	
38	046	26	0100110	%	
39	047	27	0100111	'	single quote
40	050	28	0101000	(	
41	051	29	0101001	)	
42	052	2A	0101010	*	
43	053	2B	0101011	+	

ASCII CHART

Decimal	Octal	Hexadecimal	Binary	Character	Note
44	054	2C	0101100	,	comma
45	055	2D	0101101	-	hyphen
46	056	2E	0101110	.	period
47	057	2F	0101111	/	
48	060	30	0110000	0	
49	061	31	0110001	1	
50	062	32	0110010	2	
51	063	33	0110011	3	
52	064	34	0110100	4	
53	065	35	0110101	5	
54	066	36	0110110	6	
55	067	37	0110111	7	
56	070	38	0111000	8	
57	071	39	0111001	9	
58	072	3A	0111010	:	colon
59	073	3B	0111011	;	semicolon
60	074	3C	0111100	<	
61	075	3D	0111101	=	
62	076	3E	0111110	>	
63	077	3F	0111111	?	
64	100	40	1000000	@	
65	101	41	1000001	A	
66	102	42	1000010	B	
67	103	43	1000011	C	
68	104	44	1000100	D	
69	105	45	1000101	E	
70	106	46	1000110	F	
71	107	47	1000111	G	
72	110	48	1001000	H	
73	111	49	1001001	I	
74	112	4A	1001010	J	
75	113	4B	1001011	K	

Decimal	Octal	Hexadecimal	Binary	Character	Note
76	114	4C	1001100	L	
77	115	4D	1001101	M	
78	116	4E	1001110	N	
79	117	4F	1001111	O	
80	120	50	1010000	P	
81	121	51	1010001	Q	
82	122	52	1010010	R	
83	123	53	1010011	S	
84	124	54	1010100	T	
85	125	55	1010101	U	
86	126	56	1010110	V	
87	127	57	1010111	W	
88	130	58	1011000	X	
89	131	59	1011001	Y	
90	132	5A	1011010	Z	
91	133	5B	1011011	[	
92	134	5C	1011100	\	
93	135	5D	1011101	]	
94	136	5E	1011110	^	
95	137	5F	1011111	_	underline
96	104	60	1100000	`	back quote
97	141	61	1100001	a	
98	142	62	1100010	b	
99	143	63	1100011	c	
100	144	64	1100100	d	
101	145	65	1100101	e	
102	146	66	1100110	f	
103	147	67	1100111	g	
104	150	68	1101000	h	
105	151	69	1101001	i	
106	152	6A	1101010	j	
107	153	6B	1101011	k	

ASCII CHART

Decimal	Octal	Hexadecimal	Binary	Character	Note
108	154	6C	1101100	l	
109	155	6D	1101101	m	
110	156	6E	1101110	n	
111	157	6F	1101111	o	
112	160	70	1110000	p	
113	161	71	1110001	q	
114	162	72	1110010	r	
115	163	73	1110011	s	
116	164	74	1110100	t	
117	165	75	1110101	u	
118	166	76	1110110	v	
119	167	77	1110111	w	
120	170	78	1111000	x	
121	171	79	1111001	y	
122	172	7A	1111010	z	
123	173	7B	1111011	{	
124	174	7C	1111100	|	
125	175	7D	1111101	}	
126	176	7E	1111110	~	
127	177	7F	1111111	DEL	rubout

Bibliography

American National Standards Institute. *American National Standard for Information Systems: Programming Language C.* Washington, D.C. 1989.

Bentley, Jon. *Programming Pearls.* Reading, MA: Addison-Wesley, 1986.

Gries, David. *The Science of Programming.* Springer-Verlag, 1981.

Hoare, C. Anthony R. "Quicksort," *Computer Journal* 5(1):10-15 (1962).

Kernighan, B.W., and Ritchie, D.M. *The C Programming Language.* Englewood Cliffs, N.J.: Prentice Hall, 1978.

Knuth, Donald E. *The Art of Computer Programming.* Vol 1, *Fundamental Algorithms.* Reading, MA: Addison-Wesley, 1968.

Knuth, Donald E. *The Art of Computer Programming.* Vol 2, *Seminumerical Algorithms.* Reading, MA: Addison-Wesley, 1969.

Knuth, Donald E. *The Art of Computer Programming.* Vol 3, *Searching and Sorting.* Reading, MA: Addison-Wesley, 1973.

Koenig, A., "C Traps and Pitfalls." In AT&T Bell Laboratories *Computing Science Technical Report #123* (July 1, 1986).

Pugh, Kenneth H. *All on C.* Chicago: Scott Foresman, 1989.

Pugh, Kenneth H. *C Language for Programmers.* Chicago: Scott Foresman, 1985.

Strawberry Software. *Applied C.* New York: Van Nostrand Reinhold, 1986.

GUIDE TO MAGAZINES

This magazine is devoted exclusively to the C language.

C Journal
    2120 W. 25th St., Suite B.
    Lawrence, KS 66046

This magazine contains many articles on C.

Dr. Dobb's Journal
    M&T Publishing
    411 Borel Ave.
    San Mateo, CA 94402-3522

This magazine covers many languages, but usually has an article on C in each issue.

Computer Language
    CL Publications
    650 Fifth Street, Suite 311
    San Francisco, CA 94107

This is a general journal devoted to computers and programming.

Communications of the ACM
    Association for Computing Machinery
    11 West 42nd Street
    New York, NY 10036

Index

! logical negation operator 33
!= inequality operator 31
^ bitwise exclusive OR operator 210
# operator 220
# preprocessor 167, 199, 221
operator 220
% modulus (reminder) operator 17
%= modulus assignment operator 18
& address operator 8
& bitwise AND operator 210
&& logical AND operator 31, 211
&= bitwise AND assignment operator 210
( ) cast operator 212
( ) function-call 62
( ) expression grouping 21
* indirection operator 152
* multiplication operator 17
*= multiplication assignment operator 18
+ addition operator 17
+ unary plus operator 17
++ postfix increment operator 19
++ prefix increment operator 19
+= addition assignment operator 18
, comma operator 211
, . . . ellipsis, unspecified parameters 288
- subtraction operator 17
- unary minus operator 17
— postfix decrement operator 19
— prefix decrement operator 19
-= subtraction assignment operator 18
-> structure/union pointer operator 160
. structure/union member operator 159
/ division operator 17
/= division assignment operator 18
/* */ comment delimiters 22
: colon (with goto)

329

330 INDEX

: colon (with switch)
; semicolon (with statement) 21
< less-than operator 31
< redirection 123
<< left-shift operator 210
<<= left-shift assignment operator 210
<= less-than-or-equal-to operator 31
= assignment operator 17
== equality operator 31
> greater-than operator 31
> redirection 123
>= greater-than-or-equal-to operator 31
>> right-shift operator 210
>>= right-shift assignment operator 210
? : conditional operator 211
??! trigraph sequence, | 290
??' trigraph sequence, ^ 290
??(trigraph sequence, [290
??) trigraph sequence,] 290
??- trigraph sequence, ~ 290
??/ trigraph sequence, \ 290
??< trigraph sequence, { 290
??= trigraph sequence, # 290
??> trigraph sequence, } 290
[ ] array subscript operator 91, 92
\ backslash character 207
\" double-quote-character escape sequence 207
\' singlle-quote-character escape sequence 207
\? question-mark escape sequence 207
\\ blackslash-character escape sequence 207
\0 null character 105
\a alert escape sequence 207
\b backspace escape sequence 207

\f form-feed escape sequence 207
\n new-line escape sequence 23, 207
\ooo octal-character escape sequence 205
\r carriage-return escape sequence 207
\t horizontal-tab escape sequence 207
\v vertical-tab escape sequence 207
\xhhh hexadecimal-character escape sequence 205
^ exclusive OR operator 210
^= exclusive OR assignment operator 210
{ } braces 21, 94
| inclusive OR operator 210
|= inclusive OR assignment operator 210
| | logical OR operator 31, 211
~ bitwise complement operator 210
__DATE__ macro 170
__FILE__ macro 170
__LINE__ macro 170
__STDC__ macro 170
__TIME__ macro 170
_IOFBF macro 246, 251
_IOLBF macro 246, 251
_IONBF macro 246, 251

A

abort function 245, 283
abs function 270
acos function 241
addition assignment operator, += 18
addition operator,+ 17
address, arithmetic 216
address, of variable 8

INDEX

address, operator,& 24, 67
alert escape sequence,\a 207
American Standard for
    Information
    Interchange 12
AND operator, bitwise,& 210
AND operator, logical, && 31, 211
AND (COBOL) 31
arc functions 241
argc parameter 217, 218
arguments, call by reference 67, 155
arguments, call by value 66
arguments, command line 217
arguments, function 61, 66
arguments, pointer 155
arguments, variable number of 287
argv argument vector 217
arithmetic conversions 207
arithmetic operators, unary 17
arithmetic right shift 210
array,
    and pointers 217
    as parameter 95
    character 105, 112
    general 91, 94
    index 91
    initialization 91, 110
    in structures 130
    restrictions 98
    subscript operator [ ] 92
ASCII character set 12
asctime function 279
asin function 241
assembly 1
assert macro 284
assert.h header 284
assignment,
    conversion by 18, 208
    of structures 133
    operators 17

associativity of operators 212
asterisk-slash, */ 22
AT END (COBOL) 182
atan function 241
atan2 function 241
atof function 265
atoi function 265
atol function 265
at_exit function 283
auto storage-class specifier 77
automatic variable 77
automatic conversion 19

B
backspace escape sequence,\b 207
basic syntax 3
binary stream 191, 244
bit,
    definition of 303
    most significant 303
    pattern constants 209
    shift 304
bitwise,
    AND operator, & 210
    exclusive OR operator, ^ 210
    inclusive OR operator, | 210
    operators 210
ADD (COBOL) 18
boolean variables 34
braces, in compound
    statements 21, 37
break, in endless loop 38, 42
88 LEVEL (COBOL) 35
break, in switch 45
bsearch function 269
BUFSIZ macro 246

C
call by reference 67, 155
call by value 66
CALL (COBOL) 63
calloc function 268

332 INDEX

carriage-return escape
  sequence,\r 207
case label (switch) 44
cast operator, ( ) 212
ceil function 244
char type 12
character,
  constant 15, 205
  functions 122, 192, 280
  multi-byte 290
ACCEPT (COBOL) 115, 119
character, wide 289, 290
CHAR_BIT macro 239
CHAR_MAX macro 239
CHAR_MIN macro 239
clearerr function 250
88 (COBOL) 172
CLK_TCK macro 277
clock function 278
clock_t type 277
ASSIGN (COBOL) 181
COBOL equivalents 223
comma operator, 211
AT END (COBOL) 182
comment code 171
comment delimiters, / * */ 22
comments 22
COMP (COBOL) 11
compiling a C program 297
compiling multiple files 299
complement operator, ~ 211
compound statement 21, 30, 35
COMPUTATIONAL (COBOL)
  11, 115
COMPUTATIONAL (COBOL)
  11
COMPUTE (COBOL) 17
COMPUTE 16
COMP-2 (COBOL) 11
conditional compilation 171,
  220
conditional operator,? : 210

const type 209
constant,
  character 15
  double 15
  general 15, 204
  integer 15
  string 15
continue statement 214
conversion,
  arithmetic 207
  assignment 18, 208
  cast operator 209
  general 207
COPY BOOK (COBOL) 127,
  128, 170
cos function 241
cosh function 242
ctime function 279
ctype.h header 280

D

DATA DIVISION (COBOL) 62
data types 204
data type synonyms 175
date and time functions 277
DBL_ macros 238
declarations, general 12
declaration, multiple
  variables 13
decrement operator, postfix,— 19
decrement operator, prefix,— 19
default label (switch) 44
defined directive 220
diagnostics functions 284
difftime function 278
direct I/O 264
DISPLAY (COBOL) 11, 115
div function 270
DIVIDE (COBOL) 18
div_t type 265
double 11, 15, 205
double quotation marks 109

INDEX **333**

do-while. *See also* while 39
dynamic memory allocation 215, 267

E
EBCDIC 12
EDOM macro 237, 239, 240
end of file 192
END-IF (COBOL) 21, 35
end-of-file macro,EOF 192, 246
END-PERFORM (COBOL) 21
enum type 175
enumerated data type 172
EOF macro 246
EQUAL TO (COBOL) 31
equality operator == 30, 31, 33
ERANGE macro 237, 239, 240
errno macro 237
errno.h header 237
escape sequences 15, 167, 205
EVALUATE (COBOL) 45
execution, first line 7
execution options 218
exit function 8, 15, 70, 167, 205, 245, 283
EXIT_FAILURE macro 265, 283
EXIT_SUCCESS macro 265, 283
exp function 242
exponential functions 242
expression 16
Extended Binary Coded Decimal Interchange Code 12
extern 80, 204
external,
    definition 80
    variable 77-80, 204

F
F (constant suffix) 207
fabs function 244

fclose function 183, 248
feof function 250
ferror function 250
fflush function 248
fgetc function 192, 261
fgetpos function 252
fgets function 192, 263
fields 127
file,
    buffering 250
    closing 248
    mode 182
file errors 250
FILE I/O (COBOL) 179
file manipulations 247
file pointer 182
file positioning 190, 251
FILE SECTION (COBOL) 181, 184
FILE typedef 245, 248
FILE-CONTROL (COBOL) 181, 182
FILNAME_MAX macro 246
first line executed 7, 69
flags 34
float type 205
float.h header 237
floor function 244
FLT_ macros 237, 238
fmod function 244
fopen function 182, 245, 247
FOPEN_MAX macro 246
for statement 41
forever loop 42
format specifiers 23, 116, 118, 253, 258
format string 23, 115
formatted input/output functions 191, 253
fpos_t typedef 246
fprintf function 191, 253
fputc function 192, 262

334 INDEX

fputs function 192, 263
fread function 183, 264
free function 215, 268
freopen function 245, 248
frexp function 243
fscanf function 191, 257
fseek function 251
fsetpos function 252
ftell function 190, 251
fully qualified names 128, 130
functions,
    and arrays 98
    and strings 105
    and structures 105
    arguments 61, 65
    general 61
    library 225
    names 65
    parameters 61, 65
    prototypes 65, 67
fwrite function 183, 264

G

garbage 9
getc function 262
getchar function 122, 262
getenv function 283
gets function 122, 263
gmtime function 278
GOBACK (COBOL) 62
goto statement 212
GREATER THAN (COBOL) 31

H

header files 170, 231
hexadecimal constant 205, 209
hierarchies 138
hyperbolic functions 241
hyphen 218

I

if statement 29
IF (COBOL) 29

if-else statement 35
IF-ELSE (COBOL) 35
implicit function calls 69
increment operator, postfix, ++
    19
increment operator, prefix, ++
    19
index 91
    checking 92
initialization,
    array 110
    structures 133
    variable 110
input/output,
    character 261
    conversion 255, 259
    data width 121, 255, 259
    direct 264
    flags 253, 258
    formatted 119
    functions 244
    justification 118
    precision 118, 254
    string 263
    width 118, 255, 258
int type 11
integer,
    constant 15
    long 206
    short 206
    unsigned 206
internationalization, 289
    characters 289
    monetary information 293
    time transformation 292
INT_MAX macro 239
INT_MIN macro 239
isalnum function 282
isalpha function 282
iscntrl function 282
isdigit function 281
isgraph function 282
islower function 281

isprint function 282
ispunct function 282
isspace function 282
isupper function 281
isxdigit function 281

J
jmp_buf 285

L
L (constant suffix) 207
labs function 270
LC_ALL 291
LC_COLLATE 291
LC_CTYPE 291
LC_MONETARY 291
LC_NUMERIC 291
LC_TIME 291
LDBL_macros 238
ldexp function 243
ldiv function 270
ldiv_t type 265
LESS THAN (COBOL) 31
library functions 69, 225
linking 297, 298
LINKAGE (COBOL) 62
localeconv function 293
locale.h 290
localization 291
localtime function 278
log function 242
log10 function 242
logarithmic functions 242
logical AND operator, && 31
logical OR operator, || 31
logical right shift 210
long double type 205
long int type 204
longjmp function 285
LONG_MAX macro 239
LONG_MIN macro 239
loops, break 43
loops, forever 42

LU (constant suffix) 207
L_tmpnam macro 246

M
main function 69, 70, 217
malloc function 215, 268
math.h header 240
mblen function 295
mbstowcs function 295
mbtowc function 295
members, structures 159
member-access operators, . and -> 159
memchr function 276
memcmp function 276
memcpy function 275
memmove function 276
memory,
    allocation 215, 267
    functions 275
    location 30
mktime function 279
modf function 243
modulus operator (%) 17, 79
multiple files, compiling 80
MULTIPLY (COBOL) 18

N
new-line character(\n) 8, 15, 116
NEXT SENTENCE (COBOL) 43
non-printing character 116
nonlocal jump functions 284
NOT operator. *See* negation operator
NOT = (COBOL) 31
NOT GREATER THAN (COBOL) 31
NOT LESS THAN (COBOL) 31
not-equal-to operator, != *See* inequality operator
NUL character (strings), \0 105, 106, 107, 108

null character, *See* NUL character,
NULL macro 237
NULL pointer 164, 192
null statement (;) 21

O

OCCURS (COBOL) 91
octal, character constant 205, 209
offsetof macro 237
ones's complement operator (~) 211
OPEN (COBOL) 181, 182
operators,
   arithmetic 17
   associativity 212
   comma 211
   logical 211
   precedence 212
OR operator, logical, | | 31, 211
output. *See* input/output

P

packages 140
parameters, *See* arguments
parentheses, ( ) 29
PERFORM UNTIL (COBOL) 38
PERFORM UNTIL...TEST AFTER (COBOL) 39
PERFORM VARYING (COBOL) 41
PERFORM (COBOL) 61
perror function 275
PICTURE (COBOL) 12
pointer to member operator,-> 160
pointers,
   and allocated memory 215
   and arrays 217
   and functions 155
   and strings 216
   and structures 159
   and unions 162

   arithmetic 216
   errors 163
   indirection 151
   general 151
   NULL 164
   scanf 261
   unitialized 163
   void 164
pow function 242
precedence 20, 33, 212
prefix decrement operator, — 19
prefix increment operator, ++ 19
preopened files 193
preprocessor,
   concatenation 220
   directives 219
   general 157
printf function 12, 23, 111, 115, 256
private variables 204
PROCEDURE DIVISION (COBOL) 62, 70
program, environment functions 282
prototype, function 67
ptrdiff_t typedef 237
putc function 262
putchar function 122, 262
puts function 264

Q

qsort function 269
quotes, double 220
quoting operator, # 220

R

raise function 287
rand function 267
RAND_MAX macro 265
READ (COBOL) 115, 184
READ (COBOL) 181
realloc function 268
record 187

INDEX **337**

REDEFINE (COBOL) 93, 142
redirection, I/O 123
redirect input (<) 123
redirect output (>) 123
reference 80
register storage-class 208
relational operators 30-33
remove function 249
rename function 249
reserved words 13
return statement 62
return type 62
return, implicit 62
return values 64, 67
RETURN-CODE (COBOL) 62, 70
rewind function 252
RUN (COBOL) 70

S

scanf function 12, 23, 67, 111, 119, 261
SCHAR_MAX macro 239
SCHAR_MIN macro 239
scope,
    block 203
    file 203
    functions 203
    of names 203
searching function 269
SEEK_CUR macro 190, 246, 252
SEEK_END macro 190, 246, 252
SEEK_SET macro 190, 246, 252
SELECT (COBOL) 181
semicolon (;) null statement 21, 40
semicolon (;) with statement 21
set of characters 105
setbuf function 245, 251
setjmp function 285
setjmp .h header 284
setlocale function 291

setvbuf function 245, 250
shift bit 304
short 204
short int type 204
shorthand assignment operator 18
SHRT_MAX macro 239
SHRT_MIN macro 239
SIGABRT macro 287
SIGFPE macro 287
SIGILL macro 287
SIGINT macro 287
sign extension 304
signed char type 206
signal function 287
signal handling 286
signal .h header 286
signed char 305
SIGSEGV macro 287
SIGTERM macro 287
sig_atomic_t 286
SIG_DFL macro 286
SIG_ERR macro 286
SIG_IGNT macro 286
sin function 241
sinh function 242
sizeof operator 95
size_t typedef 177, 215, 237
slash-asterisk (/*) 22
sorting function 269
source file inclusion, *See* #include
SPACE (COBOL) 224
sprintf function 256
sqrt function 243
srand function 265
sscanf function 122, 261
standard error 193, 245
standard input 193, 245
standard output 193, 245
statements,
    compound 21
    general 21

static,
   declaration 77, 204
   external 204
stdarg.h header file 288
stddef.h header 236
stderr file 193, 245, 246
stdin file 119, 192, 245, 246
stdio.h header 24, 118
stdlib .h header 265, 283
stdout file 119, 245, 246
STOP (COBOL) 70
storage,
   allocation 267
   classes 70
strcat function 109, 272
strchr function 273
strcmp function 272
strcoll function 291
strcpy function 106, 159, 272
strcspn function 274
streams 244
strerror function 275
strftime function 292
string,
   and functions 105
   and pointers 216
   comparison functions 109, 272
   concatenation functions 271
   constant 15, 110
   copying functions 271
   functions 271
   general 105
   input and output 111, 118
   length 107
   search functions 272
string conversion functions 122
string literal 110
string .h header 271
strlen function 107, 275
strncat function 272
strncmp function 272
strncpy function 108, 272

strpbrk function 273
strrchr function 273
strspn function 273
strstr function 274
strtod function 266
strtok function 274
strtol function 266
strtoul function 266
structure assignment 130
structures,
   declaration 129
   templates 129, 133
strxfrm function 292
subprograms 61
subscripts. *See also* array, index
subscripts 91, 92, 96
SUBSTRACT (COBOL) 18
suffix 19
switch general 43
system function 283

T

table (COBOL) 91
tag-type general 129
tan function 241
tanh function 242
termination, loop 43
test expression 29, 30, 34
text stream 191, 244
time, and date functions 277
time function 278
time .h header 277
time-t type 277
tm structure type 277
tmpfile function 249
tmpnam function 249
TMP_MAX macro 246
token concatenation 220
tolower function 280
toupper function 280
trigonometric functions 240
trigraph sequences 290

INDEX 339

type conversions 19
type modifier 209
typedef declaration 175
typedef reserved names 177

U
U (constant suffix) 207
UCHAR_MAX macro 239
UINT_MAX macro 239
UL (constant suffix) 207
ULONG_MAX macro 239
unary minus 17
unary plus 17
underscore 13
ungetc function 252, 262
uninitialized pointers 163
union 142
unsigned, char 206, 304
   data type 205
   integers 205
   int 206
   long int 206
   short int 206
USHRT_MAX macro 239
utility functions 265

V
VALUE (COBOL) 16
variable arguments 287
variable declaration 62
variable names 13
variable declaration 203
variable external 204
VARYING (COBOL) 92
va_arg 288
va_end 288
va_start 288
vfprintf function 289
void in prototype 66
void pointers 164

void return type 68
volatile modifier 209
vprintf function 289
vsprintf function 289

W
wchar_t 289
wcstombs 305
wctomb 305
while statement 38
white space 22
wide characters 290
WRITE (COBOL) 115

X
X3J11 2
#define,
   and array 169
   directive 25, 167
   reserved names 169
   with tokens 219
#elif directive 220
#else directive 172
#endif directive 172
#error directive 221
#if directive 171
#ifdef directive 172
#ifndef directive 172
#include directive 7, 24, 170
#include reserved file names 170
#line directive 220
#pragma directive 221
#undef directive 220
%c format specifier 116, 121
%d format specifier 8, 116
%lf format specifier 8, 116
%o format specifier 209
%s format specifier 116
%x format specifier 209

OPERATORS IN C

Precedence and Associativity

Operator	Associativity	Order of evaluation
() [] -> .	function call array element pointer to structure member member of structure	left to right
! ~ ++ -- - + *(type)* * & **sizeof**	logical negation one's complement increment decrement unary minus unary plus cast indirection (pointer) address size of object	right to left
* / %	multiplication division modulus	left to right
+ -	addition subtraction	left to right
<< >>	left shift right shift	left to right
< <= > >=	less than less than or equal to greater than greater than or equal to	left to right
== !=	equality inequality	left to right
&	bitwise AND	left to right
^	bitwise XOR	left to right
|	bitwise OR	left to right
&&	logical AND	left to right
||	logical OR	left to right
? :	conditional	right to left
=	assignment	right to left
op=	shorthand assignment	right to left
,	comma	left to right

KEY WORDS

Storage types
- auto
- extern
- register
- static

Data types:
- char
- double
- enum
- float
- int
- void

Data type modifiers
- const
- long
- short
- signed
- unsigned
- volatile

Aggregate data types
- struct
- union

Data type declarator
- typedef

Built-in operator
- sizeof

Control flow
- break
- case
- continue
- default
- do
- else
- for
- goto
- if
- return
- switch
- while